THE STORY OF URMSTON, FLIXTON AND DAVYHULME

THE STORY OF
URMSTON, FLIXTON AND DAVYHULME

MICHAEL BILLINGTON

This book is dedicated to the memory of my parents, Jim and Peggy Billington. Sadly they both died just a few months prior to the publication of this history of my birthplace, and where I grew up with them both in such a happy childhood.

Title page: The Urmston coat of arms. Urmston Official Guide 1971

First published 2018
Reprinted 2020

The History Press
97 St George's Place, Cheltenham,
Gloucestershire, GL50 3QB
www.thehistorypress.co.uk

British Library Cataloguing in Publication Data.
A catalogue record for this book is available from the British Library.

ISBN 978 0 7509 8789 9

Typesetting and origination by The History Press
Printed in Great Britain by TJ International Ltd, Psdstow, Cornwall.

CONTENTS

ABOUT THE AUTHOR

Michael Billington was born in Urmston Cottage Hospital (the single-storey white building) at 7.10 a.m. on Wednesday, 1 April 1953, and brought up in Flixton and Davyhulme. He was baptised on 10 May 1953 at English Martyrs Roman Catholic church on Roseneath Road, where his parents had been married two years earlier on 31 March 1951.

After studying for a LLB degree at Liverpool in the early 1970s he gained an Open University degree and moved into primary school teaching in the mid 1990s.

Michael's first interest in the local history of his home town came about when he was studying art A-level between 1970 and 1972 at De la Salle College in Weaste, Salford. In addition to a drawing and painting assignment there was a requirement to submit an architecture thesis. Interviews with the local council, planners and architects resulted in a thirty-six-page submission on the then recent redevelopment in 1970 that included the new precinct (which was re-redeveloped in 2012) housing, shops, council offices, the Conservative club, a public house, the new library and car parking facilities. A second phase was part of the development where the old Victoria pub used to be situated.

Michael is a humanist and, in addition to his interest in local history, he is an artist, musician, writer, bee-keeper and ex-broadcaster as a former radio presenter and producer with BBC Radio Manchester, KFM and Red Rose Radio. A large collection of renaissance woodwind instruments occupies much of his leisure time and he is known for his extensive collection of bagpipes from around Europe.

Now a semi-retired primary school teacher, Michael lives in Chorlton-cum-Hardy; he has lived there since the mid 1970s but he has never forgotten that he is, first and foremost, still an Urmstonian.

Michael is a member of the Urmston and District Local History Society.

FOREWORD

Michael Billington's history of Urmston, Flixton and Davyhulme gives an insight into the everyday life of a small community from the time of the Norman Conquest to the present day. The area has changed considerably over the last 200 years as a result of its close contact with Manchester, a city that was at one time the most important industrial centre in the world. The Industrial Revolution, the coming of the railways and the Manchester Ship Canal accelerated the changes to the lives of ordinary people living in this area. These changes are documented through the various chapters in the book dealing, among other things, with employment, housing, religion, entertainment, transport and planning development.

The four case studies illustrate how the community evolved, from mainly agricultural production and handloom weaving to a dormitory town for incoming professional, managerial and skilled workers. I would like to thank Michael Billington for including the case study of Simpson Ready Foods, which is in many ways typical of this evolution. The company was started by my grandfather, who was the son of a handloom weaver from Droylesden; he moved to Urmston to set up a food manufacturing business in 1910. Over the past 100 years the company has employed many local and incoming workers. These include people similar to George Baldwin of Case Study 2, whose parents arrived around 1890, Hungarian refugees in the 1950s and Polish workers from the 1940s to 2016. The company even employed the author's mother for a short period!

The case study of Ernest Leeming, who was a contributor to the Manchester district planning proposals of 1945, shows the influence this visionary surveyor had on the layout and appearance of the Urmston area in the 1920s and 1930s. He also foresaw the building of motorways and the Channel Tunnel.

There is plenty of detail in this book which should be of interest to anyone who picks it up. I commend it to you.

William Simpson, MD of Simpson Ready Foods, 2018

INTRODUCTION

This is not the first book about the history of the old townships of Urmston, Flixton and Davyhulme. The 1898 books by David Herbert Langton and Richard Lawson, periodically referred to and quoted from in this book, are excellent reads and have been vital source material for the initial research for this book. It would appear that these two gentlemen had originally intended to collaborate on a single book but, after a disagreement, went their own separate ways to write their own individual works. Richard Lawson was living at Rostherne Cottage, Queen's Road, in Urmston at the time of writing his book and, like this author, he spent many hours researching in Manchester Central Reference Library. Meanwhile David Herbert Langton was living at Morningside in Flixton. Nonetheless, these books are now over a century old and the histories of the three townships are in need of updating.

Alan Crossland's *Looking Back at Urmston* and Karen Cliffe and Vicki Masterson's *Urmston, Flixton and Davyhulme*, part of the 'Images of England' series, are excellent brief histories of the area, sumptuously accompanied by beautiful archival images, as is the more recent Steven Dickens book *Flixton, Urmston & Davyhulme Through Time*, which juxtaposes photographs of 'then and now' views. See the bibliography for a comprehensive list of works I have consulted, which have included some that have been in my own personal collection for forty-five years or more.

However, it is over thirty years since Alan's book and sixteen since the Cliff/Masterson volume so I thought I would tackle the challenge of an up-to-date history of my birthplace. The book is by no means intended to be an autobiography although, as an Urmstonian, it is inevitable that there have been occasions when my own memories have proved to be useful source material. I ask the reader to indulge me on the few occasions when this happens.

This book traces the history of the two townships up to the town centre redevelopment in 1970. The Urmston Urban District, now as such defunct, was made up of the townships of Urmston, Flixton and Davyhulme that now form part of the Metropolitan Borough of Trafford and, before the boundary changes, was part of the county of Lancashire. The former Urmston Urban District Council was constituted on 1 April 1933 and on 1 April 1974 (coincidentally my 21st birthday) the boroughs of Altrincham, Sale and Stretford and the urban districts of Bowden and Hale together with the rural district of Bucklow were amalgamated to form the Borough of Trafford. From that date the Urban District Council ceased to exist. It is interesting to note in passing that in some records the council is referred to as the Urmston Urban District Council but in others as the Urban Urmston District Council.

Described as a dormitory town after the coming of the railway, Urmston lies around 6 miles south-west of the city of Manchester and covers some 4,800 acres of predominantly residential housing with businesses and open spaces such as fields and parks. Put simply, the three townships are bordered by the Manchester Ship Canal to the west and north, the River Mersey to the south and the borough of Stretford to the east, now mostly demarcated by the M60 motorway. The canal was built into the River Irwell, which divides Manchester from Salford and flows from some 39 miles from the Lancashire moors. None of the three townships was mentioned in the Domesday Book.

Although seen now as a larger and possibly more important township, Urmston was originally part of the parish of Flixton and worshippers would have had to travel to St Michael's on Sundays.

The coat of arms of Urmston Urban District Council, before its abolition in 1974, is illustrated on the title page. The chevron and martlets are from the heraldry of the local families of Asshawe and Hyde, and the griffin, with a change in colour, is from the arms of the de Traffords. The oak tree alludes to the preservation of the rural aspect of the area, while the anvil and waves refer to industry, the River Mersey, River Irwell and the ship canal. The squirrel is from the heraldry of the de Ormeston family and the balance is an emblem of St Michael, to whom the parish church is dedicated. The motto *Salus Populi Suprema Est Lex* means 'the welfare of the people is the highest law'.

The heraldic terminology describes the coat of arms as:

ARMS: Per chevron Azure and barry wavy Argent and of the first on a Chevron Ermine between in chief a Griffin segreant and an Oak Tree eradicated Or and in base a Bezant charged with an Anvil Sable a Rose Gules barbed and seeded proper between two Martlets also Or.

CREST: On a Wreath of the Colours a Squirrel sejant proper holding with the fore-paws a Balance Or.

It was in 1942 that the council adopted HMS *Express* and wanted to present a plaque that, according to custom, would be affixed to the quarterdeck of the adopted vessel. At that time, however, the district had no armorial bearings, and so an application for a grant was made to The College of Arms, and a little over three months later, on 10 June 1942, the grant was obtained.

The new coat of arms, depicted below, actually the arms of Trafford Council, is a compromise of elements representing the various townships in the modern Borough of Trafford. It depicts a griffin on a shield flanked by two unicorns. The line bisecting the shield horizontally symbolises the River Mersey running through Trafford from east to west and the canals in the borough. The white legs of a lion on a red background represent the parts of Trafford previously controlled by the de Massey family, while the red body and head of an eagle on a white background represents the areas of Trafford previously controlled by the de Traffords. Both elements were taken from the coats of arms of the respective families. The fist holding bolts of lightning represents Stretford and the electrical industry; the cog on the arm represents Altrincham's engineering industry. The unicorns stand for Sale and Altrincham. The oak branches represent Urmston and the rural areas of Trafford.

So, as can be seen, Urmston retains some representation, albeit minimal, in the references to the Mersey and the oak leaves and acorns.

The Trafford coat of arms. Trafford Council

The Hyde coat of arms in stone, shown here with John Howe OBE, chair of the Urmston and District Local History Society. (John Howe)

However, a different coat of arms was rescued from Urmston Hall in the 1930s and the stonework seen above is thought to be the arms of the Hyde family. The stone slab, here shown with John Howe OBE, chair of the Urmston and district local history society, can be seen in the church of St Clement, Urmston, at the back of the church near the children's corner. The watercolour is by Norman Booth and is a speculative depiction of what the full coat of arms may have looked like.

With the dissolution of the Urmston Urban District Council and the naming of Trafford Borough Council to take its place, it is appropriate to give a short history of the Trafford name.

The de Trafford family lived in what is now Trafford Park for ten centuries. The origin of the name may be 'tree ford'; a wooden ridge through which the road to the ford runs. The River Irwell formed the northern border to the estate, which covered some 1,200 acres with dimensions of 3.5 miles by 1.25 miles. Ralph de Trafford was a contemporary of King Canute (reigned 1016–35) and was one of the king's military heroes.

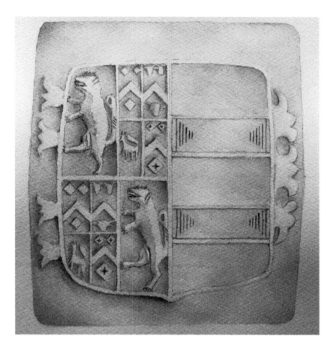

Norman Booth's watercolour showing what the complete, undamaged arms may have looked like. (Norman Booth)

Although the original family seat was at Old Trafford, a large mansion house was built during the reign of Elizabeth I.

In 1648, during the time of Edmund de Trafford, another mansion house was built and named Urmston Lodge.

It was the construction of the Manchester Ship Canal that led to Trafford Park being developed more as an industrial than a residential area. In 1897 Sir Humphrey de Trafford sold the estate to the Trafford Park Estates Company, a company formed by Ernest Terah Hooley. A large lake in the estate had been used for fishing and boating.

In 1940, during the Second World War, Trafford Hall was badly damaged by a mine and as a result it was demolished around 1946.

One

ETYMOLOGY

T he name Flixton is derived from the old Danish words *Flix* and *tun*. One theory is that Flixton was founded by a ninth-century Viking called Flikke. The wall behind the altar at St Michael's church is the original wall from the first church that was built by Flikke when he found Christianity.

However, in his *History of the Parish of Flixton* of 1898, David Langton mentions a variety of spellings such as fflixton, Fluxton, Flyxton, Flyxeton, Flixston and Flixtone. Possible explanations, he hypothesises, are Flet meaning flat, Flit being a Saxon term for 'battle strife' and Fleot + town, Fleotston or the town up to which the tide comes. Presumably the flowing refers to the nearby river. J. Eglington Bailey, in his *Old Stretford*, suggests Fleece Town; 'a derivation that refers to the old staple commodity of England'. Harland, in his *Mamecestre*, suggests that the origin might be from the Anglo-Saxon Fleax, Flex or Flax.

Another suggested derivation is Felix Town. However, this is generally dismissed as the combination of the Roman *Felix* with the Saxon *ton* is not considered viable. Both Lawson and Langton, though, seem to have preferred *Flux*, meaning 'a flowing', and thus Fluxton later corrupted to the present Flixton. Nonetheless, it is a firmly held view by local historians that the name Flixton is definitely of Danish origin with the name of Flikke combined with *ton* or *tun* meaning a farmstead.

Urm is an old Danish name and *ton* is from the old English *tun* meaning enclosure, yard or homestead; so, the home or settlement of Orm or Urm. The earliest reference to the modern spelling is in the *Testa de Nevil*, written about 1200, where we find that 'Albert Gredle, senr. gave to Orme, son of Edward [Aylward] with his daughter Emma, in marriage, one carucate of land in Eston by 10s. yearly: the heirs of Orme hold that land [Orme Eston or Urmston].' A carucate of land was as much land as a team of oxen could plough in a year. The *Testa de Nevil* also states that 'In the time of King John, Adam de Urmeston held one carucate of land, of the heir of Randle, the son of Roger. Richard, the son of Adam, granted lands in Urmston to Richard de Trafford in 1219–20.' The name was also spelled Urmyston on a 1577 map of Lancashire and Urmstone on a pre-Ordnance Survey map in 1830.

The origin of the name Davyhulme is somewhat uncertain. The old hall was the seat of John de Hulme in the reign of Henry II. This may be the origin of the name with 'Davy' being a contraction for David. Old Court Leet records show various spellings; in 1559 it is spelled Deaf Hulme, in 1566 Dewey Holme and in 1735 Davy Hulme. Other spellings show it as Daveyholme, Davey Hulme and, of course, the now accepted spelling of Davyhulme, the first reference of today's spelling possibly being 18 March 1792 as referred to by Dr Adam Clarke in his *Journal*. As if to add further confusion, the word *Hulme* is also an old Saxon word meaning a flat island in a river or the low meadow land by the banks of a curving river.

Other local place name derivations include Crofts Bank as a correction of Cross Bank. The old way of writing the letter 's' as 'f' is thought to have contributed to this. Cross Bank was considered to be the junction of four important roads.

As far as other nearby towns are concerned, Stretford derives from the Anglo-Saxon meaning the paved ford; Irlam from the Anglo-Saxon *Irwel Ham* or the Irwel House; Carrington from Celtic and Anglo-Saxon *Cathair*, a fortress. Bent Lanes means the place where the rushes grow. The River Irwell derives from the Celtic meaning *Ir* (fresh) and *Gwili* (river). The Mersey is thought to derive from the fact that the river anciently divided the Saxon kingdom of Mercia from Northumbria. However, Lawson tells us that the current spelling comes from *Meres ea* or 'the river fed by meres', which he dates to 1662.

Two

HISTORY

Flixton was part of the lands between the River Mersey and the River Ribble that William the Conqueror gave to Roger de Poitou shortly after the 1066 Norman Conquest. In turn, Roger bestowed part of these lands upon Albert de Grelly, a follower of the Norman duke.

As has been mentioned, Albert de Grelly gave one carucate of land to Orme Fitz-Siward, son of Edward Aylward, on his marriage to his daughter Emma, for 10s, and the land was known as Orme's Tun, later Orme Eston in the reign of King John (1199–1216). In turn, Richard, son of Adam of Ormeston, gave lands in these parts to Richard de Trafford in 1219 and later, in 1305, it is recorded that lands passed to Gilbert of Ashton, who was killed in a duel with John de Trafford.

The lands reverted to the Ormestons with the exception of the Newcroft estates, which remained with the de Traffords. During the reign of Henry IV

Carr's Ditch, Moorside Road. (David Smith)

(1399–1413) lands in Urmston passed to the Hyde family on the occasion of marriage between the daughter and heir of Adam de Urmston to Sir John Hyde of Norbury.

William Hyde's great-granddaughter, Susan, married Richard Hulme of Davyhulme in 1642, after which the lands passed into the Hulme family.

In 1735, Ann Hulme of Davyhulme married Thomas Willis of Bleckly in Buckinghamshire, who later sold his Urmston estates by a decree of chancery to a banker, William Allen, in 1765. Allen was declared bankrupt in 1789 and his estates were purchased by a Mr Marsden, who sold them in turn to John Miller and thence to the Ridehalgh family. It was Colonel Ridehalgh who in 1868 gave an acre of land as a gift for the building of Urmston parish church.

One feature of the area was known as Carr's Ditch, once thought to be a defensive structure of Roman origin but now established to be a medieval boundary between the townships of Urmston and Davyhulme. It served as a drainage ditch for surrounding fields. The construction of Moorside Road from Crofts Bank Road through to Bowfell Circle has now hidden the ditch from view. Nico's Ditch ran the length of Winchester Road to where Crofts Bank Road crosses and Carr's Ditch continued on the other side. Nico's Ditch is thought to run from Denton through Levenshulme and through to Stretford. It was possibly constructed in Saxon/Viking times and might have formed the border between the kingdoms of Northumbria and Mercia. It is now accepted to be the border between Urmston and Davyhulme.

Flixton

The first mention of Flixton is in the *Testa de Nevil* ('Head of Nevill') a book written about 1200. Originally in two volumes of parchment, the *Testa*, also known as the *Liber Feodorum,* is a collection of about 500 written brief notes made and added to throughout the thirteenth century, concerning fiefs held in capite or in-chief, that is to say directly from the Crown. The reference to Flixton reads 'Albert Gredle, sen; gave to Henry, son of Siward, one carucate of land in Flixton by 10s yearly. The heirs hold that land.'

Due to its geographical position, the parish of Flixton has had a quiet and uneventful history overall. It lies out of touch with the old main roads from Manchester to Warrington and to Chester, and the rivers on two sides, being unbridged, coupled with the fact that roads leading to Flixton led to nowhere else, contributed to some degree of insularity of the township. Thus changes in the ownership of land were, comparatively speaking, infrequent. Only one of its local gentry has taken any prominent part in the movements of the day, namely Peter Egerton of Shaw, an active partisan of Parliament during the Civil War.

Volume 5 of *The History of The County of Lancaster* (1911; part of The Victoria History of the Counties of England) describes Flixton thus:

> The Parish of Flixton is a compact area of three plough-lands ancient assessment lying in the tongue between the Irwell and Mersey, appears to have been cut off from Barton; the boundary between them is a straight line running east and west, while the eastern boundary is merely part of that between Barton and Stretford, also a straight line running south from the boundary of Whittleswick to the Mersey. Similarly the division between the component townships of Flixton is a straight line running southwards. The area is 2,581 acres. The geological formation consists of Upper Mottled Sandstone (Bunter series) of the New Red Sandstone.

This volume also describes the township of Flixton as measuring about 2.25 miles from east to west, with an average breadth of nearly 1.5 miles. The general slope is from from the north and east towards the opposite boundaries, the Mersey and Irwell. The population in 1901 was stated to be 3,656. It should also be borne in mind that the Mersey's course has varied from time to time and so its present course is not everywhere the exact boundary of the township as in past times.

Baines, in his 1868 *The History of Lancashire*, describes Flixton as not more than 7 miles from the town of Manchester and as 'a small part of the hundred of Salford [which is] of necessity partly manufacturing, but is principally agricultural'. Baines also tells us that the township had an area of 1,575 statute acres 'delightfully situated upon a verdant eminence', with a population of 1,302 in 1861. He also notes that the population of Flixton decreased from 2,064 in 1851 to 2,050 in 1861, which he attributes to 'the absence of manufacturing establishments in the township and the strong attraction presented by the abundant supply of labour and liberal wages of Manchester'. In his book *Labour Migration in England 1800–1850* (1926), Arthur Redford comments on the distress caused to the handloom weavers and says that they were willing to starve rather than submit to factory discipline. Nonetheless, a considerable number of handloom weavers flocked to the growing factory towns after the mid 1830s to seek employment for themselves and their children, and this exodus gave rise to the growth of such new towns as Stalybridge and Ashton-under-Lyne. Redford goes on to mention Flixton, which he refers to as a small village 7 miles from Manchester in which the population actually decreased due to the migration of handloom weavers.

Urmston

The area now known as Urmston formed part of the land between the Mersey and Ribble rivers, which were given to Roger de Poitou just after the Norman conquest of 1066. Roger de Poitou later bestowed these lands around the River Mersey to Albert de Grelly.

The land then became known as Orme's Tun, or 'the settlement or dwelling of Orme', later to be known as Orme Eston, then Ormeston and finally as its current name of Urmston. Other spellings have included Wermeston (1194), Urmeston (1212) and Ormestone (1302) as mentioned in *The History of The County of Lancaster* (1911).

In Volume 5 of *The History of The County of Lancaster* Urmston is described as a township measuring about 1 mile from north to south and 1.5 miles across

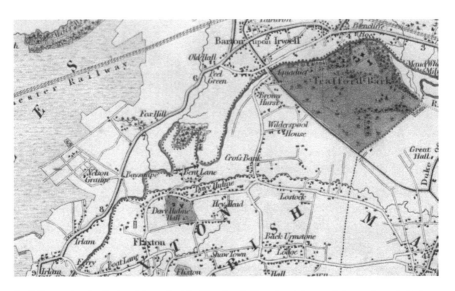

An 1830 map showing the hamlets south of the River Irwell. These hamlets were to be amalgamated into the townships of Urmston, Flixton and Davyhulme. (Manchester Central Reference Library)

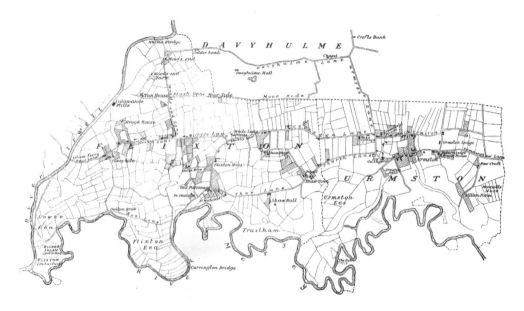

The 1846 Ordnance Survey map of Urmston, Flixton and Davyhulme. (From Langton's *A History of Flixton, Urmston and Davyhulme*, 1898)

with an area of 993 acres, the land sloping gently from north to south where the Mersey forms the boundary. The field names include Hillam, Barrowfield, Bakewell Meadow, Twines, Treeley, Rant and Woefield.

The manor of Urmston was originally part of the Marsey fee, and held of the lord as one plough-land by a family using the local surname. The earliest known holder is Richard de Urmston who, in 1193–4 gave 40s for having the king's good will after the rebellion of John, Count of Mortain (later King John). Adam de Urmston held it in 1212 but after this there is a period of uncertainty. The superior lordship was acquired by the Trafford family, who held it until the sixteenth century. In 1305 Adam de Urmston conferred all his lands in Urmston upon Gilbert de Ashton. Gilbert had several daughters and Urmston became the portion of Hawise, wife of Henry son of John de Trafford. Her heir, a daughter, married Ralph son of John de Hyde of Hyde in Cheshire. The manor continued with the Trafford family until the eighteenth century. Baines tells us in his *The History of Lancashire* that Urmston had an area of 974 acres with a population of 748 in 1861.

Maps can tell us a great deal about the growth of an area. The 1830 pre-OS map shows the area still very sparsely populated and that the spellings of Urmston and Davyhulme are spelled Urmstone and Davy Hulme respectively, although Flixton has acquired its modern form.

The 1846 map of Urmston, Flixton and Davyhulme shows how rural the three townships were and also that they had now become known by their current spellings. The railway was still some twenty-seven years away and Park Hospital was, as yet, unbuilt. The grey areas depicting houses and other buildings show the distinct nature of Flixton and Urmston, with the latter catching up the former in size but Flixton's population at the time was still some 600 greater than that of Urmston.

Stretford Road, which runs from St Clement's church towards Stretford, was called Gammershaw Lane until 1850, and then Front Urmston. Higher Road was called Back Urmston and this is shown on the 1830 map as 'Back Urmstone'. Moss Vale Road was originally known as Brook Lane and then Moss Road.

Davyhulme

The Manchester Ship Canal passes along the northern boundary of Davyhulme which, along with the four other hamlets of Crofts Bank, Bent Lanes, Dumplington and Bromyhurst, was constituted as a separate township under the provisions of the Local Government Act of 1894.

The three maps of Davyhulme above date from 1898, 1908 and 1936 and show a great deal of change within that brief thirty-eight-year period. The church of St Mary's, a mere eight years old, in the top right-hand corner of the 1898 map can be seen with Hey Head Farm just to the south. Careful scrutiny of the 1898 and 1908 maps shows very little change at all apart from the brickworks that has appeared on the 1908 map just to the north of the church on the other side of Davyhulme Road. But what a major development can be seen taking place just thirty years later with the construction of Park Hospital and a large housing estate to the south of St Mary's, which has swallowed up Hey Head Farm and Davyhulme Hall Farm. The railways had made Urmston, Flixton and Davyhulme dormitory towns and suburban sprawl was taking effect in a big way.

The 1898 Ordnance Survey map of Davyhulme.

The parish of Davyhulme was not established until 1890 with the completion of St Mary's church. Although it was three times the size of of Flixton and Urmston in area, the population only stood at 1,326 when the church of St Mary's was built.

Unfortunately Davyhulme is probably best known for the sewerage works constructed by Manchester Corporation in the late nineteenth century to reduce the amount of sewage deposited in the rivers around Manchester and to provide the town with an efficient disposal system. There had previously been no modern sewage system in Manchester and toilets were mostly ash pits needing emptying by hand. The construction of the sewage works enabled the introduction of flushing toilets. The location was due to Davyhulme being near to the canal and some distance from major residential areas. The works were opened in 1894 and the treatment was chemical precipitation and

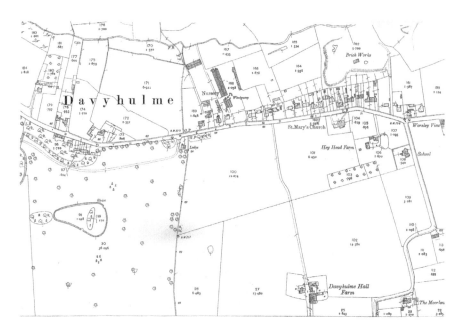

The 1908 Ordnance Survey map of Davyhulme.

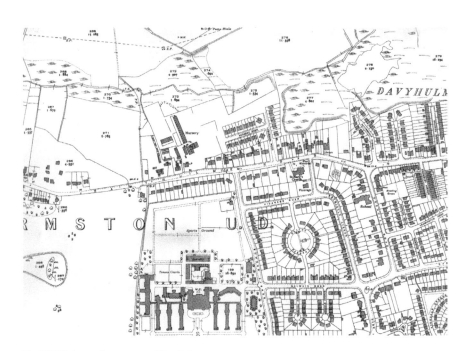

The 1936 Ordnance Survey map of Davyhulme.

land filtration. Additional sedimentation tanks and contact filter beds were installed in 1904. This enabled biological treatment of the settled sewage.

Urmston Hall

Urmston Old Hall was the home of the manorial lord and a centre of power in the area during the Middle Ages. The old hall was rebuilt in brick and timber in 1580 and inhabited by Adam de Ormeston, then by Richard, his son. In Volume 5 of *The History of The County of Lancaster* the hall is described as being 'a two-story timber and plaster building on a stone base. The principal front, which faces north, is entirely of wood and plaster under a single gable about 21ft. wide and on the east side are two timber gables with a good brick chimney between'. The description goes on to describe 'windows, each of seven lights' that had 'lost their original glazing'. Mention is also made of the quatrefoils (see photograph) being only painted on the plaster.

Urmston Old Hall. (Author)

During the reign of Henry IV (1399–1413), Adam had no male heir and so the lands passed into the Hyde family on his daughter's marriage to Ralph Hyde. Subsequently the lands passed to the Hulme family through marriage in 1642 and stayed in the family until 1765. Subsequent owners included Thomas Willis, a banker Mr Allen, Mr Marsden, and Mr Miller.

The hall was used as a farm from the mid nineteenth century, owned by the Ridehalgh family and tenanted and farmed by Jonathan Stott, then passing to the Bancroft family, who were farming the land at the turn of the century. The hall, a gabled timber and plaster Tudor building, decorated with lozenges and trefoils, was renovated in 1731. In 1790, the hall and lands were purchased by Samuel Taylor, who built Newcroft House in 1850. Newcroft House is still occupied and stands on Stretford Road not far from where the motorway crosses. The hall stood on what is now Manor Avenue between St Clement's church and Queen's Road and was demolished in 1937. Bricks and beams from the demolished hall were used in the building of a house at No.1 Carlton Crescent.

Newcroft Hall

Backtracking to 1219, Adam de Ormeston gave lands to Richard de Trafford of Trafford Hall who, it is thought, built Newcroft Hall.

Lawson tells us that one Richard Warburton lived here in 1397 before the hall was inhabited by Henry de Trafford and later by Sir John de Radcliffe of Ordsall. Sir John's descendants occupied the hall, including Richard, third son of Sir William Radcliffe, and it is this Richard, who died in 1602, who is celebrated on the brass plaque in Flixton parish church.

In August 1879, the estate, consisting of 79 acres, 1 rood and 35 perches, plus a church pew in Flixton church, was advertised for sale; it passed into the ownership of Samuel Taylor, who built Newcroft House in 1850.

In August 1888 Newcroft Hall was sold at auction for £4,000 subject to a yearly rent charge of 25s to be used for the education of children attending schools in Shawtown and a yearly rent of 2s 6d to be paid to the parson of Flixton church for a sermon. The provision for a pew at Flixton church was included in the price. There was also provision made for a 9d duchy rent and 2s 6d for the bellringers of Flixton church.

Newcroft Hall was situated where Newcroft Road lies, just opposite the Urmston public house. Dating from the thirteenth century, the original hall was surrounded by a moat, so Lawson tells us. The first recorded occupant of the hall was John de Trafford. He killed Gilbert of Ashton in a duel in a field called Barrowfield Bank behind Urmston Hall and buried his victim there and took the deeds of the manor.

Henry de Trafford was resident in 1334 and later his daughter Alice married William de Warburton and the estate passed into the Warburton family. Geoffrey de Warburton is recorded as living in the hall in 1389–90 and Richard de Warburton in 1397, after which came William de Warburton, who made a grant of some land in 1429–30 to his son on his marriage.

The Warburtons eventually moved to Arley Hall in Cheshire, after which Newcroft Hall came into the ownership of Sir John Radcliffe of Ordsal Hall in what is now Salford. Then came John's son Richard, who married Margaret, daughter of Sir Edmund Trafford of Trafford Park. Richard distinguished himself as a soldier. In 1579 his wife died and he married Margaret, daughter of John Radcliffe of Foxdenton Hall in Manchester. One of his daughters, Mary, was one of Queen Elizabeth's ladies of the bedchamber. It is this Richard, who died in 1602 aged 67, who is commemorated on the brass in Flixton church. His successor at the hall was Alexander Radcliffe. Alexander sold the hall to his half-brother William of Foxdenton Hall.

In 1662 the hall passed into the Rogers family; the Hume family acquired it next, but leased it to the Gregory family. William Allen then purchased the hall on 7 March 1765 but he later became bankrupt.

The Newcroft estate, together with a pew at Flixton church, 74 acres of land and subject to a payment of 20s for the education of poor children at Shaw Town School, 2s 6d yearly to the minister of Flixton church and 2s 6d yearly to the ringers of Flixton were put up for sale in 1789. Thus, on 23 June 1790, the hall and estate were purchased by the Taylor family from Hulme Hall, Reddish. It was about this time that the hall was rebuilt of plain brick of Georgian design and was said to have no architectural beauty whatsoever.

In 1888 the hall and estate passed into the hands of Herbert Bannister for £4,081. The Bannister family never occupied it and there then followed a series of tenants. The hall eventually fell into the hands of John, Edmund and James Chadwick, but on the death of James in 1871 and Edmund in 1877 the estate passed to John Taylor of Newcroft House.

The occupant at the 1891 census is shown as Edwin Bradshaw, a 43-year-old auctioneer from Hereford, and his wife of the same age, Elizabeth, originally from Manchester. They are shown as having three children: Daniel, aged 20,

Shaw Hall. (From Langton's *A History of Flixton, Urmston and Davyhulme*, 1898)

also an auctioneer; John, 18, a butcher; and Francis, 16, a clerk. Three servants are shown also: Thomas Alfred Lee, a 16-year-old farm servant from Nantwich; 16-year-old Mary Jane Frost, also from Nantwich and employed as a domestic servant; and 14-year-old Florence Gibson from Salford.

The hall was sold by Clifford George Bannister to the builders Longworth & Taylor on 3 January 1935 and later that year it was demolished to make way for a new housing estate.The name is memorialised in the estate containing Newcroft Road, Newcroft Crescent, Newcroft Drive and Acrefield Avenue. An interesting discovery was made when foundations for a garage were being built at No. 8 Newcroft Road in 1981; an old 20ft well.

Shaw Hall

According to Dr Leech in his article *Flixton and its Church*, Shaw Hall was built by Leonard Asshawe in the reign of James I. Other evidence supports 1603 as the date of the hall's construction. The Asshawe coat of arms, reflected in the

1942 arms, is 'argent on a chevron between three martlets vert as many crosses form fitchy of the field'.

The earliest known family resident at Shaw Town was the Valentines. Sir Ralph Valentine fought and was killed at the Battle of Bosworth Field on 22 August 1485 and, on setting out from home, is said to have remarked to his wife that he would return dead or alive. The official roll call of the battle as published by *The Richard III Foundation* shows that he fought on the side of Richard III.

Sir Ralph was slain in battle and his wish was for his body to be returned home; Lady Alice went out to meet the returning soldiers with her husband's remains. The legend runs as follows:

But o'er her form there ran
The tremor and chill of death
His face was all she saw
And sinking at his charger's feet
Died Alice of Asshawe!

Shaw Hall passed to the Asshawe family, who were related to the Valentines. On the death of the second Leonard Asshawe without male heirs, the estate passed to his daughter Elizabeth, who married Peter Egerton in 1611. Peter became High Sheriff of Lancashire in 1641 and he was on the Parliamentary side during the Civil War and played a part in the defence of Manchester when the Royalist forces marched on the city in 1642. He held many official positions locally and died on 22 May 1656. His death was recorded as a case of misadventure in that he suffered from distemper and took flour and brimstone as a medicine. His maid erroneously prepared a draught that included mercury. He was poisoned and died within hours.

The Egertons were resident at the hall until 1757. Leech comments on some of the fine aspects of the interior such as the windows, tapestries and painted ceilings; although evidence was never found, he also talks of the legend of an underground passage leading from the hall to the church, although parts of a causeway were discovered. This causeway was, in all probability, the remnants of a drain as the land was on a flood plain.

Leech also comments, with some humour, that the hall has 'more gables than an idle man would care to count on a sunny day'. Baines adds that the roof has a profusion of chimneys with a cupola removed in 1863. There were also gables and wooden parapets on the south-west and north sides.

In the early part of the nineteenth century the building was used as a school, first by Mrs Knubley, who ran a ladies' school, and then by Mr J. McDougall. Later, it was divided into two houses, one of which was occupied by Mr James Ridehalgh.

In Volume 5 of *The History of The County of Lancaster* mention is made of two pieces of tapestry in the upper rooms representing scenes from the life of Alexander and a painting on the cove of the hall ceiling representing the wife of Darius kneeling before Alexander, together with a smaller allegorical circular painting on the ceiling of the entrance porch to the north house. In his 1898 book, Richard Lawson tell us that the painting was 200 years old. Mention is also made of a good deal of seventeenth-century heraldic glass which had been removed. It depicted the coats of arms of the Asshawe and Egerton families. There was also once a moat adjoining the gardens.

The hall was demolished for an extended Shaw Hall housing estate in 1956 even after public opposition to the scheme. This was carried out by Maunders Construction.

Davyhulme Hall

Davyhulme Hall was originally built in 1154 and demolished in 1888. The image below is from 1850 and the grounds form part of what is now Davyhulme Golf Club.

The hall was the seat of the Hulme family, with John de Hulme resident during the reign of Henry II (1154–89).

The hall passed out of the Hulme family when the heiress Ann Hulme married Thomas Willis of Bleckley in 1735. The next owner was William Allen, a banker, who bought the estate in 1765. However, on Allen being declared bankrupt in 1789, the estate passed into the possession of Henry Norreys. On his death his estate was left to his daughter Mary and son-in-law Robert, who adopted the family arms and surname. Their son, Robert Henry Norreys, inherited the estate in 1844.

In 1887 Norreys died childless and his nephew, J.B. Norreys-Entwistle, inherited the estate. It was Mr Entwistle who donated land on which was built St Mary's church. In 1887 he appointed the Royal Institute of British Architects

Davyhulme Hall.

Below: Norreys' urn in the grounds of Davyhulme Hall, now Davyhulme golf course. (Author)

to organise a competition for the new church; eight architects competed for the commission, which was won by George Truefitt.

Davyhulme Hall was demolished in 1888 and the golf course now occupies the land. The large stone slab that served as the entrance to the hall can now be seen in the grounds of the church of St Mary The Virgin in Davyhulme.

There is still a huge ornamental stone urn, listed Grade II, visible from Moorside Road in the grounds of the golf course. The urn was erected as a memorial to one of the Norreys family's favourite racehorses, which is said to be buried beneath the urn. However, as it has been moved several times it cannot be said with certainty whether the horse is beneath its current location.

Very few ancient artefacts have been unearthed by archaeologists. One that deserves mention was uncovered by the South Trafford Archaeological Group in 1983; fragments of Roman pottery were found in what was Urmston Old Hall, now the site of Urmston cemetery. During construction of the Manchester Ship Canal in 1890, what were thought to be two prehistoric canoes were discovered in the bed of the River Mersey between Irlam and Barton. Also, a spearhead was found in the workings of the Irlam section of the Manchester Ship Canal, as mentioned in the *Transactions of the Lancashire and Cheshire Antiquarian Society* in 1895.

Langton mentions that a large stone celt – a type of early axe, 13in by 3.25in – was unearthed in Flixton, in an ancient bank of the Mersey, in 1846. It weighed 3lb 13.5oz. The celt had been discovered by workmen who sold it to Mr Charles Royle while he was taking gravel near Shaw Hall – presumably under the right of common of marl which; like rights of pasture, piscary, pannage; estovers and turbery as defined by the manorial courts, was a right of common enjoyed by the people.

Neolithic stone celt.

Three

FARMING

The open-field system was the predominant agricultural system in Europe during the Middle Ages and lasted, in many places, into the twentieth century. Under this system, each manor or village had two or three large fields, usually several hundred acres each, which were divided into many narrow strips of land. The strips were cultivated by individuals or peasant families, often called tenants or serfs. The fields of cultivated land were unfenced, hence the name *open*-field system. Each tenant of the manor cultivated several strips of land scattered around the manor.

The holdings of a manor also included woodland and pasture areas for common usage and fields belonging to the lord of the manor and the church. The farmers customarily lived in individual houses in a nucleated village with a much larger manor house and church nearby. The open-field system necessitated co-operation among the inhabitants of the manor.

The lord of the manor, his officials and a manorial court administered the manor and exercised jurisdiction over the peasantry. The lord levied rents and required the peasantry to work on his personal lands, called a demesne. In the Middle Ages, little land was owned outright; instead the lord had rights given him by the king, and the tenant rented land from the lord, who in turn demanded rents and labour from the tenants. These tenants had firm user rights to cropland and common land and those rights were passed down from generation to generation. However, tenants were not free to leave the land or follow another occupation unless a penalty was levied.

The open-field system was gradually replaced over several centuries by private ownership of land, especially after the fifteenth century, in the process known as enclosure. Enclosure had been used as early as the thirteenth century but this process of enclosing land accelerated in the fifteenth and sixteenth centuries and escalated further still during the eighteenth. This was the system of enclosing a number of small landholdings to create one larger farm.

Once enclosed, use of the land became restricted to the owner, and it ceased to be common land for communal use. It has been argued that rich landowners used their control of state processes to appropriate public land for their private benefit. The process of enclosure created a landless working class that provided the labour required in the new industries developing in the north of England.

The more productive enclosed farms meant that fewer farmers were needed to work the same land, leaving many villagers without land and grazing rights. The advent of machinery in the late nineteenth century had superseded much of the old skilled work, rendering such ancient skills as thatching, hedge laying and slashing, drain laying, mowing and shearing as lost arts. Furthermore, falling prices resulted in farmers economising in the use of farm labour; the neat appearance of their farms more or less suffered as a consequence.

The nineteenth century, and up to about 1918, was a period during which the lives of the working classes were dominated by the squire, who lived in his country house on the estate. Within the squire's circle was a system of affluence and leisure, while outside this privileged circle the small farmers, craftsmen and labourers of the village eked out a bare living. The squire exercised almost complete authority over his tenants in terms of punishments meted out for such misdemeanours as poaching, rent arrears and even non-attendance at church.

Many young men moved to the cities in search of work in the emerging factories of the Industrial Revolution. Ancient crafts such as the making of farm implements were compromised, as they could now be made much more quickly and cheaply due to mechanisation; the relentless progress of the machine at the expense of traditional methods and craftsmanship. There was, therefore, no point in young men learning these skills from their fathers so many would move to the cities to find work in the factories and mills. Boots and shoes too were able to be made at half the cost in the factories of Northamptonshire and so the shoemaker became virtually extinct. Others settled in the English colonies. English Poor Laws were enacted to help these newly created poor.

By the closing years of the nineteenth century men were becoming disillusioned with agricultural labouring jobs and were looking instead to opportunities offered in the city; jobs were available in factories, on the railways, building canals, on the docks and in the police force. Here they found higher wages, although poor accommodation counterbalanced this. Many failed to return to their rural roots, though, due to the greater social freedom experienced in the city.

When Queen Victoria ascended the throne in 1837 the majority of her subjects still lived in rural areas and were dependent for their livelihoods on agriculture with the attendant vagaries of of the temperamental seasons and harvest yields. Industrialisation was in its early stages, although developing quickly in the north of the country, but rural life and the village community still dominated English society. Farming was a way of life for many but rural crafts were also needed such as carpenters, wheelwrights, blacksmiths, coopers, saddlers, millers, thatchers and others who served the needs of the farmers, even craftsmen who made farming tools such as rakes, baskets, etc. The blacksmith particularly found his livelihood in jeopardy due to the new machine methods of producing the wares that he would have traditionally had a monopoly on, such as making the ironwork for the wheelwright's carts and waggons, making chisels, hammers and other tools for the village carpenters and the making and mending of a whole host of farming implements such as ploughs, mowing machines and harrows as well as farming tools such as hoes, spades, shovels, mattocks, axes, scythes and similar edged tools. Like the blacksmith, the saddler and the wheelwright were closely involved in farming life; the saddler made the harnesses needed by the horses for the various tasks of carting, pulling and ploughing.

Urmston Meadows. (Author)

In carrying out the tilling and cultivation of the soil, the harvesting of the crops and the raising of livestock, all these members of a tight-knit rural society would be mutually dependent on each other and co-operation would be the keyword to ensure the existence of themselves and their livelihoods. The very nature of farming was one of intense labour, and the whole village would turn out to ensure the bringing in of the harvest, which also depeded on on itinerant workers. Thomas Hardy reflects many country practices and customs of the time in his novels, and *Far From The Madding Crowd* (1874) includes a scene with Sergeant Troy helping out at harvest time, which he had done regularly over the years. This mutual dependence of the village community often gave rise to a parochialism that would even result in inter-village marriages being discouraged and frowned upon.

This depiction of a rural life of farming was how it must have looked in Urmston until the early nineteenth century, when weaving became a significant source of employment in the area. A study of the censuses from the latter half of the nineteenth century shows that the main employment was from these

A Flixton byway. (Bob Potts)

two occupations. In fact the growing of produce was essentially for personal consumption, with very little being made available for open sale. The average size of a farm was 30 acres; this generally consisted of meadow, pasture and arable land, and many farmers owned cottages which they would rent to the handloom weavers.

Some of the many farms in the area included Glebe Farm, where Parker's garden centre in Flixton is now situated; Bethell's Farm, dating from the eighteenth century, where Davyhulme Circle is now; Day's Farm, close to the Hulme Ferry; Guy's Poultry Farm, dating from 1717, on Bent Lanes; Stickings Farm, dating from 1723, also on Bent Lanes; Ye Old Farm, again on Bent Lanes; Boat Lane Farm, dated to 1830; Whitehead's Farm on Brooklyn Avenue; the eighteenth-century Gorse Hill Farm; Chassen Farm, the earliest date being from 1848; Little Barn Farm, the only mention of which is in the 1881 census; Brook House Farm on Crofts Bank; and Whitegate Farm on Davyhulme Road. Lime Tree Farm is where Churchgate is today; Acreage Farm, consisting of some 60 acres, was originally built in 1869; Willows Farm, Tanhouse Farm and Towngate Farm were in Flixton, as was Warburton Wall Farm. Newcroft Farm and Hillam Farm were in Urmston, as was Auburn Lodge Farm. Rudyard Farm was behind The Nags Head in Davyhulme; Davyhulme Hall Farm was near Moorside Road. Other farms in Davyhulme were Croft Hall Farm on Barton Road, Fold Farm on Davyhulme Road, Moss Farm on Redcliffe Road and Bromyhurst Farm, which was demolished as recently as the late 1990s to make way for the Trafford Centre. Shaw Hey Farm in Flixton still survives.

One interesting farm was Acreage Farm, adjacent to the Bottoms footpath, and now the municipal golf course. This farm had the only known example of ridge and furrow ploughing in Flixton. The 1843 Tithe Map shows that a field named Push Plough Field exactly covered the land with the ridge and furrow remains. These remains were levelled to create the golf course.

We can place some of the inhabitants of various farms. The 1901 census return for Upton's Farm on Irlam Road has widower James Upton still recorded as 'farmer' at the age of 79; his 37-year-old daughter is the only other resident. Also on Irlam Road was Brown's Farm, where John Brown (67) is recorded as 'farmer' with his wife Sarah (61). De Brook Farm is recorded in the 1901 census with farmer John Johnson (54) and his wife Francis (54) accompanied by three children and two servants.

The 1911 census shows Mrs Alice Whittam as head of the household of Newcroft Hall Farm on Stretford Road in Urmston. By then she was a 75-year-old widow, but the business of cattle dealer was carried on by her single 54-year-old son John and her 51-year-old married son William, whose wife, Dublin-born 40-year-old Julia, was also resident. Two servants are also shown; Eliya Jane Wilson (22) and Margaret Ellen Shaw (23). Hillam farm, also on Stretford Road, was a working farm in 1911 with Harry Steel (44) and his wife Hannah (45) in residence. There was also a cottage associated with the farm and this was occupied by farm labourer Henry Pimlott (43) and his wife Emily (33).

The holder of a rather unsavoury job was the manager of the sewage works, who lived at Sewage Farm House on Stretford Road. In 1911 this honour went to Joseph Edmondson (56) whose occupation is described as 'Sewage Wks Manager' and he was employed by Manchester City Council. His wife Emily (46) from Penzance in Cornwall was also resident along with three children. A separate census entry for this address shows Harry Graves (40) as a sewage farm labourer. His wife Jane (44) is also shown along with their four children.

Croft Farm on Stretford Road operated as a dairy farm in 1911 with John Martin (39) and his wife Sarah (38) and their four children resident. Poultryman Edward Dyer (23) is also recorded as a servant.

Large industry became competition for farmers, which also resulted in a decline in weaving as a source of employment. In 1848 the population was recorded as being 771, at a time when 80 per cent of the land was recorded as farming land. The opening of the Cheshire Lines Railway in 1873 resulted in Urmston changing its status to more of a commuter town; between 1871 and 1901 the population grew by over 650 per cent, from 996 to 6,594. It has to be borne in mind that the 1851 census proved that, nationally speaking, more people were now resident in urban rather than rural areas. Consequently, farming had virtually died out in Urmston by 1901 as the town had now become a residential area for the middle classes. Furthermore, more housing was now needed to accommodate the newly growing population and it seems that the Flixton residents were less willing to give up land for development than the Urmstonians, which was part of the reason for the population of Urmston finally outstripping that of Flixton by the census of 1881.

It also has to be borne in mind that the Industrial Revolution propelled the nearby city of Manchester on to the centre stage of world history. This industrialisation, made manifest by the rise of machine-powered industries harnessing the power of steam, mainly in the cotton industry, in turn gave rise to urban growth and the creation of the 'suburb'; the suburb to which workers could escape from their place of work. Urban growth had escalated dramatically;

between 1801 and 1841 the population of Manchester had trebled and by 1851 it was over four times larger than it had been fifty years earlier. The suburb was the answer to this population growth, and what had been sleepy agricultural villages and hamlets such as Urmston, Flixton and Davyhulme now had to accommodate an influx of workers demanding homes.

Indicative of the growth of population at the turn of the century is a postcard showing Station Road in Urmston sent to Miss Mary Watson in Bedford on 28 February 1909, which states, 'Does this view look familiar? You would hardly know Urmston now, it has grown so large.' It is signed 'Amy'.

Langton mentions a large array of flora and fauna in the area and birds seen at the time included rook, greenfinch, chaffinch, sallow, house martin, sand martin, swift, blue titmouse, thrush, blackbird, house and hedge sparrow, yellow bunting, meadow pipit, tree pipit, starling, robin, whitethroat and skylark. These he describes as plentiful; lesser-seen birds included the linnet, wren, fieldfare, partridge, cuckoo, lapwing, redwing and, surprisingly, the now ubiquitous magpie.

Langton also goes on to comment that the Mersey once teemed with fish but at the end of the nineteenth century they had all been poisoned due to the foul water pumped into the river from the factories, and the sewage.

EMPLOYMENT

Before the dawn of the industrial age, when villages were very much insular and self-sufficient, people worked the land and caught fish in the nearby Irwell and Mersey as there was no means of transport to take them to the nearest towns, and no shops at which to buy food. In later times employment was to be found in the mills that sprang up along the Irwell and also at handloom weaving.

Lawson tells us that 'Flixton and Urmston have always had a reputation for weaving', and just about every cottage had a handloom in the back. Langton adds that there would be up to four looms in the cottage loom-shed. Indeed, it was common for the farmer to carry out dual employment with the income from farming and weaving contributing to his livelihood.

The work would have come from a manufacturer in Manchester where waggons would come from time to time to deliver the warp and weft to the weavers; the waggons returned later to collect the completed work, known as 'Manchester gold'. Lawson tells us that the weaver's remuneration was 'scanty'.

The Industrial Revolution, while improving the lot of the entrepreneur and offering work to many, offered opportunities to these weavers working in solitude in their cottages, but it greatly reduced – and even stopped altogether – their independence. Consequently, the increased use of machinery in the Lancashire cotton mills drove the Flixton weavers to near-extinction. Kay's flying shuttle (1738), Wyatt and Paul's spinning rollers (1739), Hargreaves's spinning jenny (1764) and Arkwright's drawing rollers (1765) all contributed to the beginnings of automisation and the factory system. Samuel Crompton's spinning mule (1779) was the invention that was, perhaps, the most significant to sweep across the region and thereby hammer the final nail in the coffin of the handloom weaver working independently in his cottage. The power loom, invented and patented by Edmund Cartwright, (1785, with subsequent patents for improved designs) further consigned the manual weaver to the scrapheap of history.

Abraham Johnson, blacksmith to Sir Humphrey de Trafford, pictured here with his wife Emma, *c*. 1890.

To continue in employment, the Flixton weaver would now have to travel on foot to obtain his materials from Manchester and then walk all the seven or so miles back to return his finished cloth. The only alternative would have been to starve; the wages also decreased. Some left the area while others took on employment at Stott's mill in Flixton. Langton tells us that the last of the handloom weavers in Flixton was Samuel Bent, who worked his loom opposite The Bird in Hand public house.

It is interesting to note here that the changing face of the agricultural and industrial landscape in the nineteenth century and the effects on the population, especially the working classes, was reflected in and commented on by ballad writers of the day. Songs were written about the railways, the canal navigators, the coal industry, road building, ship building and, of course, handloom weaving. The decline in the fortunes of the handloom weavers is reflected in this song published in *Ballads and Songs of Lancashire*, collected, compiled and edited by John Harland and T.T. Wilkinson in 1882; they state that the song was 'of a transitional era in weaving' and was 'sung by John Grimshaw of Gorton near Manchester'.

HAND-LOOM v. POWER LOOM

Come all you cotton-weavers, your looms you may pull down;
You must get employ'd in factories, in country or in town,
For our new cotton masters have found out a wonderful new scheme,
These calico goods now wove by hand they're going to weave by steam.

In comes the gruff o'erlooker, or the master will attend;
It's 'You must find another shop, or quickly you must mend;
For such work as this will never do; so now I'll tell you plain,
We must have good pincop-spinning, or we n'er can weave by steam.'

There's sow-makers and dressers, and some are making warps;
These poor pincop-spinners they must mind their flats and sharps,
For if an end slips under, as sometimes perchance it may,
They'll daub you down in black and white, and you've a shilling to pay.

In comes the surly winder, her cops they are all marr'd;
'They are all snarls, and soft, bad ends; for I've roved off many a yard;
I'm sure I'll tell the master, or the joss when he comes in:'
They'll daub you down, and you must pay; – so money comes rolling in.

The weavers' turn will next come on, for they must not escape,
To enlarge the master's fortunes they are fined in every shape.
For thin places or bad edges, a go, or else a float.
They'll daub you down, and you must pay threepence, or else a groat.

If you go into a loom-shop, where there's three or four pair of looms,
They are all standing empty, encumbrances of the rooms;
And if you ask the reason why, the old mother will tell you plain,
My daughters have forsaken them, and gone to weave by steam.

So, come all you cotton-weavers, you must rise up very soon,
For you must work in factories from morning until noon:
You mustn't walk in your garden for two or three hours a-day,
For you must stand at their command, and keep your shuttles in play.

The last two verses are particularly significant in showing how the advent of steam looms had completely taken away the independence and dignity of the handloom weaver, once very much a part of Flixton livelihood. Perhaps this song was sung in the pubs in the area.

A study of the census of population returns is revealing, showing that Flixton and Urmston were very much rural townships: employment was of a predominantly rural nature, with very few non-manual jobs, until the coming of mechanisation and industrialisation at the end of the nineteenth century. Most people worked as farm labourers or handloom weavers. The 1851 census, for instance, shows Thomas Ramsdale, a 53-year-old lock tenter living at Lock House in Flixton. He had a 52-year-old wife, Betty, and daughters Ann, aged 24; Charlotte, aged 23; Mary, aged 21; Ellen, aged 20; Martha, aged 18; and Betty, aged 16 – all were born and bred in Flixton and all were employed as 'handloom weaver cotton'. Thomas and Betty had a large family as the census also mentions another daughter, Alice (14), who was a winder and a son Thomas, aged 12, a scholar.

Many more handloom weavers are recorded in Boat Lane (now Irlam Road), Green Lane, Penny Lane, Smithy Lane and Gails Brow, to mention just a few places. Workers were recorded as still working in their seventies, such as Joseph Howard of Boat Lane, who was 76 and still a handloom weaver.

The weaving mill owned by James and Adam Stott of Shaw Town in Flixton was built in 1851 and was situated opposite where Flixton High School for Girls is now. At the time of writing his *A History of the Parish of Flixton* in 1898, Langton tells us that there were 240 employees working at the mill, but later the workforce grew to almost 400 men and women. A 300ft well served the mill, along with four reservoirs.

The 1861 census shows that Adam Stott was 29 years old at the time of the enumeration, and that his wife Sarah was from Salford. The census is annotated that he was an 'employer of upward of 200 hands'. The Stott family were well known in the area, and six brothers in all were born between 1816 and 1833. John Stott was landlord at The Greyhound, Adam Stott built Wibbersley and James Stott built Abbotsfield. Stott's mill manufactured shirtings, nankeens, jeans, coutils and ticks, and also carried out bleaching, dyeing and finishing as well as, of course, weaving.

Although the trend was for populations to increase over time, the forty-year period from 1821 to 1861 saw the population of Flixton reduce from 1,604 to 1,302.

The *Manchester Courier and Lancashire General Advertiser* of 11 June 1886 covered the funeral of Adam Stott at Flixton and reported as follows: 'The remains of the late Major Adam Stott of Wibberley, Irlam Road, Flixton were interred yesterday in Flixton Parish Churchyard.' The report included a long list of mourners and pall bearers. It is also mentioned that the 4th Battalion LRV band played the 'Dead March'.

The same newspaper reported on the death of John Stott of Well Acre, Irlam Road, Flixton. He was described as a 'prominent member of the Conservative Party'. He was also 'noted far and near for his large-heartedness and the poor and the Church were the constant objects of his liberality'. He was also described as 'genial and full of dry humour [and he] occasionally made opponents – but never enemies'. John Stott had died on Wednesday, 17 December 1902, and the newspaper reported that the funeral was to take place at St Michael's, Flixton the following Monday.

John Stott was described as a bachelor of 69 years of age who was a member of the firm of Messrs J. and A. Stott, manufacturers. The obituary goes on to pay testament to the feelings of and his altruism towards his workforce, in that he was 'highly esteemed by the operatives [and] he provided reading rooms, a swimming bath [situated near The Bird i'th Hand public house and now demolished], and other means of recreation'.

An interesting footnote to these chapters about the Stotts is that the granddaughter of John Stott, Barbara Barker, nee Stott and licensee of The Greyhound public house in the early 1900s, commented in 1987 in a conversation with local historian Bob Potts that the first Stott to settle in Flixton was a fugitive from Bonnie Prince Charlie's army in 1745.

The mill was demolished in 1936, with the rubble being used for the foundations of the construction of Bowfell Road. Abbotsford School now occupies the site. A 1936 newspaper shows a photograph of the demolition in progress.

As the nineteenth century was drawing to a close, a greater variety of occupations was seen. The census returns of 1881 show that there were still many agricultural labourers and some cotton weavers and mill hands, but other trades and occupations included farmer, gardener, landscape gardener, market gardener, fruit salesman, shopkeeper, baker, grocer, brickmaker, bricklayer, wheelwright, blacksmith, general labourer, signwriter, joiner, coachman, tailor, seamstress, draper, bleacher and dyer, stone mason, plumber, basket maker, packer (warehouse), willow merchant, chemist, confectioner, banker's clerk, block printer, beer house keeper, bookseller, insurance agent, restaurant manager, railway excavator, railway clerk, accountant, charwoman, general domestic servant, lock keeper and boatman.

These latter two occupations refer to lock keeper John Ravenscroft, originally from Runcorn and 59 years of age at the time of the census and living in Flixton. He was married to Mary Ann, 54, who was originally from Dublin. Their son William Henry, aged 28, was the boatman. Ellen, William's wife and originally from Warrington, was 27 and a housekeeper. William and Ellen's two children were Thomas, aged 3, and Frederick, aged 12 months.

An interesting entry in the 1881 census is that of wheelwright William Lowe, aged 28, who lived in Flixton with his wife Elizabeth, aged 26, and their two children – Arthur, aged 2, and Edith Alice, who was 10 months old. The house-

Irlam Ferry.

hold included lodger William Unsworth, 65, whose trade wass stated to be a blacksmith; another lodger, John Holland, aged 23, was a carter. It is just about certain that the three men would have benefitted each other with their respective trades as William Unsworth would have more than likely made the iron bands for the wheels made by William Lowe and carter John may also have used the skills of the two Williams on his carts and waggons. National evidence also points to these crafts being closely associated.

While young girls would be entering a career of domestic service, the boys would be seeking an apprenticeship in one of the traditional village crafts. A young male apprentice would first have to learn the tools of his trade. An apprentice wheelwright would have to learn how to use saws and planes and after the first year or two would be able to make and paint a wheelbarrow before progressing on to wheels for carts and waggons as well as barrels and barley rollers. Meanwhile, the apprentice blacksmith would likewise have to become familiar with his tools and how to use them.

The smithy was often one of the social hubs of the village, where the blacksmith would enter into social intercourse with passing locals. The role of the blacksmith was varied in that he would be expected to repair a host of implements as well as shoeing horses, making hoes, sickles and scythes as well as plough shares. The young apprentice blacksmith would often be asked to lift the anvil as a show of his ability, as the trade required great physical strength.

It is interesting to note that, even at this late date of 1881, some thirty years after the 1851 census which showed that England was now a less rural and a more urban country, the vast majority of occupations still consisted of the manual trades. In spite of industrialisation, the Urmston area was still predominantly rural in nature. Chemist, clerk, bookseller and insurance agent appear to be the only non-manual occupations in 1851.

Nonetheless, at the end of the nineteenth century these old trades were being undermined by the advances of technology. In addition to the blacksmith and wheelwright, the tailor and shoemaker were being threatened by the competition of mass-produced, machine-made clothing and boots.

A wider spectrum of occupations was now being seen and the 1891 census for Flixton shows callings which include cabinet maker, shippers' clerk, bank clerk, teacher, professional nurse, certificated midwife, milliner, mill hand, wire drawer, bricklayer, paper hanger, basket maker, cashier, bleacher (cotton), grocer's assistant, office cleaner, gardener, dressmaker, warehouseman, sailor, police constable, painter, winder in cotton mill, basket maker, machinist as well as the long established farmer and agricultural labourer. The recent advent of the railways was reflected in the occupations of railway engine driver, railway engine stoker, platelayer and railway signalman. Furthermore, construction on the Manchester Ship Canal commenced in November 1887 with the canal filled on 25 November 1893, opening to traffic to Manchester on 1 January 1894, and the formal opening by Queen Victoria the following May. Consequently, a number of excavators and navvies appear in the 1891 census.

The navvies worked long hours and would live in purpose-built villages nearby. Over 16,000 men and boys worked on the canal's construction. The work was dangerous, giving rise to a series of first aid stations and three hospitals being placed along the route. Between 1888 and 1893 there were over 3,000 serious accidents.

One occupation, not as yet mentioned, is that of Frederick Hawker, a 42-year-old pianoforte tuner and repairer from Gloucestershire who lived in Park View with his 41-year-old wife and six children including 10-year-old Albert, who is also described as a piano tuner even at this tender age. No doubt Frederick and Albert would cater for the pianofortes that would be gracing the drawing rooms of the newly built villas along Crofts Bank Road and Church Road.

Also mentioned in the 1891 census living at Atherton Cottage with his four children is 74-year-old Parisian and widower Victor E.A. Chevalier, a professor of the French language. Another interesting occupation is that of lithographic artist. This was the occupation of 41-year-old John H. Hough from Cheddleton in Staffordshire. He lived with his 42-year-old wife Esther and 13-year-old daughter Mary at Whitelake View.

The last census we have access to, due to the 100-year restriction, is 1911, and we see from this that occupations included a variety of roles in the retail trade such as shop assistant, grocer, hairdresser, milliner, draper and outfitter, tobacconist, baker and butcher. Office jobs included sorting clerk, insurance clerk, shorthand typist, telephonist, shop manageress, bank cashier and furniture broker. The professions are represented by solicitors, surgeons and those in management, no doubt occupying the grand houses being built along Crofts Bank Road and Chuch Road, many by Spark the builder, who also built Urmston Cottage Hospital and the tower of St Clement's church.

An interesting addition to the 1911 census is the Holland family, comprising Thomas and his wife Amelia, both aged 24, described as 'assistant to travelling showman and roundabout proprietor' and living in a caravan off Flixton Road. They are married and have a daughter Gladys, aged 2, and a son aged 9 months. Thomas's place of birth is Pomona Gardens near Manchester and Amelia's is Stone, Staffordshire. William Harry Williams and his wife Sarah, both 25, are also resident at a caravan off Flixton Road and their occupations are stated to be 'stall keeper at fair grounds'. Other families are also recorded with the same address and occupations such as those mentioned as well as 'labourer for travelling showman' and the boss himself, George Clarke (48) from Norwich, described as 'travelling showman' with his wife Ellen (40) and daughter (17), both of whom are described as 'assisting with the business'.

An intriguing entry is that of calico print designer James Thomas Heaton (48) and family living on Queen's Road. The entry is annotated 'I have a daughter (Florence) 22 years, born at Chadderton employed in Paris, France as a fashion designer.'

Other miscellaneous occupations in 1911 included corn merchant, furniture designer, school mistress, music teacher, silver engraver, plumber, electrician, timber merchant, commercial traveller, leather merchant, pig salesman, traffic canvasser with the Manchester Ship Canal Company, and, of course, the domestic servants that were still needed to serve both the wealthy and small businessmen alike.

The railway had opened Urmston up as a dormitory town and as a desirable residential district for people with a wealth of occupations and, of course, the new residents would need not only retail outlets but also plumbers and electricians to serve the newly built villas. Indeed, the opening of the railway in Urmston and Flixton, not unnaturally, saw an increase in railway jobs among the population of Urmston and Flixton.

The increase in the occupation of clerks is an interesting point. Not only was there expansion in the manufacturing industries but also in other sectors including retail distribution, banking and insurance, as can be seen from the census returns in the late nineteenth century in Urmston; the 1862 Companies Act created a need for accountants, lawyers and other experts. Therefore the demand for clerks was such that the national figure saw a 273 per cent increase between 1841 and 1881.

Domestic service

For as long as there have been rich and poor in society there have been domestic servants to minister to the wants and needs of the well-to-do. In medieval society the best chance to obtain comfort and security would be to secure a position as a servant in the household of a noble or rich family.

As for the servants themselves, the individual was given much guidance as how to conduct themselves. *The Young Servant's Own Book*, published in 1883, was one such guide which, among other things, warned against excessive eating and drinking:

> Eating too much is bad for your health and drinking too much leads to misery. I do not think it wise for young servant girls to accustom themselves to strong tea, with a great deal of sugar; for, after a while, should they have to buy for themselves, they will find it very expensive to do so.

In other words, it was very much recommended that one knew one's position in the social hierarchy and that ideas above one's station were very much to be discouraged.

The famous *Mrs Beeton's Cookery and Household Management,* originally published in 1861, contains a section on domestic servants and their duties and, in addition to giving advice to the lady of the house on hiring her staff,

Mrs Beeton sets out the duties of such roles as housekeeper, cook, general manservant, nanny, governess, lady's maid, footman, chauffeur and butler as well as for temporary, freelance and casual staff.

The Servant's Behaviour Book was another publication advising young girls of the etiquette required when employed as a domestic servant, such as how to act and speak in the presence of her employers. Similarly, *A Few Rules for the Manners of Servants in Good Families,* issued by The Ladies' Sanitary Association in 1901, contained over twenty pages of Dos and Don'ts. The sobering reminder that 'had God seen that it would have been better for your external good that you should be great and rich He would have made you so; but He gives to all the places and duties best fitted for them' was included in the publication *Advice to Young Women on Going in to Service* issued in 1835 by *The Society for Promoting Christian Knowledge.*

During the period 1850 to 1900 domestic service employed more women and girls than any other single occupation nationwide. The 1891 census showed that in England and Wales there were nearly 1.4 million female servants, of whom 107,167 were in the age range 10–14 years of age inclusive. By contrast, male servants numbered only a little over 58,500, of whom 6,891 were under the age of 15.

Once a girl was at the end of her schooling, her mother would seek a place in service for her. It goes without saying that the wealthy and people in the professions employed servants covering a range of duties; this is illustrated by the 1911 census entry for Henry Charles David Scott (46), who was a director of a company making engineering specialities. He lived with his wife Rachel (47) at 'Arrandale', Crofts Bank Road. He had five children and employed Clara Naomi Millard, a 16-year-old general domestic servant.

Dr George Ernest Fryer, a 47-year-old physician and bachelor, employed 45-year-old housekeeper Francis Binks in his home on 25 Crofts Bank Road. He was later to live at 'Arrandale' and bequeathed his home and lands 'for the good of Urmston'. The house and land is now the site of the Golden Hill War Memorial. A stone in memory of George Ernest Fryer once stood at the edge of the park and is now in private hands. He was Medical Officer of Health in Urmston from 1838 to 1929.

Doctor of medicine Richard Barnes (47), originally from Cooktown, Co. Tyrone in Ireland, is registered with his wife Ethel (28) and four children together with Annie Bardwell (19) from Hereford, employed as governess, Agnes Dolan (39) from Kingstown, Co. Dublin, cook and domestic servant, and Edith Thatcher (18) from Lincoln, domestic servant. The household lived at The Firs, Urmston.

John Edwin Collier (50) was in the leather trade and lived at Kent Villa, Crofts Bank Road on the night of the 1911 census with his wife Ann (44) and 8-year-old son George. They employed Elsie Hurst (23) from Middlewich, Cheshire, as a domestic servant. 34-year-old timber merchant William Vernon Blake lived at 'Inglewood', Crofts Bank Road in 1911 and, in addition to his wife Lucy (33) and three children, 22-year-old Margaret Walsh is also shown as resident as a domestic servant.

Another named house on Crofts Bank Road was 'Alliston', and living here on the night of the 1911 census was surgeon Thomas Wolstenholme (30) with his wife Susan (31) and 3-year-old son John. Spinster 19-year-old Hilda Haycocks was employed as a housemaid (domestic). 'Woollhara' was another house on Crofts Bank Road and this was the residence in 1911 of building contractor George Morton (48), who lived there with his wife Sarah (also 48) and two children. Dora May Lloyd (18) was their domestic servant. 'Rosebank' was the home of 57-year-old retired builder Gideon Cooke and his wife and three children. Ester Ann Aspinall (44) was employed as a domestic servant.

Gloucester House, on the corner of Gloucester Road and Station Road, built in 1880 by the Mayne family, is still a doctor's surgery to this day and, indeed, the practice was the surgery of my childhood doctors, Dr Tennant, Dr Campbell and Dr McCormick. Back in 1911 surgeon Walter Furlong Mayne (58) was registered with his widowed mother Mary Ann Grace Mayne (82). Domestic servant Evelyn Weaver (23) was registered at the address as a general domestic servant. She was originally from Montgomery. The first doctor practising here was Dr Walter F. Mayne, who practised for some fifty years. He left Urmston in 1927.

The 1911 census also shows The College on Urmston Lane, recording 'principal of private school' widow Elizabeth Elide (52) with her staff of four teachers and two student teachers described as 'servants'. Five students are recorded as boarders and a domestic staff comprises Bessie Bates (40) from London as a cook and domestic, Catherine Jones (26) from Liverpool as housemaid and domestic and Selina Holroyd (28) from Warrington as housemaid and domestic.

Servants were often well looked after by their employers, although their duties were physically demanding and the hours long; they rose as early as 5.30 a.m. and retired at 9.30 p.m. Accommodation was often basic also. Furthermore, at the end of the nineteenth century the most generous holiday would be a fortnight during the summer, one day off monthly and half a day on Sundays. Servants would also be required to attend family prayers and service on Sundays, where the seating in church would observe a strict hierarchy. There was also the requirement to be 'neatly and plainly dressed', often facing the ordeal of an inspection by their employer before setting off for church.

Food would be plentiful, although wages were low. At the end of the nineteenth century a female servant under 16 would receive an average annual wage of £6 and 10s rising to £7 and 14s on reaching her sixteenth birthday. An under-16 kitchen maid would receive £5 and 18s and a housemaid £8.

Families with social pretensions in the nineteenth century would have seen it as indispensable to have at least one domestic servant, even if this meant recruiting a young girl from the local workhouse at a wage of 1s a week. This was what William Marsden, in his *Education and the Social Geography of Nineteenth-Century Towns and Cities*, called 'a compulsive, individualistic quest to to achieve or preserve status'.

Indeed, girls whose lot in life was poor due to circumstances often beyond their control, such as the absence of a father and a mother whose dire financial situation had led her into prostitution, were taken into one of the industrial schools in Manchester until they were 16 and trained in the basic duties of the domestic servant; this was often the only form of employment open to them. Boys in similar circumstances would be taken and trained in crafts such as blacksmithing, saddlery, bootmaking, etc.

The number of servants one employed acted as a rough guide to one's status within the ranks of the socially superior. Indeed, those who kept servants varied widely in both social position, occupation and income. The 1881 census in Urmston shows cotton print salesman Thomas Makin, aged 42, married with six children aged from 2 to 14 years old. Even with the expense that such a large family would have entailed he still employed Emma, a 15-year-old girl from north Cheshire, as a domestic servant.

In other returns from the same census, 18-year-old Elizabeth Carrol from Kildare in Ireland was employed as a servant by 48-year-old Eliza Beswick, who was a grocer and lived with her brother Michael Devine; apprentice butcher John Burgess employed 20-year-old Teresa Sponge as a domestic servant; draper William Walker employed 19-year-old Heskia similarly; tailor and hardware dealer Thomas Gillmore, aged 62, employed 16-year-old Ann Atherton from Suffolk. Frederick Perkins, described as an agent to a linen manufacturer, employed 18-year-old Emma Serris from Hereford as a domestic servant. Peter Kelly, 35, was a bookstore dealer with a wife and four children as well as his 62-year-old father in the household but even he is shown as employing five men, one woman, and one girl in the shop plus Alice Dunbarand, a 21-year-old domestic servant.

In 1911 baker Frederick Royle, aged 44, lived at Oakleigh, Crofts Bank Road with his wife and two children and could afford to employ Lily Kinsey (18) as a housemaid and Marian Latham (17) as a kitchen maid. Widower William Main, aged 50, whose occupation is shown as 'maker up and packer', lived at The Elms, also on Crofts Bank Road, with his two children and two servants; Elizabeth Meeson (38), cook and domestic servant and Emily Dean (25), housemaid. Fred Greenwood, (35) a civil engineer with the Manchester Ship Canal Company, and his wife Agnes (45) lived at Laurel Bank and employed Elizabeth Shaw (22) as a general domestic servant; Elizabeth hailed from Runcorn.

So, it can be seen that not only were those of modest occupations keen to take on domestic servants to preserve their status in the community, but that young girls came from various regions of the country and even from Wales and Ireland to take up their duties.

Case Study 1: Simpson Ready Foods

One of Urmston's largest employers for over 100 years was Simpson Ready Foods, a firm started in 1910 by William Simpson.

Born in Droylsden in 1861, William Simpson hailed from humble origins. The son of a handloom/silk weaver, his mother was illiterate and signed her name with a cross on his birth certificate. William was a cobbler's boy before securing a position in the grocery trade. He progressed quickly and was a branch manager at the age of 23. Through his meticulous work experimenting with preservation techniques and different ingredients, William founded and became manager and secretary of the Co-operative Sundries Manufacturing Society, Droylsden, in 1884. The rules were based on those of the well-known co-operative movement. In 1904 he joined Sutcliffe and Bingham as a managing director, investing £1,600, and received an annual salary of £300 plus 5 per cent of the business he generated. He was 51 years of age when he left this firm, having served seven years with them. By the time he was in his forties, William was a widower and in 1910 he married a young widow, Gertrude Rayner; together they decided to set up their own manufacturing business.

The site of the present-day factory was originally a private house built by James Howard Parkinson, a dental surgeon, who had his business premises

William Simpson. (William Simpson)

Link House from the orchard. The chimney, built by Sparks, shows the letter S for Simpsons. (Author)

in Mosely Street in Manchester. On 3 May 1889 Parkinson bought two fields called Smithfields and Gamester Field for £1,175 from John Taylor of Newcroft House. The house, named Link House, was built the same year with stables, a coach house, an orchard and a large sunken garden with poplar trees on the front of the road. These trees would be cut down when Stretford Road was widened in 1939. There was also a pond further back in the grounds.

Lemocreme vans. (William Simpson)

The 1891 census shows that 41-year-old James H. Parkinson was resident with his 3-year-old son Willie. There is no mention of a wife. Also resident were 67-year-old servant and domestic groom John Chatterton as well as 38-year-old housekeeper Sarah Chatterton and 22-year-old servant Emily Humphries. Parkinson died on 13 June 1894.

Daniel Bradshaw (30) with his wife Mary (26) plus two children and a domestic servant moved from Newcroft Hall and lived in the house until 1906, when he went to live at Derby House, Derbyshire Lane, Stretford. James Yapp then came to live at Link House but he was only in residence for four years.

Link House was acquired by William Simpson – then aged 49 – and his wife in 1910, to start their own business, which was established the following year. The 1911 census shows 50-year-old William with his wife Gertrude, aged 35, as resident at Link House. William's mother-in-law, 70-year-old Mary Taylor, is also recorded, as are daughters Immy (24) and Florence (18), both telephonists

Labelling and packing jam in the 1920s. (William Simpson)

with the GPO. Six-month-old William is also recorded, as is Florence Fradley, a 15-year-old domestic servant.

The house was altered and enlarged to make what was called Links Works. The business was first called William Simpson (Manchester) Ltd. When William Simpson started the business on this land, part of the reason, according to the memories of one of the last partners in the business, William Simpson, grandson of the founder, was that there were plans to build a railway into the back of the factory where the allotment gardens are and alongside where Bradfield Road now runs. Those plans never came to fruition.

William and his wife Gertrude lived at their place of work for a while and their older son was born in the room currently serving as a director's office. They later moved to Oak Lea on Washway Road in Sale in October 1918 and commuted into the factory in a horse-drawn carriage. Link House itself then became the company's offices.

Perusal of the board minutes book shows that no time was lost in improving the factory. Minutes for 8 June 1918 show that it was 'resolved that a 5 bowl

Lemocreme jars. (Author)

lavatory washstand be affixed in the new jam works as stipulated by the factory inspector at a cost of £36'. It was also 'resolved that the job of flagging the new works be given to Messrs Spark for the sum of £56'. Also at the same meeting it was 'resolved that a Benns Mechanical Stoker be installed on the new boiler at a quoted price of £190'. And finally it was 'resolved that the job of building the new chimney be given to Messrs Spark at the sum of £250'.

Although William overcame his humble origins and became a wealthy man, he suffered financial difficulties in the early 1920s. This was partly through the effects of Excess Profits Duty (EPD), which in 1920 was levied at 60 per cent to help deal with the post-war economic crisis. William Simpson wrote to Hesketh & Co accountants in Manchester on 24 September 1923 to point out that his life's savings were all gone and complaining that 'to be compelled to pay this money would stultify my business, prevent it from ever raising its head and would penalise me in £1000 per year for the next six or seven years'. The original shareholders of the company included Simon and Ephraim Marks and Thomas Spencer (of Marks and Spencer). Their early involvement ended in 1917 when Simon went to fight in the First World War.

In those early years a range of products were produced including Lemocreme (lemon curd), mincemeat, jelly crystals and even temperance wines as well as Christmas pudding, which remained in production right up to the closure of the factory. A secret recipe for lemon curd was one of the company's earliest successes. Lemocreme, followed a little later by Lemocurd and Lemocheese, all became trademarks of the company. Pottery jars for lemon curd (designed for return and refilling) were unearthed during modern building work for the new pouch container facility.

The First World War brought sugar shortages and problems of preservation. The preservation of fruit without sugar became commonplace and William's notebooks are full of data and formulae on questions of preserving. During the Great War Simpsons acquired its first motor lorry, which had solid tyres. Prior to this most goods were transported to Urmston station by horse and cart and forwarded by rail. After the war William bought his first car, a Daimler.

The 1920s brought the introduction of many new products, including many confectionery lines such as piping jellies, specially sieved jams, bottled fruits, pastry flours and canned sweet puddings. The Goblin ever-ready pudding was launched in four sizes and eight flavours: sultana, lemon, currant, college, ginger, date, fig and Christmas pudding – 'one for every day of the week and two for Sundays'. Mrs Simpson is said to have had a dream which inspired the brand name Goblin, which has been used on many Simpsons products since 1929.

A growing workforce enjoyed factory days out by open-topped bus to places such as Blackpool and Wales. The factory became known as 'The Garden Factory' because there was a sunken garden and orchard on the site of the cannery built in the 1960s. The surrounding area was also relatively undeveloped. Annual Morris dancing displays were practised on the spacious lawns then surrounding the factory and performed at local fetes. These dances were performed by factory staff dressed in yellow to advertise Lemocreme.

Gertrude Simpson died suddenly on 14 February 1931. Two days later William also died, aged 70. Following the death of his parents, the young William Simpson, not yet 21, found himself guardian of his 12-year-old younger brother, winding up his parent's estate and running the day-to-day business of the factory. He was advised by the family doctor to sell the family home in Sale and move into a hotel until he was more established in his new role. The two brothers moved to the Woodcourt Hotel, Brooklands Drive, Sale, then being run by Miss Catherine Gray.

Trading conditions were unfavourable during the early 1930s but William met the challenge, extending the factory and launching new products such as the highly successful 3d meat pudding in a tin in 1935. This product was in production for seventy-three years. In September 1933, the name of the firm was changed from William Simpson (Manchester) Ltd to Simpson Ready Foods Limited.

On 20 April 1936 land to the rear of the estate amounting to some 2 acres was sold to Messrs Longworth & Taylor for building purposes. In 1937, the younger son, James, entered the business and in due course was appointed a director and secretary of the company. Miss Catherine Gray, a qualified dietician, also joined in a full-time capacity and was later to appear on all the company's labels.

During the Second World War the factory was managed by Ethel Pickles and Catherine Gray while William and James went off to serve in the forces. A firebomb landed in the middle of a pile of empty wooden barrels in the factory yard but, fortunately, it failed to explode and was safely defused.

During the war years considerable quantities of ready meals and sweet puddings were canned for the War Office for distribution to the forces in Britain and overseas.

Factory workers in 1949. (William Simpson)

During the post-war period, William Simpson inaugurated a scheme of gift parcels. This provided for the dispatch of thousands of parcels containing Goblin canned meats to families short of food because of rationing. These were paid for by friends and relatives in the United States and Canada with dollars, which the country badly needed. A measure of success of the gift parcel scheme is evident by the fact that questions were asked in parliament as to why Simpsons were able to sell so many meat products while rationing was still in existence.

Several Manchester United players worked at the factory in the 1940s and, after the war, William was asked to be a director of Manchester United Football Club but turned it down. It appears that the club just wanted his money to pay for the fencing round the pitch. Louis Edwards was then approached and he accepted; the rest, as they say, is history.

Simpsons was the first company to can hamburgers, which it did in the late 1940s. They became a best seller in coal, steel and shipbuilding regions of the UK. The fruit and Lemocreme business declined and was eventually discontinued. The company began to focus more on canned meat products and ready meals. The 'ready dinner', a complete meal of selected beef, vegetables and gravy, was a great success for the company, and the meat pudding in a tin continued to be a bestseller nationwide.

In 1953 one of the first chicken-processing plants in the country was set up and a large modern refrigeration plant was installed to handle the hundreds of birds that passed through the plant daily. This project was discontinued in 1969. More innovations followed; in 1957 Simpsons introduced the flat pie can to the British market and in 1965 the company was the first to put pork pies and black puddings in cans.

The company lost two very important people in 1970. William Simpson died in April at the early age of 59, and Miss Gray died in May. The responsibility of managing director then fell on William's younger brother James, who was assisted in this task by his wife Lilias. James's two sons Andrew and William joined the company in 1971 and 1972 respectively.

In 1979, Simpsons devised a catering-sized flat can called the Caterdish, which contained a complete meal such as lasagne, chilli con carne or beef stroganoff. The manufacture of own-label products then started for the supermarkets and there also began the production of Indian-inspired foods under the brand name of Shiva, named after the Hindu god. A separate company, Simpsons Spiced Foods, was set up to develop the growing market for Indian foods.

In 1980 the sixty-two-year-old brick chimney emblazoned with the letter S was demolished and replaced by a modern one. Then in 1983, major alterations were made to the factory's offices including a new walkway on the outside of the building which could be seen from the main road. The press also reported with amusement that Simpsons had won the 'Coals to Newcastle' award by exporting Irish stew to the Irish.

In 1985 Simpsons celebrated its seventy-fifth anniversary; the same year, James Simpson and his wife Lilias retired and passed on the day-to-day running of the factory to their sons, William and Andrew. In 1986 the longest-serving employee, Miss Ethel Pickles, died. She had started with the company in 1918 and as a young secretary had received the telephone call informing the company that the war had ended. She rose up through the ranks to become company secretary.

In 1984 an association with the Veeraswamy restaurant in London resulted in more curry products and other Indian-inspired foods. During the 1990s a new brand, Sundar, was developed for a range of Indian foods. Also, the demand for own-label supermarket products grew and different products were manufactured for all the major supermarkets. Simpsons again developed a partnership with an Indian restaurant, Shere Khan, and a range of curry sauces was developed with them.

However, sales of meat puddings declined and the product was discontinued after seventy-three years. The last one came off the line at 1.43 p.m. on 11 October 2008. Canned hamburgers were also discontinued after many years in production. As to the development of food containers, the company began to manufacture foods in flexible plastic pouches in 2003. Plastic pots and tubes soon followed.

Two younger Simpsons, Mathew and Craig, sons of William and Andrew respectively, joined the family firm. The longest-serving product for the

The Simpson brothers, Andrew and William. (Author)

company was the Christmas pudding, and it was a winner of the 1919 Milan prize; a variation on the original recipe was developed. Other innovations were a new range of sponge puddings in pots under the Simpsons label, which were initially retailed in Asda and then Morrisons. There was also the launch of a new range of premium canned ready meals under the Simpsons label.

So, as can be seen, the Simpsons products of 2016 were very different and many new products and packaging formats were introduced over the years since the firm was started in 1910.

Staff working at Simpson Ready Foods during the last month of production, April 2016. (Author)

Postscript

However, there is sad end to this chapter: Simpsons, as an employer, is now no more. The last products to be produced and dispatched were in April 2016. The business name of Simpson Ready Foods and the Goblin brand were sold to a Dutch company, which continued to manufacture some of the lines, and the factory was scheduled to be demolished to make way for a new housing development.

.

The Nag's Head, late 1800s. (Bob Potts)

The Lord Nelson Hotel, 1905. (Author)

The Victoria Hotel, 1907. (Bob Potts)

Five

PUBLIC HOUSES

P ublic houses have often, if not always, been a more genial alternative to the church as a centre of social intercourse and the three townships of Flixton, Urmston and Davyhulme were, and still are, well endowed.

An interesting return was made on 4 September 1788 to 'the Worshipful His Majesty's justices of the peace in the County of Lancaster' as follows:

We the Minister, churchwardens, constables and principal inhabitants of Flixton and Shawtown within Flixton aforesaid in the Co. of Lancaster now present in accordance with your request. We do hereby make a return; the number of licensed Ale-housekeepers and Innkeepers in Flixton and Shawtown aforesaid are four, as follow.

James Tongs at the sign of the Greyhound
John Shawcross   Do   " Dog and Partridge
Edward Booth   Do   " Lion
Joseph Gilbody   Do   " Buck

which are all convenient and necessary for accommodating travellers & situated near the public roads to Manchester & Warrington. All the said houses have beds and stables fit for the reception of travellers; and we believe the said publicans never encourage or permit Cockfighting, Bull Baiting, Horse Races, Gaming, Riots, Disorders, selling liquors in short measure, Drinking during divine service on the Lord's Day after the hours fixed for shutting up the houses.

Witness our hand this day 6th day of September, 1788. Etc.

The Nag's Head was originally built in the sixteenth century and amounted in size to not much more than the average cottage. The roof was of stone tiles and latticed windows adorned the whitewashed walls. John Parr is shown as licensee in 1828. The new building was built next to the original pub before it was demolished in the 1870s. A bowling green was built behind the pub in 1895 but destroyed by a bomb in 1940. The current building reflects the Victorian style and, at one time, the entrance boasted a revolving door. The cobbled forecourt is a leftover from 1900.

Apparently the facilities were many as an 1899 advert in *The Western Telegraph* welcomed wedding and other parties with the additional attractions of billiards, bowling green and stabling. In front of the pub was Bethel's farm, on which was built the cenotaph.

The Lord Nelson was built by the Royle family shortly after Admiral Nelson died at Trafalgar in 1805. It was originally built of plain brick, but was rebuilt in 1877 by George Royle's grandson. The original site was occupied by the old Court Baron, where the lord of the manor, Colonel Ridehalgh, would sit in judgement twice yearly. The pub was still used as a courthouse in 1890 and was also used as the terminus for a local bus service.

The following year, 1891, the census shows 64-year-old widow, Catherine Fielden, originally from Rossendale, as head and licensed victualler. Her son, 36-year-old James, born in Bury, Lancashire, is shown as assistant alongside 26-year-old son John and 23-year-old daughter Mary. Also present are 26-year-old Esther Murray, servant and general domestic Michael Brock, 26, described as general domestic and groom, and 20-year-old Leeming Hancock as a general domestic. By 1901, Herbert Bannister (28) was publican with his wife Kate (20).

The Victoria. This old pub was an imposing sight and one I vaguely remember from my youth. Situated on the corner of Station Road and Higher Road opposite the entrance to the railway station goods yard, it was demolished to make way for phase two of the town redevelopment. The 1911 census shows Robert Robertson (43) from Stockport as hotel manager. He is recorded as having a wife, Maud (39) and three children. There are also two barmaids, two kitchen maids, one housemaid and two barmen recorded.

The Union Inn was in Flixton on Woodsend Road and parts are thought to date back hundreds of years. Some think that the building was originally a farm and then a workhouse. The 1881 census credits 43-year-old William

Jackson, originally from Ireland, as a 'beer retailer'. His wife, also from Ireland, was 45-year-old Bela. William's father (78) was also in the household, as was boarder 19-year-old George Hulme from Prestwich. Major alterations were carried out in 1973 when the pub was renamed The Fox and Hounds.

The Red Lion, or, as it was originally named, The Lion, was brewing its own ale as far back as 1782 by Edward Booth. Langton mentions bear baiting was once carried on here. The 1901 census shows Albert Stott, aged 49 and born in Middleton, as licensed victualler of the pub. His wife Elizabeth, aged 50, and originally from Stalybridge, is also registered along with their four children, Lena (25), John (20), Hettie (17) and Albert (13). The pub was demolished in 1967 and rebuilt. However, it closed again in 2009 and was demolished in 2011; the land is now occupied by the care home De Brook Lodge.

The Roebuck Hotel is on the corner of Flixton Road and Chassen Road and was brewing its own ale back in 1788 when it was known simply as The Buck in Shaw Town. The first licensee was Joseph Gilbody. The local delicacy, 'snig pie', made with eels from the nearby River Mersey, was served as an accompaniment to the local brew. The pub was also known for bull and bear baiting. A licensee named Holt approached the council to enlarge the pub in 1900 and a second licence was applied for in 1909 to add a billiard room.

The pub fell victim to a fire in 2007, casting doubts over the building's future, but the brewery rebuilt the affected area and added a restaurant at the rear. Gardens adorned the front originally but these have given way to a car park.

The Church Inn is next to St Michael's church in Flixton and its origins are nearly 300 years old, records being traced back to 1731. A deed for the sale of the pub dated 1830 refers to it as having once been

The Church Inn, Flixton, 1907; formerly The Dog and Partridge. (Alan Crossland)

The Red Lion, 1900.
(Alan Crossland)

known as The Dog and Partridge. In 1867 there was a brew house, stable and piggery behind the building. An 1880 directory shows William Davies as land-lord. The present inn was built in 1924.

The Bird In Hand (originally known as The Bird i'th Hand) dates from around 1881, when Ambrose Smith is shown as proprietor, although evidence suggests that there was a pub here 200 years prior to this. Smith was granted permission to rebuild in 1896. In 1901 widower Henry Thomas Street (49) is shown as 'hotel proprietor pub' and with him were resident his 19-year-old son George, his 74-year-old widowed mother Ann and 46-year-old Caroline Sleains, who is recorded as a visitor and married. Henry's 37-year-old brother-in-law John E. Lee is recorded as 'manager of hotel' with Henry's 39-year-old sister as man-ageress. Two nieces, Mary Grant (17) and Annie Grant (19), are recorded as 'assistants in hotel'. William Edwards is known to have been the proprietor in 1909. A bowling green at the rear has now made way for extended parking.

The Greyhound is next door to The Church Inn and was first licensed before 1772 to James Tong. Joseph Whitelegg was licensee in 1828 and John Stott is shown as landlord in 1893. Stabling was available for travellers in the early days. The pub was rebuilt in 1923 and was renamed The Village Inn in 2007.

The Garrick's Head. In 1881, the census tells us that 55-year-old widow Ellen Clough was the 'beer house keeper'. Her 25-year-old daughter, Annie, was the barmaid and another daughter, 22-year-old Mary Ellen, was a dressmaker. Ellen had two other children; 15-year-old pupil teacher William and 13-year-old 'scholar' Elizabeth. The pub has had many changes and was in fact totally demolished in 1928. The present building is half-timbered in design.

The Railway Tavern on Irlam Road, Flixton, is first mentioned in the 1871 census, although the tithe map of 1843 records a 'beer shop' on the site. The 1881 census shows 55-year-old Michael Tattersall, originally from Newchurch, as the 'beer retailer' of The Railway Tavern. His wife, 30-year-old Sarah, was originally from Bakewell. They had a 2-year-old daughter, Anne, at the time of the census. Michael Tattersall was still running the place in 1888 but it was Pauline Howarth who, as licensee, applied to rebuild the original cottage around 1900. She is registered in the 1901 census as a 33-year-old widow born in Montreal, Canada. Her occupation is described as Inn Keeper. 20-year-old boarder Robert Stansfield, aged 20, is also registered. The nearby Manchester-to-Liverpool railway is the origin of the pub's name.

The Moss Vale is on Lostock Road opposite the George Carnell sports centre. Its history is interesting as the present site is a result of previous applications being rejected; at the corner of Moorside Road and Bowfell Road and again at Barton Moss Vale. The first application was made by Wilson and Walker in 1937 and it was not until 1956 that the pub was built on its present site. Various refurbishments have been made including a French theme in the early 1970s. Three of the author's paintings were purchased by the landlord as part of this theme. The latest refurbishment was carried out in 2009.

The Bent Brook is a modern public house of no architectural or aesthetic worth and situated on Broadway in Davyhulme. The pub was only established around 1962 and is so named as it sits on the bend of the local brook. Refurbished in 2009, it is open once again, catering to the more youthful side of this area: modern-style music and atmosphere being proffered to attract its clientele.

The New Victoria was the public house that formed part of phase two of the redevelopment of the town centre in 1971 and was intended to replace the old Victoria Hotel. It was a modern, soulless building and of no architectural or spiritual worth at all and, in 2017, was still lying vacant among the rest of, for the most part, untenanted retail outlets in the complex.

The Urmston was built in 1939 in the ubiquitous half-timbered style. The land had been purchased from the Constantine family of Victoria Villas. The purchaser was the brewers Messrs Walker & Humphreys. The pub was extended in the 1960s, thereby losing part of its gardens to accommodate extra parking space.

Six

OLD HOUSES

U rmston could, in its heyday, boast many fine and impressive houses, just about all of which have now been demolished to make way for the M60 motorway and housing estates. Industrialisation created new wealth for entrepreneurs, who used their money to build impressive houses in the leafy suburbs of Manchester. These are just a selection of what were, in their day, magnificent residential houses occupied by the wealthy of the district.

Urmston Lodge, built in 1648 by the de Trafford family, was situated at the corner of Gammershaw Lane and Brook Lane, now Stretford Road and Moss Vale Road. The house was known as Pineapple Hall after three carved stone pineapples positioned over the front door. The pineapples were thought of as a symbol of welcome.

The grounds covered more than 9 acres and at the rear there were a coachman's house, stables and an orchard. The lodge was extended with a maple-wood double staircase and a grand entrance hall. There was also a priest hole and a cellar with a vaulted roof. The de Traffords were Roman Catholic and there was a mahogany altar in one of the rooms. The last resident of the family was Miss Clementine Trafford, sister of Sir Thomas de Trafford. She died on 30 March 1834.

There then followed various tenants, including cotton broker Henry Matchett, and James Cunningham, also a cotton broker. Solicitor John Henry Law was tenant from 1841 until 1863, after which Peter Hogwood Moore took up the tenancy. In the census for 1871 the record shows another solicitor, Edward Atkinson, and his wife Louisa in residence.

The property and land was sold on 10 November 1874 by the then owner Charles Cecil de Trafford to Christopher Sparrow, a textile merchant and man-ufacturer, at a purchase price of £6,200. Sparrow, previously owner of Highfield

Urmston Lodge, 1900; also known as Pineapple Hall. (Alan Crossland)

House, installed stained-glass windows with his initials engraved in them. In 1884 Christopher Sparrow and his wife Eleanor moved to the south of England but left their son Walter and his wife Mary in residence. Indeed, it is 29-year-old Walter Sparrow who is shown as Home Trade Manufacturer and head of the household in the 1891 census along with his 29-year-old wife Mary. A large household included Arthur Sparrow and Walter's 33-year-old brother, who was a barrister. Also shown are Walter Sparrow's 4-year-old son Walter, 2-year-old son Richard and 6-month-old Arthur. A domestic staff included 21-year-old housemaid Clara Lathbury from Hanley in Staffordshire, 21-year-old waitress Harriet Conway from Willenhall, Staffordshire, 31-year-old cook Maria William from Wolverhampton and 23-year-old nurse Gertrude McIrod from just down the road in Altrincham, Cheshire.

After Christopher died in 1893 and his wife later the same year, the estate was left to their sons Arthur and Walter. On 24 March 1920 Arthur and Walter sold the lodge together with 2 acres, 3 roods and 13 perches of land for £2,000 to Mabel Ann Marshall Hird. During the Second World War Mrs Hird converted the large front lawn into a potato field and gave the crop to charity. She was a member of the ARP and regularly patrolled the area. Her husband, Maurice, died shortly after the war. Mrs Hird was very upset in 1957 when she was informed that Urmston Lodge was to be subject to a compulsory purchase order at a price of £3,790. The building was demolished in October 1958 to make way for the M62, now the M60 motorway. The lodge had occupied the site for 310 years.

Local historian Alan Crossland, author of *Looking Back at Urmston*, rescued one of the stone pineapples and it is situated above his front door in Humphrey Park.

Auburn Lodge was built about 1740 and one famous resident is thought to have been Mrs Henry Wood, the Victorian novelist. Around 1780, the house

Auburn Lodge. (Alan Crossland)

was enlarged, making a total of twenty-two rooms, two front doors and two staircases. An orchard and duck pond were to the rear.

The Stevenson family, farmers and landowners, owned the lodge in its early days and the family sold the building and grounds in 1790 to the Faulkner family. John Faulkner is shown as the owner in 1841 but cotton merchant James Pollitt is shown as tenant in 1851. Incidentally, Stevenson Square in the centre of Manchester, just north of Piccadilly Gardens, is named after William Stevenson.

William Shore was the organist at Cross Street Chapel in Manchester and he lived at Auburn Lodge with his wife Mary until shortly after 1861. Various tenants followed. Henry Wood, possibly the husband of the Victorian novelist who wrote *The Channings*, *East Lynne* and others, was resident until 1882. The 1891 census was taken on 6 April and Auburn Lodge is shown as 'not occupied'. Mr Mellor followed as tenant until 1893, after which John Foulkes moved in. He was to leave in about 1908. The 1911 census shows master builder Robert Wheeler (40) as resident with his wife Louisa (42) and their three children but their tenancy seems to have been a short one as Samuel Leathem became resident in 1917, after which the lodge was known as Leathem's Farm.

Census returns are unavailable for inspection after 1911 so subsequent residents cannot be ascertained with accuracy. However, it is known that the Faulkner family sold Auburn Lodge in 1964 for housing development and the building was demolished the same year.

Highfield House was built in the 1860s and situated opposite Urmston Lodge on the corner of Stretford Road and Moss Vale Road. The name comes from 'High Field' as the field in which it was built is, at 68ft, one of the highest points above sea level in Urmston. It was built in about 1865, possibly by the Taylor family of Newcroft. The Taylor family, if they were not responsible for the construction, were certainly the owners sometime before 1900.

The grounds covered some 5.52 acres and the estate included coach house and stables, as well as plenty of fruit trees. The house itself boasted a large central staircase with large rooms on either side. There were twelve upstairs rooms. Christopher Sparrow was the first known resident in 1866, with his wife Eleanor and their family, and he was a well-known local personality and benefactor. He made donations for various church buildings in the area and paid for an annual New Year party for the old people of Urmston. The next occupant was John Chappel in 1879, followed by James Caulfield. One resident was

Marshall Stevens, who was one of the founders of the Manchester Ship Canal. He moved in in 1883 with his wife Louisa.

The 1891 census shows a 39-year-old Marshall Stevens, described as an executive officer for the Manchester Ship Canal Company, as residing here with his 39-year-old wife Louisa. Originally from Plymouth, Stevens is shown as having four children aged 15, 8, 6 and 4 months at the time of the census. Also declared are Florence Prince, aged 18, a domestic servant from Over Darwen in Lancashire; 32-year-old Mary Ann Gaiter from Wellington, Shropshire, employed as nurse and cook; and 20-year-old Mary Ann Poole from Brierley Hill, Staffordshire, whose duties were domestic servant and housemaid.

The house was later used as a private kindergarten by Mrs Smith. It became a residential home once more in 1904 when the Taylor family bought it, and Henry Cross moved in as tenant in 1904. He was a justice of the peace and gave apples from his orchard to children passing by on their way to school. Henry Cross died on 20 October 1927, aged 74, and is buried in Urmston cemetery.

The 1911 census shows a 58-year-old Henry Cross from Bristol described as an dealer in antique furniture. Also registered is his wife Anne Cross (56) and three children all described as 'assisting at shop'. They were Henry (28), Rosalind (24) and Elsie (21). Kate Fegan (23) is also resident as general servant

The interior of Highfield House. (Alan Crossland)

domestic. After this Ernest Nash-Eaton, who built the Curzon cinema, and family were the occupants. The Nash-Eaton family moved out in 1937 and Thomas Gaskell resided in the property for about two years.

The house was empty during the Second World War and a subsidiary fire station was in front of the house. Urmston Council bought Highfield House on 21 June 1948 and it was demolished in the same year. The council sold the grounds on 18 January 1951 to Lancashire County Council, who built Highfield Primary School in what once were the grounds. The M60 motorway also covers part of what was the estate.

Urmston Grange dates back to 1590 and was originally called Brook House, covering some 68 acres. A small lodge welcomed the visitor, after which a long drive led up to the house. The interior boasted a beautiful maple-wood staircase and a private chapel with angels carved into the beams.

The kindly Henry Cross, who gave apples to children on their way to school. (Alan Crossland)

The Stevenson family, farmers and landowners, were one of the earliest known residents from 1790 or possibly earlier. William Stevenson and his wife Maria lived at Brook House in the early 1800s and in 1806 they donated the sum of £5 for the bells at Flixton church. William died on 5 December 1847, aged 69, and his wife Maria died in 1850, aged 66.

John Tomlinson Hibbert became resident in 1851 when the house was renamed Urmston Grange; he became an MP for Oldham in 1862 and the first chairman of Lancashire County Council. Hibbert is best known for founding the first church schools in Urmston in 1859 and making a donation to the construction of Urmston parish church. He also donated the pulpit as a gift to the newly consecrated church of St Clement and also obtained the first organ at a cost of £15. Some years later he also donated £50 to the church enlargement fund. Another of his altruistic acts was to start an annual treat for the old people of Urmston by holding parties, the first taking place in 1873. This he did in conjunction with Christopher Sparrow, then of Highfield House.

Hibbert was a true philanthropist and did much for the good of Urmston. He became the first president of St Clement's Cricket Club in 1874 and president of Urmston Football Club during the 1880/81 season.

The 1901 census shows mahogany merchant John Ashton (48) with his wife Elizabeth (44) as resident, along with their sons John (21) and Roy (12) and daughters Lucy (19) and Ruth (8). Servants Lucy Mason (47), originally from Tunbridge Wells, and Mary Davies (47), born in Haverford West, are also recorded. George Woods purchased the property in 1919 and it was then known as Grange Dairy Farm. Woods eventually converted the house into flats.

For most of its life the house was lit by gas and there was talk of a ghost haunting the rooms. It has been speculated that the reason for this may have been the fluctuation in the gas pressure, which may have resulted in lights dimming as 'the presence' moved from room to room. The construction of the M62 (now the M60) motorway was, again, the reason for the building's demolition in 1958.

The Grove. This house was in Urmston and should not be confused with a thoroughfare in Flixton of the same name. No photographs have come to light as yet of this house but what is known is that Thomas Chadwick was the highest bidder at auction for land comprising 9 acres, 2 roods and 42 perches on which he built a large mansion which he named The Grove. The price paid was £1,960 and Chadwick also had built a coachman's cottage, keeper's house and summer house. The house was almost as large as the nearby Longford Hall, on the Stretford–Chorlton border, also now demolished.

The Grove had three floors and a cellar, and inside guests would be treated to such delights as a large staircase, numerous chandeliers and a minstrels' gallery in the dining room where musicians would play for special events. In addition to two vineries the gardens boasted lilac, hawthorn, laburnum, peonies, honeysuckle, flowering currant and mock orange, and were flanked on one side by an ivy-covered high wall.

Thomas Chadwick owned the firm Thomas Chadwick & Sons Cotton Spinners of Arkwright, and Victoria Mills in Manchester. He was a philanthropist, as was his wife Ruth, and gave many donations to the Church and the local community; indeed, he gave £100 towards the building of Urmston parish church and, later, a further £100 to the church enlargement fund. Also, Ruth gifted a brass pulpit desk to the church in 1873. Thomas donated £10 for the rebuilding of the church tower at Flixton in 1877.

Thomas and Ruth had eight children in total. Ruth Chadwick died on 26 April 1886 and a stained-glass window in her memory can be seen in Flixton parish church, a gift from her widowed husband. Her sister, Jane Taylor, similarly gave a gift of a stained-glass window in the same church.

Thomas Chadwick donated the east window in St Clement's in her memory. The road from Moss Vale Road to to Humphrey Lane became known as Chadwick Lane and he would use this route to travel to Urmston with his horse and carriage. As will be seen later, it was a disagreement between Thomas Chadwick and the Taylor family that led to the building of Summerfield Terrace, now known as Gorsey Brow, although Gorsey Brow was the name of the hamlet before it was swallowed up by the Humphrey Park estate.

Five years before his death, 67-year-old widower Thomas Chadwick is listed as head of the household at the 1891 census. His occupation is stated to be 'Magistrate to the Borough of Salford; paper maker and cotton spinner'. His daughters; Sarah Chadwick, 36, Jane Chadwick, 32, Elizabeth Chadwick, 30, and Ruth Chadwick, 24; are also shown as residents along with Jane Taylor, a 61-year-old relative 'living at her own expense'. Alice Sarah Gerrard, 26 and originally from Norwich in Norfolk, is the only servant in the household.

Thomas Chadwick died on 5 April 1896, aged 71, and is buried in the family vault in Flixton churchyard. The vicar of Urmston, Rev. Elijah Harwood Cooke, in his Easter morning sermon referred to the deceased in affectionate terms, saying that 'The Church and people had lost a most generous and loyal friend, always willing to give both money and advice.' After his death, Thomas Chadwick's still-unmarried daughters listed above continued to live at The Grove. The late Mrs Chadwick's sister, Jane Taylor, also continued living there until her death on 3 April 1902.

It was intended to use the house as a hospital on the outbreak of the First World War, but eleven uninhabited years had taken its toll on the building and it was found to be suffering from dry rot. The house remained empty for many more years, acquiring the reputation of being haunted, and was finally demolished in 1926. Before demolition a large door and some stained-glass windows were rescued and used in the building of a bungalow in Blinco Road behind the post office.

Of all the houses in the area The Grove was unique, in that it was built by and occupied by only one family, the Chadwicks. The coachman's cottage remained and was called Grove Cottage, occupied by Mr and Mrs Heath and later by their married daughter and son-in-law Mr and Mrs Smith from 1930 to 1933. The Grove was demolished, and the land was eventually sold on 22 March 1933 by Samuel William and Sarah Chadwick to Messrs Longworth & Taylor for building purposes.

Manor House was probably built in the early 1800s on the east side of Humphrey Lane on land occupying 33 acres, 1 rood and 24 perches. William Allen had originally purchased lands in this area in 1765 but became bankrupt before being able to develop it. John and Hannah Joynson were possibly the first occupants and they had four children, Sarah, John, Martha and Hannah. Sarah married Charles Reade in 1827 and the lands became part of the Reade family estate. The couple had five children; Charles died on 20 March 1853 and his part-ownership of the land was divided between his wife and children. Sarah Reade died on 9 October 1880, aged 75, and is buried at Flixton church. The estate was left to her daughter Sarah Margaret Reade who, on 30 May 1882, married Colonel George Henry Gray of Stretford and they continued to live at Manor House. As with the Chadwicks of The Grove, the couple were philanthropists and gave donations to the Church. They had no children; Sarah died on 13 September 1914, aged 68, with George following on 25 April 1918, aged 72. Both are buried in Urmston cemetery. The estate passed to George Gray's nephew Joseph Edmund Smith and his niece Emily Smith, who rented the property out.

The house and grounds were sold to Messrs Longworth & Taylor on 27 April 1934 and in 1936 Manor House was demolished to make way for a new housing estate; Clevedon Avenue now passes over the site where it once stood.

Wibbersley. This grand mansion was built in 1881 by Adam Stott, who was a partner in Stott's mill. The 1901 census shows widow Sarah Stott (66) as head of the household with her niece Clara Walker (29) and two servants, cook Hannah Leigh (50) and housemaid Mary Leigh (15).

The building was used as an auxiliary hospital by the Red Cross during the First World War. The owners of this private residence, Dr and Mrs Smith of Altrincham, kindly placed the house at the disposal of the Red Cross Committee and the hospital's first casualties were a contingent of thirty-three wounded Belgian soldiers who arrived for treatment on 14 October 1914.

Wibbersley in 1915, with a Red Cross nurse. (Bob Potts)

Five rooms acted as wards, accommodating twenty-six beds; this grew to eighty-two beds, and the staff included 120 nurses and 100 orderlies on the outbreak of war. Generous donations of food, clothing and money were made by local residents and even pipes, tobacco and cigarettes. The following May, 1915, the Flixton Institute was likewise utilised for the care of the wounded and was officially known as Wibbersley 2.

A grand concert held at Urmston Public Hall on Saturday, 9 October 1915, and a garden party and fete held on Saturday, 22 July 1916, as well as other fundraising events, contributed further to the running costs of the hospital. Wibbersley acted as a hospital until the end of March 1919, when it was no longer needed; some 2,300 patients had passed through the wards. Incredibly, only one patient failed to survive his injuries.

Sadly, the building was demolished in 1927 and Wibbersley Park off Irlam Road, built in 1928, now occupies the site. One or two local residents claim to have experienced seeing the ghosts of dead soldiers on the site. In the 1960s one woman said she saw the apparition of a uniformed First World War soldier coming through her living room door. She was so traumatised at her experience that she put the house up for sale and moved out.

Flixton House, a Grade II listed building, was built in 1806 by Justice Ralph Wright, whose family had grown to be wealthy landowners in Flixton, partly at the expense of the Egerton family who owned Shawe Hall. The house was built as an addition to his existing farmhouse.

The census of 1851 records a William Worthington Wright, aged 48, as 'proprietor of land 57 acres 8 lab.' His widowed mother, Mary Worthington, aged 70, is described as a 'gentlewoman' and also in residence. There were also two servants living in the house, Mary Worthington, aged 27, and Mary Hughes, aged 31.

The 1901 census records Samuel W. Wright, aged 41, as head of the household and living off his own means. With him was his 39-year-old brother, Thomas W. Wright, also living off his own means, with sister-in-law Elizabeth, aged 34. There were three servants recorded also: housekeeper Mary Johnson (56), housemaid Lilly Hartley (19) and kitchen maid Alice Burgess (18). All three servants were single and born in Flixton.

The last squire, Samuel Worthington Wright, built the ballroom extension. He died in 1934 and the following year, on 5 March, Urmston Council bought the house and grounds, amounting to some 218 acres, opening them to the public on 28 September. A tablet to this effect was unveiled by Councillor T. Forsyth JP, chairman of the parks sub-committee.

There is a walled formal garden to the rear of the house with sensory gardens, paths and a pond. The wall itself has Grade II listed status and can be dated back to 1806. It has a cavity through which steam was piped from the main house to the greenhouses. On the front lawn is a tree known as the Seven Sisters Beech, which is actually seven saplings that were planted close together so that they grew into one tree. The individual trees can be counted quite easily. The story that a previous owner of the house planted a tree for each of his daughters that grew and wove into one is apocrythal. The arbour in the garden was the brain-child of Ernest Leeming, whose achievements and contributions to the area will be explored further below. The barn and outbuildings are also listed as Grade II.

In 1827, Squire Ralph Worthington Wright closed several footpaths across the estate to which the public previously had access. Some twenty years earlier Wright's park consisted of a number of fields, partly inherited and partly purchased, along which the footpaths ran and they were concealed from his house by hedges. Wright levelled the hedges to give an uninterrupted view from his house but found that people using the footpaths intruded on his privacy. Some footpaths were closed and others diverted, and his neighbours put up with these inconveniences at first, even though Wright had not obtained a magistrate's order. However, he eventually diverted the roads beyond his estate boundaries, preventing the public from crossing his property at all. He had applied for a magistrate's order, but went ahead with his plan before being granted permission and even ploughed up the old footway and sowed the land with oats. One neighbour, Samuel Wood, had had enough at this and decided to take the law into his own hands and, with the help of some of his neighbours, he unblocked the obstructions and trod down the oats, thus restoring the original road to the public.

Wright went before the court at the Salford Michaelmas Sessions on Monday, 29 October 1827 to answer the appeal of Booth and Others, appellants. The whole cost of these trials to the public reached the sum of £750. The case was stated to be 'an appeal against four orders signed by Mr. Brierley and Mr. Fielden, for stopping up certain foot roads, alleged to be "unnecessary", that ran through the park of Ralph Wright Esq. in the parish of Flixton'. The bench of eight magistrates was chaired by James Norris Esq.

Space does not permit a detailed account of the case as the document runs to some sixty pages. Indeed, there are several testimonies taken from various locals, including William Millat of nearby Millatt's Barn, James Barlow, William Walkden, James Harper, Thomas Harper, Jonathan Royle, George Daniel, Jacob Arrowsmith, William Smith, William Taylor, John Upton, John Gratrix, Thomas Pennington, James Shawcross, Thomas Warburton, Charles and Alice Irlam, schoolmaster Rev. John Hunter, farmer James Renshaw, schoolteacher Harriet Knubley, weaver Joseph Howard, workhouse governor William Eccles, farmer John Walkden, lock tenter Thomas Gilbody, 76-year-old John Owen, joiner and carpenter Peter Bennett, cotton manufacturer James Marsh, estate manager Charles Carrington, weaver Matthew Taylor, cow doctor Allen Cragg, bailiff John Daine, carpenter Thomas Yates and shoemaker John Hartley as to whether they thought the footpaths were used much and therefore as to whether they were necessary or not to the local people. All testified as to the uselessness of the paths in their opinion, although some confessed to having used them on occasion.

In fact it was stated by Mr Ashworth, speaking for the Respondents, that the footpaths could not be useless as people often used them, especially in going to church in times of flood. This was corroborated by Samuel Thorpe, James Pollitt, John Whitehead, George Kay, Timothy Astbury, James Walthew, George Royle, John Bowker, Peter Johnson, Thomas Johnson, John Shawcross, John Watmough, David Bradburn, Anne Royle (servant to Mrs Knubley), William Hesketh, Alice Rogers, Lucy Booth, Ann Taylor, John Harrison, Charles Royle and John Owen, who, when cross-examined, all testified as to the usefulness and necessity of the footpaths.

An interesting, if not humorous, quote from the trial document states that:

In floods, if these footways are shut up, the people at Woods and Shawcross's farm would have to go 680 yards round, to get to church and this, if they went twice a day, would be a mile and a half round, and this for no other purpose than to make Mr. Wright's park more parkish.

Mr Ashworth also stated that:

In short, though they say the roads are useless, they all use them and facts speak a much stronger language than mere declarations. The footpath is used by them all, except those who live at such a distance from it that they have no occasion to use it at all. It falls to the ground, for the witnesses say one thing and do another; they say the road is useless and they travel over it.

He also went on to say that:

> The more I have considered the case the more I am convinced, that if those orders are confirmed, it will be as flagrant an act of injustice as ever was performed; and I feel compelled, as part of the public and representing the public, to say, that if these paths are stopped, justice will be sacrificed at the shrine of power.

So Wright had to give way, the court stating that his actions were 'on general principles to be regarded as an invasion of the rights of the whole community'.

However, Wright is on record as saying, via counsel for the Respondents, Mr Courtenay, that he regretted wasting public time with this action and that:

> Had he not been kept in the dark as to the body of evidence respecting the public utility of this road, he should never had taken the steps he has done. That he is the last man in the world to infringe the rights of the public, and never would have attempted to do so, had he known the whole truth of the matter. He therefore begs that the order be set aside as to all the paths, with the exception of the path from Darbyshire's cottage to Jones' house.

The court accordingly quashed three of the orders and confirmed the fourth.

Nonetheless, *The Manchester Gazette* of 10 November 1827 was not in sympathy with Wright's comments that he had been kept in the dark as to the evidence regarding the usefulness of the roads. *The Gazette* was of the opinion that Wright only declared this after it was obvious that he was going to lose the case and that:

> He who for twenty years together had striven to deprive his neighbours of a valuable right, and who for twenty years had experienced their manly and determined resistance, and to the last hour had refused to listen to any conciliatory overture; could HE expect to be believed when he declared himself to be the the last man in the world to seek what was not his own?

The Gazette went on to say that his 'declaration was an insult and an outrage to the common sense of the court and of the public', and it went on to bestow 'hearty commendation on the inhabitants of Flixton, and particularly on the appellants, […] for their spirited resistance to most flagrant attempts to deprive them of their rights'.

The National Footpaths Association was born out of this dispute. There was a blue plaque commemorating the dispute mounted on Flixton Station but after the demolition of the building, which had by then become a public house, the plaque was lost. The citation read:

BOTTOMS FOOTPATH
The stopping of this footpath by
'SQUIRE' WRIGHT
resulted in a successful court action
instituted and entirely funded by
the people of Flixton.
It was followed by the first
comprehensive legislation
giving rights of way
to the public.

Sponsored by Goddard & Staines (Coachcraft) Ltd

There has been a successful application by Urmston and District Local History Society for a duplicate plaque to be mounted on Flixton House.

Ralph Wright's monument is in St Michael's churchyard.

Wilderspool House was situated amid Wilderspool Woods on land now occupied where the Travel Inn near the Trafford Centre stands. The Ordnance Survey map for 1895 (Lancashire Sheet CIII.15) shows the house among woodland in its own grounds just to the east of Barton Road and to the north of Moss Lane. Bent Cottage and Rose Cottage are just a short distance to the north-west. The house is also a short distance north of Crofts Bank, the area now more colloquially known as Davyhulme Circle or The Nag's Head. The farm was way off Crofts Bank Road but it was the closest address registered. The house, recorded in 1781, was centrally between the Nag's Head and Barton Bridge. Before any of the changes in this area it was all Wilderspool Woods. It was a gentleman's residence at the outset and became a farm later in life. The house was demolished in 1963 and the lands became part of the farm.

The farm, which was south of the hall, had Peter Warburton in residence there from 1894 to 1898. The farm was demolished in 1963.

Newcroft Hall was originally a moated hall dating probably from the thirteenth century; it was in 1219 that Adam de Ormeston gave lands in the area to Richard de Trafford. The first known occupant of the hall is John de Trafford, who killed Gilbert of Ashton in a duel in a field called Barrowfield Bank behind Urmston Hall. Gilbert's body was buried there and John took the deeds of the manor. Henry de Trafford is the next known resident in 1334, after which his daughter Alice married William de Warburton and the estate passed into the Warburton family. Geoffrey de Warburton is the next known resident in 1389–90, where it is recorded that he acknowledged a debt of £20 to Adam de Levy. Richard de Warburton lived there in 1397 and William de Warburton in 1429–30. The Warburton family eventually moved to Arley Hall in Cheshire, after which Newcroft Hall came into the possession of Sir John Radcliffe of Ordsall Hall.

Sir John's son Richard Radcliffe then resided at the hall with his wife Margaret, who was the daughter of Sir Edmund Trafford of Trafford Park. Margaret died in 1579, after which Richard married another Margaret, the daughter of John Radcliffe of Foxenden Hall, Manchester. His first wife gave him three sons and he had two sons and six daughters by his second wife. Richard died on 13 January 1602, aged 67, and was buried at Flixton church, where there is a brass tablet on the south-west wall to commemorate him.

Alexander Radcliffe succeeded Richard as resident of the hall; he married Clemency Hawarded of Woolston. Alexander and his brother Francis sold the hall in 1609. The purchaser was their half-brother William of Foxenden Hall, although Alexander continued to live there. Clemency died in 1615 and Alexander in 1628; both were buried in Flixton church. Newcroft came into the hands of the Rogers family in 1662, after which it passed to the Hulme family of Davyhulme but was tenanted by the Gregory family. William Gregory donated a field to the church in 1731, the annual income of which was to be given to the poor of Urmston; the field, known as the Manchet Field, was adjacent to Chadwick Lane, now Bradfield Road.

The Taylor family purchased the estate in 1790, after which the hall was rebuilt. The new hall, in the Georgian style and constructed of brick, was built round the foundations of the old hall. Samuel's son, also called Samuel, inherited the estate and by 1842 more land had been bought to expand the estate. Samuel died on 21 February 1850, aged 68, and his son, another Samuel, took on the mantle.

It was during the mid nineteenth century that Samuel built Newcroft House for his brothers John and Edmund, with Highfield View and Highfield Villas being built for his daughters and relatives when they married. Jane married James Chadwick, who then went to live at Urmston Bank, and Louise married Nathan Parr of Eccles in 1876. The third Samuel died on 23 October 1866, aged 43, and was also buried at Flixton church.

John, Edmund and James Chadwick eventually inherited the estates to the north of Stretford Road and also the estates to the south on the death of Samuel. James died in 1871 and Edmund in 1877, leaving the whole estate to John Taylor of Newcroft House. Eventually Herbert Bannister bought the hall and lands to the south of Stretford Road in 1888 for the sum of £4,081. The Bannisters never occupied the hall, preferring to lease the hall to tenants. Cornelius Edwin Bradshaw was the first, followed by his two sons Daniel and Harry, followed in turn by John Whitham, a cattle dealer. In 1918 another cattle dealer, Sam Teggins, moved in, followed by Edward Robert Saxton in 1922. Dairy farmers Mr and Mrs Lowe followed as tenants in 1927.

This was the end of the hall as a place of residence as the estate was pur-chased by the building firm of Longworth & Taylor on 3 January 1935, after which the hall was demolished. Cottages on the estate were also demolished some six years later and the Newcroft Road estate was built with Newcroft Road, Newcroft Crescent and Newcroft Drive all named after the estate. The hall was situated in the area between numbers 6 and 8 Newcroft Drive.

There were a variety of other smaller houses in the area. Highfield Bank is one such that was impressive enough to include a billiards room. It was built in the 1860s by the Taylor family on Highfield Avenue, now Bridgnorth Avenue. The house was badly damaged in the 1941 and 1943 air raids and the house had to be demolished. Highfield View was another house built in the 1860s, again by the Taylor family. The property consisted of two semi-detached houses and they became vacant in 1974. A small private chapel now stands on the site.

Two tall semi-detached houses were built in the 1860s, again for the Taylor family. These were Highfield Villas and several tenants were in occupation before the houses were used as a dairy farm from 1934 to 1969. A builder, Mr Ward, then purchased the property and carried out enlargements.

A house that is still standing and very impressive to look at from the out-side is the aforementioned Grade II listed Newcroft House. It is not as big as Urmston Lodge, The Grange, Highfield House and Newcroft Hall and the like but it boasted a large garden, stables and coach house when it was built in 1850 by Samuel Taylor for his two brothers John and Edmund. The date 1850 is etched into a beam in the roof. The 1891 census shows that John Taylor was resident at this time, aged 63, from Urmston, and 'living on his own means'. The only other resident was 22-year-old Marie Chadwick, cook and domestic servant. Ten years later the 1901 census shows John Taylor as resident still, with 46-year-old widow and servant Elizabeth Boddington the only other resident. John Taylor died on 11 March 1902, at the age of 74, and the house passed to his son John Edmund Taylor and his two unmarried daughters.

The owners and occupiers of Newcroft House at the time of writing are Don and Marlene Fry, who have assiduously and lovingly maintained the property and kept written and photographic evidence of the work done. This has included a new roof and the rebuilding of the lean-to greenhouse as a conservatory, the 100-year-old original of which had collapsed soon after they moved in. The current conservatory covers a third of the space originally occupied by the greenhouse. The cellar still includes a large stone slab on brick pillars which would have been used to keep meat and other foods cold.

Mr Fry has kept up an interesting tradition which is evident from the front of the house. The central upstairs window contains a model yacht, which is in a small box room that may have originally been a storage room for trunks and hat boxes. The yacht was originally put in the window by a previous owner, a Mr Prescott, and subsequent owners have since inherited it and displayed it accordingly. Mr Fry only takes the yacht down at Christmas when he puts a Christmas tree in its place for the duration of the festive season. Sadly, Mrs Fry passed away in 2017.

The house was listed as Grade II on 30 June 1987 and English Heritage describes it as follows:

Early C19. Flemish bond brick with slate roof. Double-depth central-staircase plan with 3 bays and 2 storeys. Symmetrical elevation with central door and stone plinth. Bays 1 and 3 are slightly advanced, 6-panel door with leaded fanlight. Total of five 16-pane sash windows with first floor sill band and flat brick arches. Projecting eaves gutter. Gable chimney stacks. Lean-to greenhouse against left return. Horizontally sliding sash windows to rear. Interior retains panelled doors, enriched plaster cornices and a dogleg stair with plain balusters.
(English Heritage Building ID: 212998)

The driveway at the side of Newcroft House was originally the driveway to Urmston Bank, built in 1770 and demolished in 1957. The house boasted stables and a coach house, and was occupied by James Swift, a farmer and pork butcher, although his son Matthew actually owned the house. Matthew also built Gammershaw House, where he lived with his family.

The ubiquitous Samuel Taylor of Newcroft Hall then moved in and, later, James Chadwick, who lived there after his marriage to Jane Taylor of Newcroft. His brother, the mill owner Thomas Chadwick, may also have lived here but he is known to have moved to the nearby house called The Grove, which he had had built after his marriage to Ruth Taylor. Indeed, the commemorative marble plaque on the north wall in St Clement's church, erected by his workers on his death, states Thomas Chadwick to be 'of The Grove'.

Occupiers also included tenants Ephraim Boucock in 1892, George Lowe in 1896, John Newton in 1898, Martha Currie in 1920 and Tresillian Ransome in 1922. John Yates followed in 1930, Eliza Marrs in 1936, Mrs Curry in 1938 followed by Robert Banks in 1942. Lancashire County Council purchased the house and grounds in 1957, demolishing the house to build Urmston Grammar School for Boys, which opened in 1961. The drive was used as a school entrance as it was considered a public right of way. After the school was demolished in 1991, permission was sought, and granted, to have the entrance closed and it became part of the gardens of Newcroft House. In 1991 a housing estate called Grammar School Gardens was built on the site of the demolished school.

Another interesting house is Buggard House near the Stretford–Urmston boundary. Parish register entries show that John Hamper lived here from 1753 to 1757. There is a famous story associated with the house that gave rise to the legend of the Gammershaw Boggart or bogey-man. It is said that an old woman lived in the house and she is thought to have had a hidden treasure of gold. One night, two travellers called, asking for a drink of water. While her back was turned one of them sprang upon her and cut her throat. The old woman's grandson was in the house and, on hearing her screams, he ran and apprehended the murderer, who was later charged with the heinous crime and sentenced to death by hanging. Legend has it that he was hung in gibbet irons in the lane where the deed was done and it is said that strange illusions and noises were seen and heard along the lane. One theory is that it is the ghost of the murdered old woman, who walks abroad accompanied by rattling chains. Less believing cynics were of the opinion that the noises were that of an owl hooting and the rattling no more than the chains of a tethered goat.

The house was pulled down and Gammershaw House was built on the site in 1853 by Matthew Smith, a farmer and pork butcher. Matthew's wife was said to be eccentric and she would steal apples from neighbours' gardens and then knock on their doors and try to sell them. Gammershaw House was eventually renamed The Anchorage when Thomas Buchan, a sea captain, moved in. Anchorage Road now commemorates the spot and a gatepost stating 'Private Road to Ellastone Hill' still stands on the roadside of Stretford Road just opposite Simpsons' factory. The Anchorage was sold in 1966 and demolished for the building of new houses.

Reade House was a large mansion house on the corner of Western Road and Flixton Road. Flats now occupy the site as the mansion was demolished in 1937. Samuel John Reade married Sir Bosdin Leech's sister Eliza in 1862 and

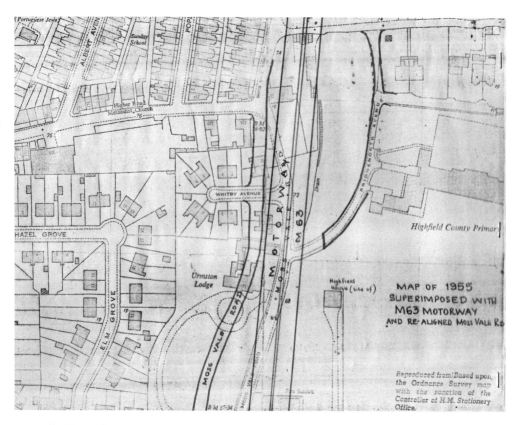

The M63 and Moss Vale Road realignment. (Alan Crossland)

moved in soon after. Reade was a philanthropist and made donations including £100 towards the building of Brook Road Chapel in 1905. He also bequeathed £300 to Flixton church and £100 to the Flixton Institute. He died in 1906.

As discussed, some of Urmston's grand houses were demolished to make way for the construction of the M63 motorway and the map (previous page), made by Alan Crossland, shows the 1955 realignment of Moss Vale Road and the new road bends to the left. As can be seen, the realigned Moss Vale Road passes over the site of the demolished Urmston Lodge (Pineapple Hall).

Highfield House can be seen on the right of the motorway. Auburn Lodge and The Grange are just out of the picture at the bottom.

Sadly the construction of the motorway was not without its incidents and tragedy. In December 1958 one man was killed and forty injured when a crane working on the new railway bridge at Moss Vale Road toppled on to the railway track. Power cables and telephone wires were severed, causing two trains to collide with the fallen crane and resulting in the fatality and injuries. Then, in February 1959, girders toppled, killing three workmen; the following December another four men were killed when another girder toppled. This latter incident caused shipping to be halted for weeks, thereby delaying the completion of the motorway, which was eventually opened in October 1960.

Seven

HOUSING

The census returns of the nineteenth century in Flixton and Urmston show the area as predominantly agricultural in nature; occupations were mainly in farming and other labouring jobs and the housing, farmhouses and labourers' cottages showed a modest character that reflected incomes of modest means.

Apart from the halls and the large houses of the wealthy, housing in Victorian England, and indeed Urmston, Flixton and Davyhulme, varied in quality from one-room mud-and-thatch hovels to four- and five-roomed dwellings built of substantial brick with slate roofs.

Ciss Lane was originally a narrow lane with tall hedges on either side. The lane would have run from Stretford Road to Higher Road. The thatched cottage in the photograph below stood at its junction with Higher Road. However, one thing that Langton got wrong was that he stated in his book that in line with other roads that had already been renamed, Ciss Lane and Jack Lane would 'be rechristened to suit the fastidious taste of suburban villa owners'. He was wrong; Ciss Lane and Jack Lane have not been rechristened and retain their historic names.

As industry grew in the area, particularly in Trafford Park, there was a similar growth in the need for housing. There were a mere 142 dwellings recorded in the 1851 census, which grew dramatically in just fifty years to 1,445 in the 1901 census. Much of the farmland characteristic of the area for centuries was gradually built on, with estates comprising semi-detached houses springing up during the late 1920s and 1930s to provide housing for the workers. The railway had turned Urmston into a dormitory town with many workers travelling into Trafford Park to work and commuting into the city centre. Between 1933 and the outbreak of the war the council provided 364 permanent homes and

Ciss Lane cottage, 1879. (Bob Potts)

in the post-war years up to the early 1970s, a further 1,856. During this period 180 unfit properties were demolished and in the post-war years a further 237.

In 1933 the Rothiemay estate in Flixton was advertised as being just 'one minute from Flixton railway station and bus routes off Flixton Road'. The cost was £425 for a house with two entertaining rooms, scullery, larder, three bedrooms and a bathroom. Applications were invited on site or at the builders, who were D. Franklyn trading at 423 Moorside Road in Flixton. The cost was 16s 11d per week after a £30 deposit. Houses were also available at a cost of £345 and £465.

Part of this building programme was carried out by local builders Albert Locke Ltd of Lostock Road in Davyhulme. The *Manchester Evening News* reported on 10 March 1939 that the builders had just completed the Hartford estate and houses would include two entertaining rooms, three bedrooms, a tiled bathroom with panelled bath and separate WC. A kitchenette and larder were also included together with coalplace and hall with panelled staircase. There was also garage room and a large garden to every house. There would be no road or legal charges or extra costs and, as an additional incentive, it was pointed out that the 11 and 11x bus services would run from Parker Street. The cost of the houses was advertised at £425 and terms were offered at 16s 11d per week payments after a £21 deposit.

An aerial photograph of 1929 shows Sevenoaks Avenue, near Davyhulme Circle, had been built but the land beyond was still fields. A similar aerial photograph of 1935 shows that the park, Canterbury Road, and many other roads and houses on the Hartford estate had now been constructed.

The Aldermere estate includes Derwent Road off Goldsworthy Road in Flixton and Conways advertised semi-detached and detached houses for sale in 1935 at a cost of £335 and £365 respectively. £5 would secure the property with payments following at 13s ½d or 14s 3½d. All road costs, stamp duties and legal charges were included in the cost. The council purchased the Stott estate, amounting to some 106 acres, on 31 October 1945, and the resulting building programme provided 900 dwellings on what is now the Woodsend housing estate.

Many houses were demolished in 1959 to make way for the construction of the motorway, which opened the year after. Three impressive houses – Highfield House, Urmston Grange and Urmston Lodge – were also casualties.

During the Second World War many households had been left homeless, the Blitz being responsible for the destruction of around 500,000 homes nationwide. One solution was the construction of prefabricated houses, known as 'prefabs' for short. They were a fast and cost-effective, albeit temporary, solution to the housing shortage and, in many cases, provided a standard of living higher than many were used to; they were also seen as providing homes for occupants as part of a programme of slum clearances. An indoor toilet and bathroom were standard features, not something that many in Britain had experienced at that time.

A typical 'prefab' would have had two bedrooms, a living room and a kitchen as well as an indoor toilet and bathroom. The houses retained a coal fire, but contained a back boiler to create both central heating and a constant supply of hot water. For a country used to the pleasures of the outside lavatory and tin bath, it was a treat that the bathroom included a flushing toilet and man-sized bath with hot running water. In the kitchen were housed such modern luxuries as a built-in oven, refrigerator and Baxi water heater; items we now take for granted. A small garden would also be standard with a shed. In comparison to the slums, where people would live two to a room with shared toilet facilities, the 'prefabs' would be seen as something of a luxury.

These houses were built under the Housing (Temporary Accommodation) Act of 1945 by the government. The Act led to the building of about 160,000 temporary bungalows across Britain between 1944 and 1948 and were only intended to have a ten-year lifespan, although many were still standing many years later. This was a scheme envisaged by Winston Churchill and devised by Lord Portal, Minister of Works, to relieve the post-war housing shortage at a time when more usual materials such as brick were unavailable and wartime industries needed a new peacetime function.

Davyhulme's prefabricated housing estate was at the bottom end of Broadway near Bent Lanes. The site was only demolished in around the early 2000s, apparently due to the discovery of methane, and is now occupied by a small housing area known as Prestwood Close, Davyhulme Medical Centre and Lloyd's Pharmacy. Another prefab estate was situated on Kingsway Park.

Summerfield Terrace; also known as Gorsey Brow and Spite Cottages. (Author)

The Spite Cottage
letter. (Alan Crossland)

When discussing housing in the area, mention must be made of the erroneously named Gorsey Brow, a row of four tall cottages on Humphrey Lane built in 1870 by John Taylor of Newcroft Hall.

Gorsey Brow was the name of a hamlet of just a couple of farms and cottages in the area now occupied by the row. The houses are actually called Summerfield Terrace and were also nicknamed 'Spite Row' after a quarrel between John Taylor of Newcroft and Thomas Chadwick, who had built a large house called The Grove in 1868 on the south side of Humphrey Lane after purchasing land previously occupied by Manor House, Manor Farm and Manor Cottages. Chadwick had amassed his fortune as a mill owner. He was in the business of cotton spinning and his firm, Thomas Chadwick and Sons, was based at Arkwright and Victoria Mills in Manchester.

The land is today occupied by Berwick, Clevedon, Darnford and Hartland Avenues, most of Firwood Avenue, a portion of the curved section of Humphrey Lane, the nearby portion of Bradfield Road and, due to the re-routing of the modern day Humphrey Lane, a portion of Humphrey Crescent.

The reason for the Taylor–Chadwick quarrel is now lost in the mists of time but it may have been a family matter as Thomas's wife Ruth, buried with her husband in the family vault in Fixton churchyard, was a Taylor before she married. The quarrel ended up in the courts, with Thomas Chadwick coming out the winner. As a result, John Taylor built these very tall cottages deliberately to spoil the view of orchards and fields for Thomas Chadwick.

John Taylor let the unfurnished cottages rent free to poor people. He even tried to continue inconveniencing Thomas Chadwick by trying to close the narrow dirt track named Chadwick Lane (named after Thomas Chadwick), which Mr Chadwick used to go to church and attend to business in his horse and carriage. The lane, now Bradfield Road, was the means of access from the cottages through to Moss Road, now Moss Vale Road. It was cobbled for a stretch leading up to Moss Road. In early photographs the lane was referred to as Lovers' Walk.

However, a law stated that a lane was a public right of way and unable to be closed if a corpse had been carried down on its way to a funeral. Taylor did the next best thing and made the lane narrower. Another lawsuit followed, which John Taylor won, and he celebrated his victory by giving flags to the tenants of Summerfield Terrace so that they could wave and jeer at Mr Chadwick as he passed in his horse and carriage. The cottages remained in the ownership of the Taylor family until 1943 and were then sold to Efficiency Garages (Manchester) Ltd, who in turn sold them to the tenants.

The Chadwick family vault is in Flixton churchyard. Alongside Thomas Chadwick, who died on 5 April 1895, aged 71 years and 9 months, is his wife Ruth, who died on 26 April 1886, aged 58; Jane Taylor, Ruth's sister, who died on 3 April 1902, aged 72; Thomas and Ruth's eldest daughter Sarah, who died on 7 January 1925, aged 70; and Thomas Taylor Chadwick, the Chadwicks' eldest son, who died on 29 December 1919, aged 65.

Eight

CHILDREN AND EDUCATION

Provision for public education in the area can be traced back to the seventeenth century, in a 1643 indenture providing for a schoolhouse for Flixton, on the north side of Flixton churchyard, for ninety-nine years. The indenture was entered into between Peter Egerton of Shagh and George Smyth, John Warburton, Thomas Walkden, Laurence Lee and John Lee. In the indenture it is clear that Peter Egerton was keen to promote literature and learning through the teaching and instructing of children in the parish. The nominal rent to Mr Egerton was 'thirteene pence' paid half-yearly 'att the feast day of the Nativitie of St. John Baptist and that of St. Martin the Byshop in Winter'. Another consideration for the lease was 'the rendering yearly to the lessor and his representative [...] one day drawing of Turves with an able p'son and one day reapinge or shearinge of corn with an able reaper or shearer of corn in and upon the Demeasne lands of the said Peter Egerton'.

Sadly the schoolhouse was demolished; the date of demolition is not exactly known but it seems that it was prior to 1773 as the sale of some land to Thomas Darbyshire to widen a road resulted in a causeway being discovered and presumed to be one of the approaches to the school.

1662 marks the year when another school was built, this time on land opposite The Roebuck Inn on Church Road. It would seem that this school ceased to operate around 1802. It lasted well over 100 years even though made of thatch; the churchwardens would have had to have had it regularly repaired. A larger school was built opposite St Michael's church on land donated in 1861 by William Worthington Wright.

Parliamentary returns for 1786 show that William Gregory gave £10 for bread for the poor of Urmston. This return seems to have been made possible by the purchase of a field called The Maunchet Field consisting of between twenty and thirty perches (a perch was 8 yards). Returns of 1786 also show that

George Hayward gave £10 to Shawcroft School, which yielded 10s per annum. Similarly, in 1786 it is shown that Peter Coupe gave £30, giving a yearly yield of 30s for the school. A will made by William Newton on 30 September 1800 made £100 available upon trust in order to pay for the teaching of children of the poor in the township.

There were other wills that made provision for the education of the less fortunate children of the townships. In 1846 land was donated by Lawrence Fogg on which was built the Wesleyan school on Moorside Road. A Sunday school operated here until 1938, when a new school was built on Brook Road. A Wesleyan school was also opened in 1911 on Delamere Road.

St Clement's School was on Higher Road and originally built in 1888 after the foundation stone was laid on 30 June of the same year; it opened on 4 February 1889 with spaces for 680 pupils. The school was enlarged in 1 912 and a four-day bazaar helped to fund the extension. The school was originally built to replace the first Church school on Stretford Road. The school was demolished and the land is now occupied by housing. The path at the side is still there and leads to the bridge over the railway station and on to Railway

St Clement's School. (Author)

Road opposite Westbourne Park. There are two stone tablets, originally from the school, set into the modern walls. One states: 'This stone was laid 30th June 1888 by the Rev. E. Harwood Cooke M.A. vicar of Urmston.' It is quite worn but still legible. The other tablet reads: 'St Clement's Parish Church Schools, Built by public subscriptions A.D. 1888, treasurers of the building committee, E.Harwood Cooke M.A. Vicar, Michael Benson Richard James churchwardens, John Robinson Hon. Secretary'. This second stone is in much better condition and the placing of both tablets is a fitting reminder of the now demolished school.

Church schools are the earliest credited schools in the area. Although there were free places for the poor children of the town, attendance at the school was dependent on payment.

Thomas Chadwick of The Grove was a local philanthropist and in 1891 he set up 'The Chadwick Scholarship' at the Church schools; two prizes for intellectual attainment and good conduct. The prizewinners benefitted to the tune of two years' free schooling, book prizes and a money prize. Four winners were chosen in 1892 and this remained until his death.

Coming into more recent times, another school demolished and now no more was Urmston Grammar School for Boys on Bradfield Road. A new housing estate, Grammar School Gardens, now occupies the site. The connection with the Chadwick family lives on, with one road leading into the estate being called Chadwick Road.

As a footnote to this section on education, I think it informative to mention my first primary school: the privately run Whitelake School, formerly called Whitelake House (now demolished) and situated on Flixton Road opposite Ambleside playing fields. I had originally spent my nursery school days at a house that is now a B&B business known as Chesham House, on Church Road. Next door is the Little Acorns Nursery, which was formerly Cauis House Preparatory School, whose pupils wore bright red blazers and caps.

A gentleman call Houghton owned Whitelake House in 1858, where he ran a small nursery. It became the Sewell's home around 1890 and was converted into a school. Adverts for the school show it as being established in 1892.

The 1901 census shows John C. Sewell (80) as a retired manufacturer of cotton goods with his wife Annie (64) resident in the house. Their two sons and three daughters are also present on census night, daughters Edith (34) and Jessie (33) are recorded as single and with occupations recorded as 'schoolmistress (private)'. The school taught from kindergarten to General Certificate.

Whitelake Junior School, 1958. The headmaster, Mr Wesley (centre), sits among children and staff; the author is on the bottom row seated cross-legged, third from the left. (Author)

Miss Sewell with Miss McKee went on to teach at the first Urmston Junior School. The school took the ground floor, while the family lived in the upper area.

Whitelake House was a classical double-storey building. Probably built around 1850, it had a central front door with windows each side, as can be seen from the school photograph. A stairway led from the front to a landing continuing on to the three bedrooms and a bathroom.

The later years of its life were in the hands of a family called Wesley, with the house completely taken over as the school. Mr Wesley was the headmaster; his sister Mrs Webber and his wife Mrs Wesley were class teachers. Miss Kershaw was another teacher on the staff. The two front rooms were occupied by infants, who graduated to the upper floor as they grew older. The lower floor had two large living rooms and a third room to the rear. In the school days these living rooms were used as the classrooms for the two youngest classes. The rear room was used as the children's dining room. A few small steps downward led to a small room used as the children's cloakroom.

The grounds had a wild approach to the back with a more traditional and formal lawned frontage. This back area, with a dilapidated outhouse, was used as a playground for the younger children while the older children would use the front garden to walk around.

My first classroom, which would be 1958, Mrs Webber's, was the ground floor room on the left of the photo and my next teacher was Miss Kershaw, whose classroom was the ground floor room on the right. Memories are much faded now but I do remember open fires in the classrooms where the children would arrange their milk bottles in a semi-circle to warm them in winter.

Mrs Webber's class c. 1958; the author is pictured in the centre of the middle row. (Author)

The author's school report from 1958. (Author)

WHITELAKE SCHOOL

REPORT · Apr 1958

Name:— Michael Billington

Figures	Improving	M Webber
Arithmetic	Pleasing progress	"
Tables	Quite good	"
Reading	Progressing	"
Writing	Is working hard	"
Colour Work	Good	"
Hand Work	Quite good	"
Drill	Keen	"
Games	Good	
Scripture	Quite good	
Poetry	Good	
Singing	Good	

Times Absent 33 · Times

Headmaster's Remarks:— A Stead
with reasonable progress
subject.

A school fees invoice from 1958. (Author)

WHITELAKE SCHOOL,
FLIXTON.
July 1958

To Mr Billington

School Fees are now due on behalf of your Son, Michael for the term commencing Sept 9th

Cheques should be made payable to "Whitelake School."

B.B. WESLEY,
Head Master

	£	s	d
Tuition	6	6	0
Elocution	1	1	0
Dancing			
Games		10	6
Swimming			
Books:- Exercise 4 @ 11d		3	8
3 @ 10d		2	6
Suess for the Young		2	6
Rea...		7	10
Total	£8	14	0

Today's preoccupation with health and safety and risk assessments would preclude this quaint custom, effective though it was.

The report above from 1958 shows a very pleasing assessment of the author's youthful endeavours and indicates promising progress in spite of a fair degree of absence. It is interesting to note that for 'writing' the comment is 'working hard'. The report also shows remarks made by the headmaster, Mr Wesley. The invoice for tuition fees is stated to be 6 guineas with an extra guinea for elocution. As will also be noted, parents had to purchase exercise books. My first teacher, Mrs Webber, lived next door to the school in a house that still remains standing to this day.

Eventually the Whitelake School building and land was cleared by 1980 for housing. The official Urmston town guide for 1958 lists Whitelake School as one of 'two private schools within the district which maintain a high standard of education'. The head teacher is stated to be B .B.Wesley, Esq. and the number of pupils is eighty (mixed). The other school was stated to be Caius House on Church Road, with the headteacher as Miss S.M. Winstanley and the number of pupils here was sixty (mixed).

Caius House, c. 1935. The classrooms at Whitelake were very much the same in appearance. Notice the open fire. (David Smith)

The school, originally at 20 Lyme Grove (now Wendover Road), was founded in 1909. It moved to Abbotsford on Church Road, taking over the building from Urmston College, in 1932. An advertisement in 1937 boasted numerous successes in scholarships, public school examinations and other examinations. The school was a kindergarten and preparatory school for boys and girls aged from 5 to 14 and offered games, swimming, football, cricket, tennis and physical training as well as the more academic subjects. The uniform was an eye-catching red blazer and caps for the boys. The girls wore red blazers with grey skirts and red bowler hats. In summer they would wear red and white gingham dresses with a straw boater with a red ribbon around the crown'.

The school later changed the name to Abbotsford Preparatory School for Boys and Girls when it moved to Flixton Road in 1997. The building was formerly Flixton Drill Hall and later Urmston College of Adult Education, where local historian Bob Potts was a history teacher in the 1980s. Abbotsford Preparatory School still flourishes to this day.

Case Study 2: George Baldwin

Looking at the wider picture nationally, The Philanthropic Society, formed in September 1788, was initiated by a group of reformers anxious to improve the morals of the poor and to improve the fortunes of London's vagrant and destitute children. They were also instrumental in providing instruction in useful skills to the inmates of prisons and reform schools.

The Victorian age was one not only of philanthropy towards making education available to poor children but also one of rescuing children from a homeless start in life, especially when there were either no parents or parents of dubious character. There are many instances in the Manchester Industrial Schools Register of children being sent to one of these schools until the age of 16 and thereby preparing them for respectable employment in life. Locally the industrial schools were in Sale, Heaton Mersey and Ardwick Green. Girls would be prepared for a life in domestic service while boys would be given training in a craft such as saddle making, boot making or blacksmithing, or were sent to one of the armed services. Children sent to these schools came predominantly from urban areas, such as Salford, Chorlton-on-Medlock, Gorton, Hulme and Ancoats but also from further afield such as Portsmouth, Nottingham and London. Comments on their charge sheets would invariably indicate parents of bad character, with mothers often in prostitution and fathers absent, a drunkard or in prison. The children really were starting life on the back foot and their 'transgressions' would often be recorded as 'wandering', 'vagrancy' or 'theft'; the latter often being the stealing of something as insignificant as a loaf of bread, apples or turnips. The character of parents would often be described as 'bad', 'very bad', 'indifferent', 'careless', 'questionable' and in circumstances such as 'poor', 'very poor' and 'wretched'.

However, instances of such children being taken into the industrial schools from the still rural townships of Urmston, Flixton and Davyhulme are very rare. One such case, nonetheless, involved young George Baldwin. George was just 11 years and 5 months old when he was taken to the Barnes Industrial School in Heaton Mersey and, at the time, was living at 46 Stretford Road, Urmston, as stated on his charge sheet. George is described as being 4ft 1¼in tall, of proportionate figure, 4st 7¼lb, fresh complexion, fair hair and blue eyes. He is recorded as having attained the educational state of second standard. Children were graded in six standards; one being basic attainment and six being the best attainment. To attain the second standard George would have been able to read 'one of the narratives next in order after monosyllables in an elementary reading book used in school'. He would also have been able to 'copy in manuscript character a line of print' and his arithmetic attainment would require him to calculate 'a sum in simple addition or subtraction and the multiplication table'. These standards were laid down by the education department in London in the Revised Code of 1862. A child of George's age, however, would have been expected to have been working within the fifth and sixth standards.

His parents are described as respectable and in fair circumstances, with his father stated to be in employment as a platelayer and his mother a washerwoman. His religion is stated to be Church of England and for the section on the charge sheet that requests to 'state if illegitimate', the notation declares 'no'.

George was admitted to the school on 21 December 1900 for a term lasting until 11 July 1905 under section 15 of the Industrial Schools Act of 1866; his charge was stated to be theft, although we are not told the nature of what was stolen. Although on the face of it Urmston may be assumed to have been a quiet, peaceful backwater, *The Guardian* newspaper reported the area as being a rough place to live at this time with murder, robbery, suicide and accidents an almost daily occurrence.

George's father was William Baldwin, born in Crowden in Lincolnshire in 1849, and his mother Jane, who was born in Hammersmith, London. We do not know how William and Jane met but we do know that they lived in Lincolnshire

When Baptized.	Child's Christian Name.	Parent's Name. Christian.	Surname.	Abode.	Quality, Trade, or Profession.	By whom the Ceremony was performed.
1891 July 5 No. 885	Ernest Son of	William Elizabeth Jane	Baldwin	Urmston	Plate Layer	E. Harwood Cooke Vicar
July 5 No. 886	George Son of	William Elizabeth Jane	Baldwin	Urmston	Plate Layer	E. Harwood Cooke Vicar
July 5 No. 887	Stanley Son of	William Elizabeth Jane	Baldwin	Urmston	Plate Layer	E. Harwood Cooke Vicar.

Baptism certificate for George Baldwin and five of his siblings; all six were baptised on 5 July 1891 by Rev. Elijah Harwood Cooke. (Manchester Central Reference Library))

July 5 No. 882	Arthur Son of	William Elizabeth Jane	Baldwin	Urmston	Plate Layer	E. Harwood Cooke Vicar
July 5 No. 883	Walter Son of	William Elizabeth Jane	Baldwin	Urmston	Plate Layer	E. Harwood Cooke Vicar
July 5 No. 884	Clara daugh. of	William Elizabeth Jane	Baldwin	Urmston	Plate Layer	E. Harwood Cooke Vicar

after they married, around 1869, after which their first child, Rebecca was born in 1870. The young family then moved to Glossop in Derbyshire, where two more children were born; Eliza in 1872 and James in 1874. A further move was then made, this time to Droylsden, Manchester, where another two children were born; John in 1878 and Arthur in 1880. This is where an important historical pattern becomes evident. Many agricultural workers and their families at this time were migrating to the towns looking for work in the mills and factories and the new construction industries such as canal navigation and the railways as work on the land was becoming scarce.

The first railway in England was opened in 1825 but it wasn't until 1873 that the railway came to Flixton and Urmston. It is significant then that the Baldwin family moved to Urmston in 1881 as the census of the same year shows William as a platelayer and Jane as a washerwoman, as corroborated on the aforementioned charge sheet. The family had presumably relocated to Urmston to avail themselves of more reliable and regular employment on the railway. A further six children arrived to William and Jane, all born in Urmston; Walter (1882),

George Baldwin's charge sheet under section 15 of the ISA 1866. (Manchester Central Reference Library)

Clara (1884), Ernest (1887), George (1889), Stanley (1891) and Annie (1895). Annie died on 10 March 1902 aged just 7 years and she is buried with her parents in Urmston cemetery.

George, born on 12 July 1889, is recorded as being baptised on 5 July 1891, just seven days short of his second birthday, at St Clement's church, Urmston. George's siblings Arthur, Walter, Clara, Ernest and Stanley were all baptised with George on the same day with consecutive record numbers of 882 to 887 inclusive. Rev. Elijah Harwood, first vicar of St Clement's, is shown in the records as officiating at the baptism.

The family was still resident at 46 Stretford Road for the 1901 census – minus George, of course, but with the addition of 51-year-old Mary Hinchcliffe, described as a visitor with the occupation of housekeeper (domestic).

The subject of our story, George, did not go into the armed services, nor did he acquire a trade; the next we hear of him, in the 1911 census, is that he is single, aged 22 and working, after his term at the Barnes Industrial School had ended, as a carter for a coal merchant. The family are living at 25 Lorne Grove off Higher Road, where George's brother Stanley, aged 20 and also single, is shown as being employed as a blacksmith. Their mother, Jane, 59, is recorded as being a widow. She had lost her husband, William, earlier the same year. The only other resident in the household is Jane Lyson, single, 22 and shown as a boarder and a servant girl originally from Leeds in Yorkshire. His mother had left 46 Stretford Road by 1911 as the census for this year shows another family in residence.

George and Jane, this same Jane Lyson, were married at St Clement's church on 22 April 1911 and their marriage certificate shows them as both living at

9/1	Marriage solemnized at _The Parish Church_					in the _Parish_	
	of _Urmston_				in the County of _Lancaster_		
ns.	1	2	3	4	5	6	7	8
	When Married.	Name and Surname.	Age.	Condition.	Rank or Profession.	Residence at the time of Marriage.	Father's Name and Surname.	Rank or Profession of Father
9	_April 22nd_	George Baldwin	21	Bachelor	Carter	25 Lorne Grove	William Baldwin	Plate-Layer (deceased)
	19 11	Jane Lyson	22	Spinster	House-maid	25 Lorne Grove	William Lyson	Labourer

rried in the _Above Church_ according to the Rites and Ceremonies of the _Established Church_ by — or after _Banns_ by me

a Marriage { _George Baldwin_ } in the { _Stanley Baldwin_ _W. Driver_
solemnized
tween us, { _Jane Lyson_ } Presence of us, { _Emily Bromley_ } Curate.

George and Jane Baldwin's marriage certificate. (Manchester Central Reference Library)

25 Lorne Grove. Most of the houses on Lorne Grove were demolished in 1957 to make way for modern houses. Just two of the original houses remain; Mary's View and Rose View. Both houses have plaques declaring the names with the date 1873. George's occupation is still shown as a carter and that of his bride a housemaid. His father, William, is shown as deceased at the time of the wedding.

The last we hear of George is that he is employed as a builder's labourer living with his wife, whose occupation is described as 'unpaid domestic duties'. They had three sons: Norman, born in 1913, and George and Eric (presumably twins) born on 1 April 1916. In a later street record of 1939 return Eric's occupation is recorded as a coalman.

Later George and Jane are found living in a flat on 25 Atkinson Road. Atkinson Road, a very short road, now contains just a few houses that would have been standing during George's lifetime. One is a hairdresser's and the other two residential. The road also contains Morris Hall and the back of The New Victoria public house. The 1939 register shows George and Jane still at this address;

Lorne Grove, where George Baldwin lived with his widowed mother and his fiancée Jane prior to their marriage. (Urmston Official Guide 1971)

George as a builder's labourer and Jane as a housewife whose employment is still described as 'unpaid domestic duties'. One other member of the household in this register is watchman Arthur Ackerley (born 22 August 1886).

George died the following year on 10 January 1940, aged just 50. His death certificate shows that he died at home of cardiac failure and his wife, Jane, present at the death, registered the death the very same day. Interestingly, although he is described as a builder's labourer the year before, the death certificate describes his occupation as coal carter. He is buried in Urmston cemetery in the same grave as his mother and father and sister Annie. Also in the grave is William's grandson Arthur Norman, aged just 2 years old; he had died on 16 March 1902. Sadly the gravestone lies on the ground broken in two pieces with the plinth still standing.

There is no mention on the gravestone of George's wife Jane. As George was only 50 when he died, and Jane just one year older, it would be conceivable that she could have remarried. However, further research shows that she died on 25 June 1950 still with the surname Baldwin. She did, in fact, die at home at 27 School Road, Stretford, where she lived with her son Eric. Her death certificate shows that she died of a disease of the mitral valve and that she is described as the 'widow of George Baldwin, coal roundsman with the Co-operative Society'. She was buried in Stretford cemetery in the council-owned public paupers' graves under the shade of a sycamore tree. However, although she is buried with three other named deceased, her name and date of death are marked. A payment, presumably by her son Eric, would have had to be made for this inscription. There could well be others in the same grave whose names do not appear due to the lack of this payment. In some areas of the country, these graves were known as 'guinea graves' as that is how much payment was needed for the inscription. This avoided the indignity of being buried in an unmarked grave. This system was originally instituted in Leeds in the 1850s.

As a footnote, George's first Urmston address, 46 Stretford Road, would possibly have been where the Shell filling station now stands opposite the Lord Nelson public house; the next house number after Trafalgar House, 36 Stretford Road, is number 48. This, of course, would only be the case if the numbers followed the same order then as they do now.

RELIGION

Old records tell us that before the Manchester Ship Canal opened in 1894, Flixton parish 'partakes much of the character of a Cheshire parish lying in the small portion of the hundred of Salford and of necessity partly manufacturing but principally agricultural'. Flixton was once a prebend of Lichfield Cathedral and curacy records trace the parish church of St Michael back to 1198 but it is, in all probability, much older.

People were baptised and married in the parish church, which was the centre of social life. Saints' days provided relief from the hardships of everyday life as they provided an excuse for merrymaking in the church grounds.

However, a favoured subject for sermons was to impress upon the congregation the fact that God, in his infinite wisdom, had appointed a place in society for every man, woman and child and it was their bounded duty to remain contentedly in their places. Anyone denying this concept was offending against the divine order, an order which was, incidentally, reflected in the seating arrangements in the church itself. The families of the clergy and the squire would sit in specially appointed pews, carefully segregated from the rank and file of the worshippers. There was even a hierarchy within the realms of the 'rank and file' as farmers and tradesmen were kept apart from cottagers, who were considered the lowest of the low and placed at the back of the church or in the side aisles.

St Michael's, Flixton

The earliest reference to St Michael's is in the Domesday Book, and Christians have worshipped on the site for some 900 years. This makes it the oldest church in the area and there are records of priests going back to AD 900, which indicates that there must have been a Saxon church in the area.

The Normans acquired the land in the area soon after the 1066 invasion and there is evidence of Norman carving above the east window on the exterior of the church. Roger de Poitou had given the land to Albert Grelley, lord of Manchester, who gave away the church as a dowry for his daughter, Emma, who married Orme Fitz-Ailward de Torboc in 1150. The church itself was founded by Emma's nephew Robert de Lathom, who gave it to Burscough Priory in 1190, and by 1500 the church had reached its present length. However, only the east wall of the chancel remains of this medieval building.

The nave and aisles were built in 1756 and the tower was rebuilt in 1731, at a cost of £300, after the churchwardens had levied a compulsory rate from parish householders. The present tower dates from 1889 as a result of rebuilding to commemorate Queen Victoria's jubilee. The tower was taken down and rebuilt in the same style but 3ft higher to better accommodate the bells. The bells were partly retuned in 1888 and fully retuned in 1938. The chancel had to be partly rebuilt in 1815 when one of the piers gave way and the wall fell in. The north-east vestry was built in 1851. Nineteenth-century additions include the stone reredos and pulpit, which were added in 1877.

St Michael's parish church, Flixton. (Author)

Langton, in his *A History of the Parish of Flixton,* mentions that in the seventeenth century the church porch was used as a place in which to redeem mortgages: 'the porch, no doubt, being sacred, lending additional weight to the transaction'. The current porch, which looks much newer than the adjacent walls, was donated by George Bolton Stott in 1919. He also donated the communion rail in 1901.

In Volume 5 of *The History of The County of Lancaster,* the church is described as standing 'at the east end of the village on high ground about 250 yards north of the River Mersey with a very extensive view from the churchyard southward over Carrington Moss'. The chancel is described as being:

27ft by 17ft., with north vestry and organ changer, nave 36ft. 6in. by 17ft. 6in. with north and south aisles, and west tower 13ft. square. These measurements are all internal. The south aisle extends the whole length of the nave and chancel and is 61ft. 4in. long by 12ft. 3in. wide. The north aisle is the same width and 37ft. 10in. in length.

The church has been so much rebuilt that little or nothing of the original work remains except in the reconstructed walling, the lower part of which appears to be old or entirely rebuilt of ancient masonry.

Apart from a seventeenth-century oak chest in the vestry, generally speaking, all the fittings of the church are modern, mostly dating from 1877 or later. The chest is accompanied by the description as follows:

In consequence of the 'laxity' shown by certain clergy in the registering of christenings, marriages and deaths an order was made in 1603 to provide each parish church with a chest with three separate locks.

This should be opened every Sunday in the presence of the Wardens and clergy to keep a record of baptisms, marriages and burials.

Each entry had to be witnessed by both of the wardens and the rector, each of whom possessed a separate key to the chest.

Formal parish registers had been introduced in 1538 during the reign of Henry III and the chest was provided to keep the registers safe under lock and key. Registers found there date back to 1570.

Baines describes the church as 'a small plain edifice of modern date, placed at the eastern extremity of the village, pleasantly situated upon an elevated site'.

He goes on to describe the windows as being semicircular at the top and the tower as being handsome, though not lofty, with an embattled parapet surmounted by small pinnacles. The interior he describes as being 'if possible, more plain than the exterior'.

St Michael's has impressive stained-glass windows. We start on the north wall just to the left as you enter the church. The first window shows a scene of Christ the Good Shepherd holding a shepherd's crook in his right hand while cradling a lamb in his left arm. At the bottom, two angels unfurl a scroll 'To the Glory of God and in Loving Memory of Albert Warburton. Died March 8th 1950. This window is given by his wife.' The next window shows Jesus with Martha and Mary. The dedication reads 'To the Glory of God and in Loving Memory of Eliza Frances Reade this window is erected by her husband A.D. 1899'. The window was made by Mayer & Co. Munich.

The last window in the north wall depicts a young man showing the empty tomb to the three women carrying jars of anointing oils, Mary Magdalene, Mary the mother of James and Salome. (Mark 16: 1–8) 'This window is erected by the children of Charles and Sarah Reade to the Glory of God and in loving memory of their parents. Also in affectionate remembrance of their grandparents John and Hannah Johnson. A.D.1881.' Again, the inscription tells us that the window was made by Mayer & Co. Munich & London.

We now come to the east wall with the altar surmounted by a large three-panelled window separated by stone mullions with the scene depicting the Crucifixion on the centre panel and the SS Michael and Thomas in the adjacent panels. St Michael is shown driving his spear into the recumbent dragon while St Thomas is depicted hiding a spear and book. The symbols of the four evangelists are also shown.

'He ascended into Heaven' is the inscription under the dramatic depiction of Christ's Ascension, also in the east wall and to the right of the main window. Here Jesus ascends on clouds, arms wide and flanked by the four evangelists all holding books. The window is 'Dedicated to the Glory of God in memory of Thomas Rogers of Liverpool who died 2nd March AD 1858 in the 64th year of his age'. The window was manufactured by R.B. Edmundson & Son of Manchester.

The window to the left of the main window in the east wall is not visible to the congregation as it is behind closed doors, behind which is the vestry. It is a two-light window separated by a stone mullion; in the left-hand light Mary is holding lilies in her right hand with the infant Jesus on her left arm; he is holding a dove in his left hand while his right is in the act of giving a blessing. In the right-hand panel is St Joseph, who is holding lilies in his right hand and a staff in his left. The dedication reads 'In memory of Emily Marianne Gregory who died the XXVI of May MDCCCLIII aged XIII years.'

Jesus with the children is the subject of the first window in the south wall with the legend 'Suffer little children to come unto me. Of such is the kingdom of Heaven' running underneath. The dedication runs:

> To the Glory of God in memory of Ralph William aged 4 years who died on the 7th of Alice Amelia aged 2 years who died on the 24th and of Margaret Ann aged 6 years who died on the 26th November 1858 children of William Wright Worthington Wright and Margaret Amelia his wife.

The roundel in the upper part of the window depicts the Ascension of Jesus with three soldiers cowering. He holds a banner declaring 'I am the resurrection and the life'. The window was manufactured by R.B. Edmundson & Son of Manchester.

The next scene is that of the baptism of Jesus by his cousin John with the inscription 'Thou art my beloved son in thee I am well pleased,' and the window is 'Dedicated to the Glory of God in affectionate remembrance of the late alderman John Kay Esq by his nephew Richard Kay.'

The next window depicts the scene with Mary Magdalene washing and anointing the feet of Jesus in the house of a Pharisee, who looks on in disdain. (Luke 7: 36–50). The legend at the top of the window proclaims 'I am the resurrection and the life' and the dedication runs as follows: 'To the Glory of God and in loving memory of Ruth Chadwick of The Grove Urmston who died April 26th 1886 this is erected by her sister Jane Taylor' (the U of Urmston is written as a V). Two angels unfurl a scroll with this dedication. Both Ruth and Jane are buried in the churchyard.

The last window in the south wall shows the Angel Gabriel with huge golden wings, right arm raised and holding a trumpet in his left hand. Below, Jesus raises Lazarus from the dead. The inscription runs 'To the Glory of God in memory of Arthur William Whitnall Lord of the Manor of Flixton: Born July 3rd 1848: Died Febry 20th 1890'. Here also the letter U is shown as V.

There are no stained-glass windows in the west wall.

A window often overlooked is the small window in the north porch depicting St George. The porch itself was built in 1919 by George Bolton Stott and his wife Ann. A bronze plaque in the porch lists the names of First World War dead

Flixton . .
Church . . .

A drawing of St Michael's church. (From Langton's *A History of Flixton, Urmston and Davyhulme*, 1898)

and the inscription runs 'To the glory of God and in grateful memory of the undermentioned officers and men from this parish who gave their lives for their country in the Great War 1914–1918'. Another bronze plaque in the porch lists the dead of the Second World War with the citation 'To the glory of God and in memory of the men of this parish who gave their lives in the World War 1939–1945'. Various marble plaques in the church pay testament to the Wright Family of Flixton House.

Until 1806 there were four bells, of which one, known as the poor folks' bell, was subscribed for by the villagers. Three of the bells bore the motto 'Jesus be our speed' and the fourth 'Leonard Asshawe, Peter Egerton, Esq. 1624'. The bells were recast in 1806 by John Rudhall of Gloucester and four new ones added by public subscription. The first peal was rung on 25 January 1808. The bells were met at Stretford by a band of musicians, who played all the way as they processed on eight carts decorated with flags led by the churchwardens to Flixton. When the bells arrived at the church the tenor bell was upended, placed in a field and ten guineas' worth of double-strong ale put in 'for the population to regale themselves with'. The beer was consumed within an hour.

In 1558 Leonard Asshawe had left money in his will for the purchase of bells for the church and the inscriptions bear witness to his bequest being carried out. The 1624 recasting was at the expense of Peter Egerton of Shaw.

Before Carrington church was built a bell, called 'the pudding bell', was rung every Sunday at 1 p.m. and again at 2 p.m. to let the people of Carrington know that there would be a service at Flixton in the afternoon.

The plate was described as consisting of a flagon, 1776, a gift of William Allan, esq., Davyhulme, a chalice and two pattens and a large almsdish, 1875. Perusal of the churchwarden's accounts can reveal some very interesting information. In 1705 payment for such items were as follows:

Besoms for the church 6d, glazing for the church and school 6s 8d, candles 3d and three farthings, hooks and nails 4d, ringing the bells on 5th November 6s 6d, bell ropes 5s, lime and hair 1s 4d and 3d for a school lock.

In 1724 payments were made for:

Bread and wine at Christmas 5s 4d, bread and wine at Michaelmas 5s 9d, bread and wine at Palm Sunday 5s 9d, bread and wine at Whitsun 5s 9d, a pound of candles 6d, wire for clock 6d, three hundred laths and carriage 8s 6d, ringing on 5th November 7s 6d, parchment for writing a List of Births etc on, mending the church gates 4d, washing the surplice 2s, oyl and besoms 2s 6d, and timber 13s 8d.

Other expenses included £7 10s agreed with the painter for his work and £3 2s 4d for the 'Joyner's' bill.

However, St Michael's has not lasted to this day without courting controversy and the churchwardens were severely brought to task, as this report from *The Wiltshire Independent* newspaper on Thursday, 27 June 1839 makes clear. Under the heading 'Seats in Churches', the report states that:

It has been often stated that all parishioners have a right to be accommodated with seats in their parish church, and this point was recently decided in the Chester Consistory Court on the hearing of a suit instituted by Mrs Kembley [the surname is wrongly quoted in the newspaper; the correct name should be Mrs Harriet

Knubley] against the Churchwardens of Flixton, Lancashire, for not providing her and her family with seats in the church according to their condition in life, she being an inhabitant and parishioner. The chancellor said, the Church of Flixton seemed to include most of the errors prevalent with respect to seats. He observed – 'We find pews sold when no legal sale can be effected – pews let when persons had no right to let them – pews devised by will when the parties had no property in them – pews claimed by non-parishioners who are precluded as such from occupation – pews considered an apartment to Estates when they never can be. And churchwardens, in violation of their duty, suffer all these irregularities to take place under their eyes without feeling that they are at liberty or bound to correct them'. The Chancellor directed the Churchwardens to appropriate a particular pew to the plaintiff and her family, &c., the persons dispossessed by this arrangement to be accommodated elsewhere.

Harriet Knubley took this further; as a teacher at Shaw Hall she wanted seating for her staff and pupils as well. An earlier law of 1836 declared that the sale of pews was illegal but it took several years to get everyone to comply. Langton refers to the aggrieved lady as Mrs Knubley who kept a ladies' school in Shaw Hall in the early part of the nineteenth century.

Another interesting story involving a disagreement concerned a stove situated opposite the the door on the south side near the communion table, originally placed there in 1814 for the comfort of the Sunday school children. In 1823 Mr Norreys of Davyhulme complained that the stove was too near his pew and he requested the churchwardens to remove it. The churchwardens refused, at which Mr Norreys applied to the lay rector, Mr Gale, who lived in York and had the authority to intervene; he ordered the stove to be moved by force. The churchwardens then sued Mr Gale for trespass and damage to the stove. An appeal was entered at the Sessions and the decision reversed. Mr Gale then took the matter to the Lancaster Assizes where he, likewise, brought an action for trespass against the churchwardens where Judge Holroyd decided against them with damages of 1s with 40s costs.

There is a mural tablet to the memory of Mr Norreys in the north aisle. His name was originally Harris but he married the heiress of Davyhulme Hall, who claimed to be descended from the Norreys of Speke.

Another story involves a Mr Taylor, who wished for a grave to be dug in the chancel for his brother to be alongside one that had already been dug for his wife. The sexton began digging but this was within 3ft of a pillar; and 3ft down was encountered a child's coffin near the foot of the pillar. On removing the coffin a trickle of soil resulted. The sexton dug down to a depth of 5ft, after which he broke off for his tea. However, his meal was disrupted when he was called back to the church to find that the pillar had collapsed with the result that the whole chancel roof caved in. The Taylor family was sued for damages but lost as the sexton was employed by the church.

The first record of an organ was in 1843 and a new organ was built at a cost of £700 in 1900. The organ was modernised and rebuilt in 1966. Local craftsmen made the brass chandelier, dedicated to Ethel Collier, in 1968 and the design represents the corn and wine of Holy Communion and the crown of thorns.

In Volume 5 of *The History of The County of Lancaster* the church materials are described as 'being built of red sandstone, the roofs of the chancel, nave and aisles being covered with stone slates, and that of the vestry with green slates'. This volume goes on to mention the 25in by 19¾in brass plaque on the south-west wall known as 'The Radcliffe Brass'. It states:

At the west end of the south aisle was formerly a brass to the memory of Richard Radcliffe of Newcroft (died 1602), but during a recent decoration of the church it has been removed to the vestry. It bears the figure of Radcliffe in armour and his two wives, kneeling at each side of a book desk, with the three sons of the first wife, and the two sons, three daughters, and three infants (swaddled) of the second. The first wife, Bridgett (Caryll) widow of W. Molyneux, kneels with her three sons opposite to Radcliffe, while the second wife and her children kneel behind him. Over the desk is a shield with the arms of Radcliffe of Ordsal with helm, crest, and mantling, and on each side a shield with the arms of Radcliffe impaling those of his wives.

Those who are recent visitors to the church will know that the brass is now back in the main body of the church. Lawson tells us that it was impossible to take a rubbing due to the incised lines being 'filled in with pitch or some other substance'. Interestingly, the last two lines were replaced with a separate strip of brass with the words 'departed this life' being replaced with the words 'deceased'. The bottom line in full reads, 'of 67 years, deceased the 13th of Ianvarie in Ano. Dom. 1602'.

St Michael's is said to accommodate two ghosts. A female figure is said to be seen often sitting in a rear pew, arriving and departing before she can be recognised. The second is a hooded monk who has the habit of periodically walking down the main aisle.

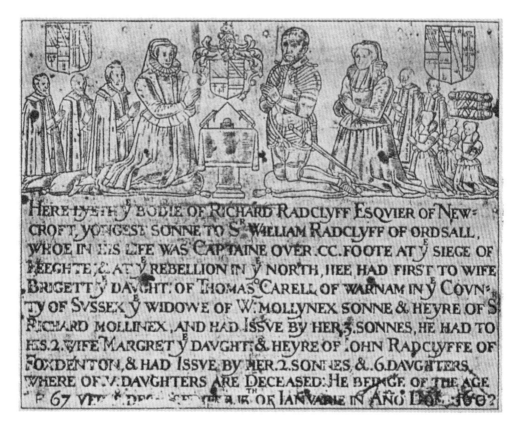

The Radcliffe Brass. (From Langton's *A History of Flixton, Urmston and Davyhulme*, 1898)

There is also the tale of the ghost of Sir Ralph Valentine, who was killed in battle at the Battle of Bosworth Field in 1485. He vowed to return dead or alive and his wife is reputed to have dreamed that she ran over the fields to meet him only to find that he was dead and still wearing his armour. Legend has it that a figure walks between Shaw Hall and Flixton church.

Table 1 shows a contrast in statistics from the parish register which started in 1570.

AD	Baptisms	Marriages	Burials
1570	11	2	7
1571	8	3	3
1831	81	3	103
1832	62	8	88

Table 1: Selected statistics from the parish register.

Restoration work was undertaken in 1964 which saw the plasterwork taken down to reveal the original stonework. St Michael's church is a Grade II listed building of outstanding interest.

Vicars of Flixton parish church are listed in Table 2.

1198	Henry de Worekid	1610	John Jones
1230	Andrew of Burscough	1613	George Byrom
1246	William of Burscough	1622	Edward Woolmer BA
1270	William Burnell	1660	Thomas Ellison
1305	William Wykeham	1664	John Isherwood BA
1316	Henry de Staunton	1693	George Smallbridge
1322	John de Kinairdly	1709	Edward Sedgwick
1326	Thomas de Clopton	1723	John Jones MA
1338	Richard de Chapliff	1752	Samuel Bardsley BA
1350	William de Wickham	1756	Humphrey Owen BA
1361	John de Waltham	1764	Timothy Lowton MA
1367	William de Newton	1771	Thomas Beeley
1383	Nicholas Shirbus	1807	Samuel Stephenson
1387	William de Boull	1816	Henry Burdett Worthington MA
1400	Richard de Kington	1823	William A. Cave-Brown-Cave MA
1425	Thomas Brown	1842	Arthur Thomas Gregory BA
1435	Andrew Holes	1863	Charles Barton BA
1442	John Bolde	1873	Richard M. Reece BA
1443	Gregory Newport	1884	Arthur E. Robinson
1459	Henry Grene	1886	William J. Hill
1472	George Downe	1892	Arthur William Smith
1482	John Yotton	1912	John Jolly
1492	John More	1936	Hugh G.G. Herklots
1502	Hugh Humphrey	1942	Joseph C. Wansey

1529	Nicholas Darlington	1945	Wilfrid Preston
1541	Nicholas Smyth	1952	Peter A. Ettrick MA
1547	Ralph Birch	1961	John C.K. Freeborn
1552	Edward Smyth	1973	Thomas E. Kennaugh
1563	Robert Radcliffe	1984	William James Twidell
1565	Richard Smith	2001	Susan J. Smith
1588	Nicholas Higson	2010	Victoria Louise Johnson
1604	William Hodgkinson	2016	Rev. Huw Thomas

Table 2: Vicars of Flixton parish church

St Clement's, Urmston

The foundation stone of St Clement's, a Grade II listed building, was laid on 16 March 1867 by the first Bishop of Manchester, Bishop Prince Lee, and the consecration of the building took place nine months later. *The Manchester*

St Clement's church, 1874, before the tower was built. (St Clement's parish church)

Courier and Lancashire General Advertiser reported the laying of the stone in it's edition of Saturday, 16 March 1867, commenting that Urmston 'is a pretty country village approached by a lane from Stretford from which it is two miles distant'. The article goes on to explain that the vicars from the church in Flixton had held divine service for some time in the Urmston schoolroom.

Urmston had, up to this date, been part of the parish of Flixton and in the mid nineteenth century the population was some 730. The people worked mainly on the land or in the cottage weaving industry and, at this time, there was no railway. St Michael's in Flixton was some 2 miles away from Urmston and the distance somewhat discouraged regular church attendance by the Christians of Urmston. It was with the intention of solving this problem that Rev. Charles Barton, rector of Flixton from 1863 to 1873, was joined by a local Urmston resident, Mr John Hibbert, to provide a local church for the Urmston flock. Mr Hibbert lived at Urmston Grange, which was to be demolished many years later to make way for the M60 motorway. Mr Hibbert had already been instrumental in promoting Christian worship by acquiring a building on Stretford Road for use as an infants' day school and Sunday school; Sunday services were also held in the building.

So it was that in the 1860s the feeling was held, by clergy and parishioners alike, that the time had come for a church to be built in Urmston itself. On 3 February 1865 a meeting was held in the Church school and an agreement was made to proceed with the plan. Various sites were considered, and the site chosen was an acre of land that originally formed part of the Urmston Hall Estate offered by Colonel Ridehalgh.

The cost of building the church amounted to over £2,600 and the sum was raised almost entirely by public subscription. Subscriptions amounted to £2,466 0s 6d, the ladies' fund £68 5s 6d and collections at opening services £75 9s 7d. Together with bank interest of £18 14s 4d the total raised came to £2,628 9s 11d.

The cost was broken down as follows.

	£ s d
Mark Foggett, Builder	2,125 00 00
ditto	128 04 02
ditto	57 18 11
Mr Burder, Legal Expenses	34 17 06
Mr J Medland Taylor, Architect	146 10 00

Heating Apparatus	35 00 00
Fencing	7 00 00
Stretford Gas Co	4 17 06
Gate and Posts	3 00 00
Thorns	1 12 06
Burnt Metal and Carting	3 01 06
Boundary Stones	0 13 00
Labourers forming Churchyard	9 12 00
Sundry Gifts to Workmen	3 12 00
For Scraper and Stone	0 17 06
Tiles	0 02 06
Bank Interest	12 02 05
Printing	6 19 11

The total cost of these disbursements came to £2,628 9s 11d.

The church building is of York stone in the decorated Gothic style. The roof slates are of two colours with a six-sided slender slated spikelet bell-turret at the east end. This is the sanctum tower that houses the sanctum bell.

The church was originally built for 300 worshippers with an anticipated future north aisle to take a further 200 souls; this extension was completed in February 1888, as were the foundations for the tower. The body of the church consisted of nave and south aisle divided from each other by an arcade and four arches resting on pillars with moulded and floriated capitals. The main entrance was through the north porch, later to be incorporated with the tower built in 1903 by local builder Joseph Spark at a cost of £1,600, although the final cost rose to £1,690 2s 0d. It had been originally intended for the tower to mark the turn of the century so that Urmston could celebrate the beginning of the twentieth century with a completed church. The clock, manufactured by Messrs W. Potts and Sons of Leeds, was added in 1906, a gift from the relatives of Mr Tom Reade in his memory.

Heating was originally by means of a coke-fired hot water boiler. The original gas lighting by fish-tailed burners giving an open flame was replaced by incandescent gas lighting in 1885. Incandescent mantles followed in 1905. Electric lighting was installed in the church in 1933 and a new oak pulpit replaced the old stone one. In 1952 the south porch was transformed into a columbarium for the interment of ashes. The garden of remembrance was created in 1963 and is situated to the south of the church.

The large arch entering the chancel once had decoration including the words 'O worship the Lord in the beauty of holiness fear before him all the earth'. This, and other decoration, has been whitewashed over.

Various gifts were bestowed upon the church on its consecration and official opening from benefactors, including the aforementioned acre of land from Col G.L. Ridehalgh; two silver communion chalices, flagon and paten from Ruth Chadwick of The Grove; Caen stone pulpit from Mrs J.T. Hibbert

The Chadwick silver. (Author)

(since replaced by an oak pulpit); stone font from Miss Hibbert and Mr Percy Hibbert; Caen stone reredos and decoration for the chancel walls from Mr Joshua Deakin (since replaced by a wooden reredos); velvet communion cloth from Mr J. Webster; oak fitting for the chancel from Mr J.E. Cockrell; two oak chairs for the chancel from Mr E. Atkinson; churchwarden's silver mounted staves from Mr John Faulkner; church bell from Mr Thos. Royle Higginson; oak gates for the churchyard from Mr Charles Schofield; evergreen shrubs for the churchyard from Mr H. Bent of Flixton; needlework for sedilia, cushions and kneeling stools for the chancel from Mrs J.E. Cockrell; the tiled chancel floor a gift of the daughter of H. Galloway, Esq.; a bible and prayer book for the reading desk from Rev. Charles Barton; and even gravel for the churchyard from Mr James Smith.

A brass lectern was also donated by Mrs Ashcroft to commemorate her late husband and the inscription runs 'In affectionate remembrance of the late John Ashcroft of Crofts bank who died Sep 9th 1867. Presented by his widow to St Clements Church in Urmston on the consecration 4th January 1868.' There is also a stone and marble credence table to the left of the altar and is inscribed 'In memory of Eliza Anne Hibbert'.

The first vestry meeting, held on 17 April 1868, decided on a yearly salary of £16 to Mr Henry Besford, who was appointed parish beadle. His duties included attending to and cleaning the church, ringing the bell and washing surplices. Organist John Bethell was appointed on a salary of £6 10s and choir-master Mr Towers on a yearly wage of £3 6s. Lighting the church for this first year of 1868–69 was £5 15s 11½d.

The first vicar was Rev. Elijah Harwood Cooke, of whom little is known, although he may have been born in Wales as the early part of his ministry was spent there. Cooke had studied at Trinity College, Dublin, where he obtained his BA. *The Bury and Norwich Post* announced on Tuesday, 2 June 1863 that he had been 'ordained (Deacon) by the Lord Bishop of Ely in the chapel within the Episcopal Palace of Ely on Sunday last', which would make it 31 May. His ordination as priest followed the year after, on Sunday 25 September 1864, by the Lord Bishop of Llandaff in the cathedral church of Llandaff, as reported in *The Monmouthshire Beacon* on Saturday, 1 October.

The Northwich Guardian reported on 17 November 1866 that 'the Bishop of Manchester has licensed the Rev. Elijah Harwood Cooke BA to the stipendiary curacy of the parish of Flixton and to officiate in a licensed room in Urmston'. This room would have been the school on Stretford Road where

Rev. Elijah Harwood Cooke, first vicar of St Clement's. (St Clement's parish church)

Sunday school and services would have been held prior to the construction of St Clement's church.

Cooke's first post was as curate of St Mary's church in Cardiff in 1864. He was curate at St Michael's church in Flixton in 1866 and must have seemed the likely choice to be the first incumbent at the new church in Urmston. He was 36 years of age when he took office at St Clement's on 9 November 1866. *The London Evening Standard* reported on Friday 17 January 1866 in the list of appointments that 'Elijah Harwood Cooke [had been appointed] to the incumbency of the new church of St. Clement Urmston'. Rev. Harwood Cooke was also involved in parish life and was vice-president of the Entwistle Golf Club, which was formed in March 1893. He proved a popular vicar and in 1891 he celebrated twenty-five years in the parish and received a gold watch, a pair of silver candlesticks and a silver inkstand from his parishioners, for which he reciprocated by giving a tea party to the children; 450 are said to have sat down to the meal. In 1891 the vicar became a member of Urmston Urban District Council. *Crockford's Clerical Directory* for 1897 reports the value of the living at £350 per annum.

The 1901 census shows Cooke resident at the vicarage with 49-year-old Elizabeth Mayor from Freckleton, who was employed as 'general servant (domestic)'. On 9 November 1916 he celebrated his golden jubilee. This milestone was commemorated by the parishioners who set up an appeal to raise funds. £750 was raised to purchase a ring of bells. They were installed in 1920 and rung for the first time on 19 February the same year.

The congregation grew steadily in the early years and within a year of opening its doors, the church obtained its first organ and organist, the aforementioned Mr John Bethell. The organ was second-hand and purchased for £15 from Mr John Platt MP. However, the purchase plus installation pushed the total cost up to £42 5s.

Reverend Cooke was to remain vicar of Urmston for sixty years until he died peacefully, sitting in his chair, on 11 January 1928 at the age of 98. He is buried in Urmston cemetery and his grave is an impressive grey granite cross in front of the chapels. The inscription reads 'Sacred to the memory of Elijah Harwood Cooke M.A. first incumbent of this parish who fell asleep January 11th 1928 in his 98th year after sixty two years faithful and devoted service among the people of Urmston. Curate in charge 1866–1868 Vicar 1868–1928.' Elijah Harwood Cooke left a substantial sum of money in his will for the use of the church.

A marble plaque can be seen in the entrance porch above the stairs leading to the tower. It is a commemoration of Rev. Cooke and runs as follows:

1866–1916

THE PEAL OF BELLS IN THIS TOWER
WERE PUBLICLY SUBSCRIBED FOR
AND ERECTED TO COMMEMORATE
THE JUBILEE OF THE
REVD E. HARWOOD COOKE. M.A.
THE FIRST VICAR OF URMSTON
AND IN WHOSE TIME THIS CHURCH
WAS BUILT AND TWICE ENLARGED

H.P. NAYLOR
J.F. AIDLEY
CHURCHWARDENS

Thomas Bache took over the curacy of St Clement's in 1925 and one of the first changes made after his incumbency was the installation of electric lighting in 1933 and a main drainage system.

As has been mentioned, the 1851 census had shown nationwide that for the first time in England's history, with the advance of industrialisation, over half of the population now lived in urban rather than rural areas. The opening of the Cheshire Lines Railway in September 1873 had resulted in Urmston becoming a desirable residential area. Between 1870 and 1891 the population had grown from 2,200 to 4,042. Consequently, with this growth in population the church needed to be enlarged. So, in 1873, the public were invited to subscribe and a bazaar, held at Stretford Town Hall, raised some £1,100 with attractions such as a display of mechanical singing birds, stereoscopic views and a musical box. The enlargement went ahead with the addition of the north aisle. The seating was increased from 360 to 552; further work enabled another 327 seats to be offered in 1888. Bishop James Frazer reopened the church on Easter Sunday, 27 March 1875, and the vicarage was completed the same year.

By 1900 many changes had taken place in Urmston and it was looking altogether a different place. The recent opening of the Manchester Ship Canal had also contributed to the transfer from a rural to an urban community and the population had grown to over 6,000. This milestone was marked by plans to build a tower, and subscriptions and bazaar efforts raised sufficient funds. By 1906 the tower bells and clock had been installed. The maker's name, W. Potts and Sons Leeds, is shown on the clock workings with the date 1906.

An interesting fact is that in January 1876 a gift of six brass collecting plates was given to replace the existing wooden boxes. The church magazine admonished thoughtless parishioners whose contributions had not been in the 'coin of the realm!'

The parishioners are understandably very proud of the church's stained-glass windows; there weren't any originally, but they have been donated by worshippers over the years, mainly in remembrance of departed loved ones.

The subject matter on the great east window covers the story of the Redemption, which includes various scenes. The Last Supper, in the lower part of the centrepiece, shows the usual scene of Jesus at table with his disciples with a crestfallen Judas as the only one without a halo holding the bag of thirty pieces of silver. The chalice and patten are on the table with the flagon in front of the table; the donation made by Ruth Chadwick when the church was consecrated. The Crucifixion is depicted in the upper central panel with Mary Magdalene shown with long, yellow, flowing hair – the mark of the prostitute, and in contrast with the more modestly attired Mary, mother of Jesus. St John the beloved makes up the three mourners at the foot of the cross. The rising from the tomb with the angel sitting by the slab slid back and the sleeping guard is in the left panel and the Ascension into heaven in the right panel. The Trinity is also represented in the form of three trefoils at the top of the centre panel containing the hand, the lamb and the dove.

The legend 'I am the resurrection and the life. If I be lifted up will draw all men unto me. I go to prepare a place for you' runs in a band separating the upper from the lower scenes. This, the largest window in the church, was given by Thomas Chadwick in memory of his wife Ruth, who died on 26 April 1886.

On the south wall the Lady Chapel windows were given in memory of the St Clement's Church Lad's Brigade, who gave their lives in the First World War, and shows the two Archangels Gabriel and Michael. The side panels are made from mosaics. The left-hand inscription reads 'To the Glory of God and in memory of the dear boys of St Clement's Church Lads' Brigade who gave their lives in the Great War 1914–1919. This window is dedicated'. Unlike the Boys' Brigade, which was interdenominational, the Lad's Brigade, formed by Walter M. Gee in 1891, was an Anglican youth organisation.

The right-hand panel runs: 'James Adshead, Malcolm Barlow, Stanley

Benson, John Bennett, William Gomersall, Walter Grundy, Geoffrey Y Heald, William H Kember, John Maskrey, William L Muskett, Roy Moorhouse, John Martell, William Nutter, Eric Norbury, Charles Smethurst, Ernest Sanderson, Stanley Smith, "I have fought the Good fight".'

The next window tells the story of Jesus visiting Mary and Martha, the sisters of Lazarus. The window carries the dedication 'In memory of Bessie R.A.B. Constantine died 15th October 1947 aged 91. Also Joseph A Constantine died 4th July 1945 aged 87 and Martha H Constantine died 10th Dec. 1903 aged 42'. This window carries the maker's name of Shrigley and Hunt, Lancaster in the bottom right-hand corner, a well-known and well-respected maker of stained-glass and art tiles. The business began in the 1750s as Shrigleys, with control passing to Arthur Hunt in 1868, and they made stained-glass for use throughout the UK and further afield in Europe. From 1878 the firm became known as Shrigley and Hunt. The firm only closed as recently as 1982.

The next window shows Jesus blessing the children with the dedication 'In memory of Annie M. Constantine, died 26th March 1929 and John Constantine, died 5th Feb. 1889. aged 38. also, Mary Elizabeth Constantine, died 6th April 1871 aged 19. This window is given by their sister Bessie Constantine.' This window also carries the name Shrigley and Hunt clearly written in the bottom right-hand corner.

The small window on the left of the west wall shows Jesus holding a lamb in his role as the good shepherd. The dedication reads 'In memory of John Constantine died 25th December 1891 aged 75 years, and Agnes Constantine died 20th November 1887 aged 68. This window is given by their daughter Bessie Constantine'. It is thought that, stylistically speaking, this window was also made by Shrigley and Hunt, although there is no signature.

The west window shows Jesus in the Sermon on the Mount. It is a large and impressive window composed of a large mullioned and transomed centre panel flanked by two smaller panels. Jesus is shown preaching to the people including children. The scene shows the poor, the sick and the lame as well as the wealthy; also the scribes and Pharisees who look on disapprovingly in the right-hand light. At the very top are shown the figures of St Clement, with his attribute the anchor, and St George. The dedication reads 'To the Glory of God and in loving memory of Thomas Chadwick of The Grove Urmston died April 5th 1895. This window is erected by his Sons and Daughters'.

The north aisle window shows a Christian knight receiving the Crown of Light from Jesus. The dedication is:

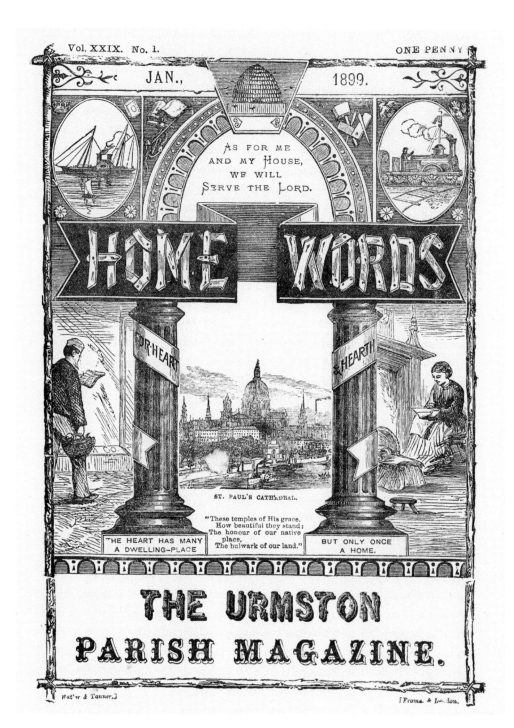

A parish magazine cover. (St Clement's parish church)

To the Glory of God and in memory of Lt. Corporal Stanley Benson MM. of the 7th Field Ambulance who was killed in action at Monrhu France, May 3rd 1917, aged 27 yrs. The third year of the Great European War. He was formerly Colour sergeant of the Urmston Church Boys' Brigade and devoted church-man. This window is erected by his loving parents Michael and Amelia Benson.

The last window in the north wall is a smaller window consisting of two panels near the organ pipes showing Jesus in the parables of the Good Samaritan and the Master of the Vineyard. The dedication reads 'In memoriam John Aitken J.P. Died Iuly XXIX MDCCCLXXXIII'. This window may also be by Shrigley and Hunt, although there is no signature.

Finally, we come to the round rose window above the organ pipes. This window was installed when the church was first built and contains a series of floral designs and the letters SC, standing for St Clements. There are the three emblems stand-ing for faith, hope and charity; the cross, the anchor and the heart.

As has been seen, Thomas Chadwick provided the funds for the east window in memory of his wife Ruth. When Thomas himself died in 1895 he was buried in the family vault in Flixton churchyard. In addition, a marble tablet in the middle of the north wall reads 'To the memory of Thomas Chadwick, J.P., of The Grove, Urmston, who died 5th April 1895 in his 72nd year and was interred in the family vault at Flixton Parish Church April 9th. Erected as a token of esteem by his *Work* people'.

St Clement's church was very proactive in organising and supporting such groups as the Urmston bible society, the girls' friendly society, athletic club, school cricket club, St Clement's brass band, men's club, the church mission-ary society and the literary and debating society, who met weekly. This latter group, in addition to debating, went on visits to such places as Owen's College Museum and the City Art Gallery, the latter of which contained, and still does to this day, many Pre-Raphaelite paintings of a moral and didactic nature such as Holman Hunt's *Hireling Shepherd* and *The Light of the World*; also Ford Maddox Brown's work, which would have appealed to the church-sponsored group. The debating society carried on into the 1930s.

St Clement's parish magazine was first published in 1873 in conjunction with Flixton parish. The first issues were printed on a single sheet then inserted into the monthly issue of *Home Words,* a magazine of stories of a moral nature. The cost was a penny and the magazine was circulated to 200 homes within the parishes of both Urmston and Flixton.

The debating syllabus, according to the parish magazine for October 1898, set out the topics for debate including such titles as 'The man of the past, present and future', 'Are the planets inhabited', 'The novel with a purpose' and 'The progress of democracy'.

The following year the subjects for debate included 'Was the French Revolution beneficial?' and 'Is an Anglo-Saxon alliance feasible?' Papers delivered included 'Thackeray', 'Carnivorous plants' and 'Modern church music', the last of which was assisted by 'a choir of ladies and gentlemen' and we are told that 'their singing was much appreciated and considerably helped to a very enjoyable evening'.

Other lectures and papers delivered included 'Is individual freedom attainable with our co-operation?', 'The hand of God in history', 'Woman's life in the East', 'Some old manuscripts', 'Some of Shakespeare's heroines', 'Was the Deluge partial or universal?', 'The development of church music', 'Further jaunts with the camera' and 'Wm. Morris – poet and socialist'. Also mentioned in the Urmston parish magazine for December 1899 is a report of the Church of England Temperance Society, who met monthly.

The parish magazine for January 1899 reports that on 1 December 1898 Rev. A.W. Davis spoke 'words of encouragement and warning' and that 'the Temperance society had a *special* sin to fight against, a sin which marred, debased and ruined the soul as well as the body'. He went on to remind his audience that St Paul, speaking of drunkards, had warned that they 'shall not enter the kingdom of heaven'. He explained that intemperance was due to idleness, the unattractiveness of the home and trouble and disappointment.

The guest for the March meeting was Rev. A. Dewhurst, who told the story of St George and the dragon and used the dragon as an analogy for the evils of drink and that 'to escape the dragon we must keep out of his way'. Reverend Dewhurst also pointed out that as much barley used in a year for the brewing of alcohol could be used to feed 3 million people. Furthermore, £90 million was spent annually on drink and 60,000 committed suicide through drink every year in England, Ireland and Scotland. It appears Rev. Dewhurst didn't have any statistics for Wales. However, he also mentioned that in the parish where he lived he could count from eight to twelve public houses in every street.

May's special guest was Rev. B. Davis of Stretford, who referred to the 'enslaving energy of the Lilliputians' in *Gulliver's Travels* in an effort to impress on his audience how easy it was to acquire habits and how difficult to break away from them. The August meeting was noted for Mr. E.J. Spafford JP, who warned the audience that when foreigners wished to describe someone who was drunk they would would say 'he is as drunk as an Englishman'. He acknowledged that this was a 'national disgrace'.

On 2 November they boasted a very good attendance with 'the large room being well filled'. Rather surprising, though, is the report of the speaker for the evening, a Mr J.M. Matthews of Oldham, who gave 'a rather lengthy address on the "converting of Barley into Malt", "The Brewing of Ale" and "The Making of Ale"'. He also illustrated how alcohol was taken from wine. The vicar proposed a vote of thanks and thirteen new members joined the society after the meeting. Cynics would, no doubt, be of the opinion that the new members may have been hoping for more home brewing tips at future meetings.

Reverend Harwood Cooke did find himself in hot water on one occasion. He had opened a working men's club in Urmston in connection with the men's bible class, which allowed a limited amount of alcoholic drinks. The Urmston and District Total Abstinence Association issued a strong protest against 'another plague spot in Urmston'. They went on to state that:

> For several years the Vicar, along with other gentlemen, has been actively engaged in preventing any new licences being granted in Urmston and district and yet he takes an active part in the formation of a club with which is associated the sale of intoxicating drinks and against which the residents of Urmston have no power to object.

This was reported in *The Bolton Evening News* on Thursday, 14 January 1904.

The parish magazine for 1899 casts much light on the societies and their events with the support of the church. In addition to the debating and temperance societies, the January magazine reports on there being a long-held view to form a Boys' Brigade, an interdenominational organisation for boys founded in Glasgow by Sir William Alexander Smith on 4 October 1883 to develop Christian manliness. The decision to form the 1st Urmston Group Boys' Brigade was made only six years later and very soon the group had grown to 150 boys who met every Wednesday evening for drill; by May the numbers had increased to 160, with twelve officers. Uniforms cost 5s per boy and donations were solicited. Very soon £23 17s had been paid or promised towards the £50 needed. The March 1899 magazine reported that all the boys had now been 'furnished with full equipment of cap, belt, rifle and haversack'

The Boy's Brigade in the school yard of St Clement's school, Higher Road. (Alan Crossland)

(see the 1900 photo above, courtesy of Alan Crossland). Interestingly the emblem of the Boy's Brigade is the anchor, also the attribute of St Clement.

Also mentioned in the magazines were the annual New Year old folks' tea parties and the Whitsuntide festivities, which included tea parties and games for the Sunday school children. Older children would be taken on outings accompanied by parents and teachers and destinations would be the likes of the Yorkshire Dales or one of the resorts in North Wales.

General parish notices are also listed including births, deaths and marriages, and also at what times these services were held. Baptisms would be free and held at 2.30 p.m. on the first and third Sundays of the month. Marriages would be at 10.30 a.m. or 2.30 p.m. on any day except Sunday unless by special arrangement. As for funerals, they would be held at 4.30 p.m. for nonconformists and 5 p.m. for church people. Other times would require special arrangement. Mention was also made regarding harvest festivals, congregational tea parties, children's services, Sunday school, a volunteer parade service, vestry meetings, the distribution of Sunday school prizes and the old folks' dinner.

Table 3: Vicars of St Clement's church.

1868–1928	Rev. Elijah Harwood Cooke, MA
1928–1945	Rev. Thomas Bache, LTh
1945–1956	Rev. Thomas Gregory, ALCD
1957–1973	Rev. Leslie Rhodes, BA
1974–1985	Rev. Herbert Dunwoody, MA
1986–2000	Rev. Alan Tiltman, MA
2000–2010	Rev. Christopher Brown, LLB
2011–2014	Rev. Cath Faulkner
2014–	Rev. Karen Marshall, MA, BSc, BA, Dip HE

At the time of writing, further restoration work is ongoing on the church roof, including stonework, lead work, gutters and timber replacement. There is also a proposal to move the font into the north east corner of the church and for a public convenience and kitchen area to be built along the west wall

The old vicarage was demolished and a new one built in the 1980s. Three stained-glass windows, a wooden and marble fire surround and a number of doors from the old vicarage were salvaged and incorporated into the interior design of the new vicarage.

It should also be mentioned that, with the expansion of the township, the Humphrey Park estate had been built in the 1930s on the Urmston–Stretford border. It was decided that provision needed to be made for the worshippers occupying some 800 houses just built. It was therefore decided to provide facilities for the congregation. Thus was born the St Clement's branch church, which held its inaugural service on the first Sunday in January 1939. The venue had been rented but the opportunity came to buy the building in September 1940 at a purchase price of £2,250.

Christ Church on Lostock Road Davyhulme is now, as of 2015, part of the benefice that includes St Clement's. The building was consecrated on Saturday, 4 October 1969 to serve the parish of East Davyhulme in the diocese of Manchester.

Just before the Industrial Revolution Davyhulme was a small hamlet of farms and remote cottages. However, with the expansion of housing due to accommodation needed for the new workforce necessitated by nearby Trafford Park, a new congregation sprang up and a new church was needed to serve their needs.

Skilled workers came from all over to work in Trafford Park and housing was also needed to accommodate them. Until 1930 Davyhulme remained the more rural area but in the 1930s an expansion in building took place. First of all, in the late 1920s the three long parallel roads, Lostock Road, Canterbury Road and Winchester Road, were constructed with eventually smaller roads connecting them. The Second World War halted building for about a decade and the estate was completed in the 1950s.

The population of the area had grown so much that in 1959 it was obvious that it needed to be a parish in its own right and the conventional district of Christ Church, Davyhulme was formed. In 1963 the first meeting of the new church committee took place and by 1964 various plans were considered. In 1965 the new site on Lostock Road was given planning permission. Around this time in the late 1960s the land of Moss Farm between Kingsway Park and the motorway was developed as a new housing estate, increasing the size of the parish still further.

The foundation stone was laid by the Duchess of Kent on the Feast of Corpus Christi on 25 May 1967; on Saturday, 4 October 1969 the new parish church of Christ Church, Davyhulme was consecrated by the Lord Bishop of Manchester.

An interesting feature of the church is the four modern stained-glass windows. These were designed by Mr K.G. Bunton, AMGP, and each one represents an 'I am the …' saying of Jesus as recorded in St John's Gospel. They are:

I am the good shepherd.
I am the bread of life.
I am the way, the truth and the life.
I am the resurrection and the life.

Over the sanctuary is a large modern cross made in perspex and wood. This cross was designed by the sculptor Josaphina de Vasconcellos (1904–2005), an English sculptor of Brazilian origin who worked much of her life in Cumbria. The cross was made by five boys in residential care. For several years it hung in St Martin's in the Fields in London, and was then exhibited in St Paul's Cathedral, London, and Liverpool Cathedral. De Vasconcellos has produced many sculptures including 'The Holy Family' in Liverpool Cathedral and a bronze cast of 'Reconciliation' in Coventry Cathedral's ruined nave. She died on 20 July 2005 in a nursing home in Blackpool, a few months after her 100th birthday.

St Mary the Virgin, Davyhulme

St Mary the Virgin is a Grade II listed Anglican church designed by the architect George Truefitt (1826–1902), a Mancunian who had made his name and fortune in London. It is constructed of sandstone with a tiled roof. The church was built in 1889–90 and the foundation stone was laid by Mrs Moorhouse, wife of the Bishop of Manchester, on 13 July 1889, followed by the consecration on 23 June 1890. Two contrasting stones are used; a cream-coloured sandstone from the Lancashire coal measures and a red desert sandstone from the Triassic deposits of Cheshire.

The church was built at a cost of £4,000, the funds being raised mainly by bequests from the local Norreys family. The land was donated by Robert Henry Norreys and the church is dedicated to Robert, a bachelor, and his two sisters, Mary and Isabella. Electric lighting was installed in 1925 and the choir vestry in 1952. A church hall was added in 1990. In plan, the church is irregular cruciform with a short nave, shallow transepts and an octagonal tower. There is an inscription on a stone on the outside wall of the east end of the church, which reads:

St Mary the Virgin church, Davyhulme. (Author)

The church was built to the Glory of God and to the memories of R.H. Norreys, Esq., of Davyhulme Hall and his sisters Mary Norreys and Isabella Bowers, wife of the Very Rev. G.H. Bowers, D.D., sometime Dean of this Diocese. The cost was defrayed chiefly from bequests made by them to their nephew, J.B.N. Entwisle, Esq., of Foxholes, who founded the church and gave the land.

St Mary's is not as well endowed with stained-glass windows as St Michael's, Flixton and St Clement's, Urmston. They were all made by Bennet's of Old Trafford during the first third of the twentieth century.

As you enter the church and leave the narthex to proceed down the main aisle, the first window is on the north wall and the scene is that of Jesus the healer curing an ashen-faced invalid lying on a litter with a second invalid on crutches in the background. The legend reads 'Come unto me and I will give you rest' (Matthew 11:28). The dedication reads as follows: 'To the Glory of God in loving memory of Louisa Edwards "Sweet Green" Urmston who died March 6th 1929. This window is erected by her son and daughter.'

The east wall does not contain a Crucifixion scene as many other churches do. There are five tall windows set into the wall above the main altar. The taller and central window depicts Jesus carrying a lamb and lantern, combining the symbolism of Christ as Good Shepherd and Light of the World; the pose is very reminiscent of the painting *The Light of the World* by the renowned Pre-Raphaelite artist Holman Hunt.

To the right are two windows representing the Annunciation and the Archangel Gabriel. The windows to the left depict scenes of sowing and reaping where a man is sowing seeds from a large, shallow basket and an old man reaping the ripe corn with a sickle. These scenes illustrate the passage from Galatians 6:7, 'As you sow, so shall you reap.' The left window contains the dedication, 'This window is erected to the Glory of God and in affectionate remembrance of' and the text is continued on the right window 'William Faulkner who entered unto rest on May 11th 1901 by his loving sister'.

The south wall contains two stained-glass windows; the first depicts the image of Jesus as the good shepherd with the inscription 'I am the good shepherd and know my sheep' (John 10:14). There is a dedication here which runs as follows: 'In gratitude to God for the life and work of Edwin Wolfe, Priest and beloved vicar of this Parish 1923 to 1932. Died Feb. 15th 1932. Aged 66.'

The second window depicts the parable of the talents (Matthew 25:14–30 and Luke 19:12–25). The master is shown praising one of the three servants with the inscription 'Well done thou good and faithful servant'. One mysterious and anachronistic image in this window is the apparent inclusion of a modern-looking suitcase on a table.

There is a dedication on a brass plaque below this window as follows: 'To the Glory of God and in affectionate memory of The Reverend Thomas Dugdale Harland M.A. L.L.M. first vicar of this Parish 1881 to 1919. The above window is presented by a number of his friends and fellow worshippers associated with him in Christian faith and effort'.

The west wall contains two long and narrow windows. The left window shows the shepherds visiting the Holy Family in a nativity scene (Luke 2:8–18) in the top half with the lower half containing the scene of the presentation of the infant Jesus to the aged and long-bearded Simeon in the temple at Jerusalem (Luke 2: 22–35). The right-hand side window contains, in the upper section, the scene with Jesus and the children calling to mind the quote 'Suffer the little children to come unto me' (Matthew 19:14, Mark 10:14 and Luke 18:16). The lower section contains the scene of the Baptism of Jesus by John as recorded in all four gospels (Matthew 3:13–17, Mark 1:9–11, Luke 3:21–22 and John 1:29–34). This window too is dedicated to the first vicar of St Mary's and the dedication on a framed plaque below runs as follows:

To the Glory of God
And in ever-loving memory of Thomas Dugdale Harland MACCM
The first Vicar of this Parish
Called to Higher Service on Sunday morning 1st Feb 1920
Where I am there shall also My Servant be
This window is given by his dearly loved and loving wife Mary Harland

The lectern is an eagle standing on a globe carved in oak, donated in 1890 when the church was consecrated. The stone pulpit came from the church of St Mary in Deansgate, Manchester, when it was demolished. The sand-stone is of a different, finer-grained cream sandstone than that used in the church walls.

Within the sanctuary there is a carved oak reredos behind the altar. This incor-porates five statues in relief: Christ the King is the central figure flanked on either side by the four evangelists, Matthew, Mark, Luke and John. St John is shown holding a scroll and chalice while the other three hold their gospels.

There is a granite Celtic cross in the gardens between the north wall and Davyhulme Road. This was erected in 1922 as a memorial to those who died in the 1914–18 war. The choir vestry on the south side was built in 1952 as a memorial to those who died in the 1939–45 war.

The original wrought iron cross was taken down from the top of the church during March–April 1995 when it was nearly blown down in strong winds. Its precarious nature was due to the soft pine wood that supported it being rotten. The poorly designed socket that it stood in had allowed water in. It was about to be sent for scrap until Rev. Stuart Winward and the deputy warden, Mr Frank Firth, rescued it and it now stands in the garden of remembrance at the front of the church. A similar cross has now been set in oak in its place on the rooftop above the lantern tower. Another item rescued, and situated under the north wall behind the flower beds at the front of the church, is a large stone slab that once formed the entrance to Davyhulme Hall.

In his book *The Buildings of England*, Nikolaus Pevsner described St Mary's as 'a building of considerable character'.

Table 4: Vicars of St Mary's Church.

1890–1919	Rev. T.D. Harland MA
1919–1920	Rev. M. R. Smith
1920–1923	Rev. R.H. Bowen
1923–1932	Rev. E. Wolfe BA
1932–1945	Rev. F.W. Rideal LTh
1945–1952	Rev. J. Lowrey DTh MA
1952–1960	Rev. A. Noble ALCD
1961–1978	Rev. W. Bould TD
1978–1988	Rev. J.M. Sinclair BSc
1989–1998	Rev. S.J. Winward BA
1999–2004	Canon N.W. Dawson BD AKC
2005–	Canon C.S. Ford PhD. AKC

All Saints, Barton-upon-Irwell

The Roman Catholic church of All Saints, a Grade I listed building (and the only building to carry the Grade I designation in the three townships) was built in the architectural style known as thirteenth-century geometric / Early

English Gothic and designed by Edward Welby Pugin (1834–75), son of the eminent architect Augustus Pugin (1812–52). French influences include the rose window, bellcote and chantry.

The earliest date in the All Saints archives is 1793, when Fr James Haydock was chaplain at Trafford Hall. The chapel, although small, had been adequate for the congregation. However, by 1818 the congregation had increased substantially so that a decision was made to build a church suitable for the new flock. The chapel of St John at the hall was pulled down and the materials used for the new church. The original building included 320 free seats, 117 others and standing room for 100. The congregation totalled in the region of 300 parishioners between 1825 and 1850.

Building on All Saints started in April 1865 and construction, by the builder Mr Glaister of Liverpool, took over two years, the church finally being completed in 1868. The cost was in excess of £25,000, the sole beneficiaries being Sir Humphrey de Trafford and Lady Annette (nee Talbot) de Trafford, founders of the church. The opening of the church took place on 18 June 1868, a drizzly day by all accounts, and the Most Reverend Henry Edward (later Cardinal)

All Saints church, presbytery and gardens. (Author)

Manning was present to deliver a sermon. The consecration had taken place on 9 June by Right Rev. William Turner, the first Bishop of Salford. The church lies on the corner of Redclyffe Road and Old Barton Road at the extremity of the boundaries opposite to the Barton swing bridge on the south bank of the River Irwell, now the Manchester Ship Canal. *The Manchester Guardian* (Friday, 19 June 1868) reported on the opening and commented on the architectural beauty, especially the chancel. 'The pavement' of the chancel, commented the reporter, 'is enriched with encaustics of rare beauty'. He goes on to report that 'the communion rails consist of solid brass' and the altar 'is formed of Carrara, Sicilian, Sienna and Devonshire marble and Caen stone'. Mention was also made in the report of 'exquisitely carved angels with uplifted hands' on the tabernacle and also of the stained-glass by Messrs Hardman and Powell of Birmingham. The clerestory was also chosen for special mention as having 'considerable beauty'.

After Sir Humphrey died, Lady Annette continued to donate to churches in the area including St Mary's, Eccles, St Theresa's in Irlam and English Martyrs in Urmston. Sir Humphrey and Lady Annette are buried in the crypt of All Saints. Also buried there is their son Gilbert, who died aged 19, and also Sir Humphrey's siblings Belinda and Charles Cecil. Canon Kershaw, first parish priest of All Saints, also lies in the crypt. They are commemorated in the church's stained-glass windows described below.

The crypt lies below the de Trafford chapel, a small chapel where the de Trafford family would hear Mass at the front of the nave overlooking the sanctuary apart from the congregation. There is a small altar in the chapel with an effigy of the crucified Christ lying prostrate underneath framed by three arches supported by pillars. The tiles in front of the altar consist of fleur de lys motifs in green, blue and white with the words 'Sanctus, Sanctus, Sanctus, Sanctus'.

The tiled floor of the chapel consists of alternating tiles: one design showing the initials DT and the other the red griffin, emblem of the family, holding a blue shield emblazoned with a white griffin. The wooden doors leading to the chapel from the nave also have glass panels showing the same initials and griffin design. There are three stained-glass windows in the chapel; the first shows two lights surmounted by a cinquefoil light and the left panel shows the sacred heart with the initials IHC. The right-hand light shows a phoenix rising from the flames. The next window likewise shows two lights surmounted by a cinquefoil light. The subject matter here is the raising of Jairus' daughter in the left light and Jesus talking to his disciples in the right. The third window shows the same light and cinquefoil pattern; the left light shows workmen building the church and the right depicts a winged eagle. There is a small inscription at the bottom of the right light which reads 'This window was rescued from St John the Evangelist Eton, by the London Stained Glass Repository 1911'.

The main body of the church is supported by pillars of alternating coloured stone. These are Runcorn red sandstone and Painswick white limestone now painted in similar colours; reddish brown bands alternating with cream bands. The tiling in the main body of the church is plain cream and terracotta colours. All the tiles in the church were manufactured by Minton.

The stained-glass windows were removed for safe keeping during the Second World War and the records of their original places have been lost, so there is some speculation as to whether they were put back in their original places. The windows and brass memorial plaques on the north wall commemorate the de Trafford family while the corresponding south wall windows and plaques com-memorate past priests of the church.

The first plaque on the south wall is under a plain window and states 'Canon Kershaw, first rector of this church begs the prayers of the faithful for the repose of the soul of his mother Elizabeth Green who died June 22nd:A:D:1874, aged 77 years. R.I.P.'

The next plaque is under a stained-glass window depicting St Elizabeth and St John the Baptist. The plaque reads 'Of your charity pray for the eter-nal rest of John Kershaw, first rector of this church domestic prelate of His Holiness Pope Leo XIII, and Canon of Salford who departed this life May 31st A.D.1890, aged 73 years. R.I.P.'

The third plaque is under a plain window and states 'This window is placed here in affectionate remembrance of the Revd Thomas Sharrock, Rector of St Marie's, Eccles, by the members of the de Trafford Family. He died January 24th A.D. 1893. R.I.P.'

The next plaque is under a stained-glass window depicting St Charles the Good and St Thomas. The dedication reads 'This window has been erected in affectionate remembrance of The Right Reverend Monsignor Charles Joseph Gadd, Y.6.,M.R. by The Lady Annette de Trafford and the members of her family. He departed this life at Barton July 1. 1907. Requiescat in Pace'.

On the west wall there is a wooden plaque which is 'In memory of George Aloysius Moorhead died 18th July 1965 age 59. Miriam Moorhead died 12th September 1993 age 89. Father into your hands I commend my spirit. R.I.P.'

The de Trafford chapel, All Saints church. Sir Humphrey and Lady Annette de Trafford are buried in the family vault immediately below the chapel. (Author)

The commemorations on the north wall start, from left to right, with a plain window; the commemoration reads 'This window has been erected by Lady Annette de Trafford and Henry de Trafford in memory of Belinda Theresa de Trafford on whose soul sweet Jesus have mercy. Born Nov 29 1816. Died Feb 12 1900. RIP'. Belinda was Sir Henry's sister and she is buried in the crypt.

The next window depicts SS Theresa of Avila and Cecilius. The dedication reads 'Pray for the repose of the soul of Charles Henry de Trafford who died December 15th: A:D:1878, aged 57 years. Requiescat in pace.' Charles was Sir Henry's brother and is also buried in the crypt.

The next window depicts St Gilbert of Sempringham and St Joseph, under which the dedication reads 'Of your charity pray for the soul of Gilbert Talbot Joseph de Trafford. who died July 14th 1890. Aged 19 years.This window is erected in affectionate remembrance by his mother, brothers and sisters. Jesus Mercy! Mary and Joseph Help!' Gilbert too is buried in the crypt.

The next window depicts SS Roch and Gertrude and the dedication reads 'Of your charity pray for the repose of the soul of Sir Humphrey de Trafford of Trafford Park, Bart. May he rest in peace. This window is erected by his children in loving remembrance of their father.'

St Francis and St Augustine are depicted in the next window, the dedication reading 'Sir Humphrey de Trafford Bart: founder of this church. Died May 4th 1886 Aged 78 years. This memorial is placed by his sorrowing widow in the hope that pious prayers may be offered for the repose of his soul. Jesus Mercy! Mary Help!'

The final window depicts Our Lady of Dolours and St Clare. The dedication reads, 'Lady Mary Annette de Trafford died July 1st 1922 aged 88 years. This window is erected in loving memory by her devoted children. May she rest in peace.'

All the brass plaques on the north wall have the griffin crest with the motto 'Gripe griffin hold fast' accompanying the dedications. All, that is, save for the Lady Annette de Trafford plaque which depicts two shields; one traditionally shaped shield and one lozenge shaped. The left shield depicts the de Trafford red griffin holding the white griffin in a blue shield with another shield, this time depicting the Talbot lion rampant; this celebrates the marriage of Sir Humphrey and Lady Annette. The second shield, lozenge shaped, depicts the Talbot lion rampant surmounted by a crown. The family motto is absent.

The west wall rose window originally depicted the twelve signs of the zodiac, the elements and seasons. The glass panels were taken down during the Second World War and, sadly, lost. It was extensively renovated in 1990 and a new design created by Design Lights of Wigan was installed named the Angelus window. The construction was undertaken by Charles Lightfoot Ltd at Brookside Glass Works in Manchester. The design comprises light and dark blue and yellow and orange lights within the existing stonework tracery.

The church ceased to function as a parish church in 1961 as it was deemed to be in the wrong locality as there was, and still is, very little domestic accommodation in the immediate area. Over a period of time the area was becoming more of an industrial area with the building of the power station and the canal. The building of the swing bridge was also an obstacle to the congregation arriving to Mass on time. The church has been looked after by the Friars Minor Conventual since 1962 and the parish church of Holy Cross, Patricroft has served the parishioners ever since.

The ceiling in the sanctuary was painted by Joseph Alphege Pippet, an employee of Hardman and Powell, the stained-glass and ecclesiastical metal manufacturers based in Birmingham, and includes roundels of angels playing instruments including flute, cittern, viol, rebec, harp, portative organ, tambour, tambourine, drum and pig snout psaltery. The nave includes carvings of angels playing a variety of instruments such as cittern, harp and portative organ.

On the south wall of the sanctuary there is another Pippet painting depicting the Adoration of The Lamb in which appears Sir Humphrey and Lady Annette de Trafford and seven of their eight children. Gilbert hadn't been born when the painting was executed and so wasn't represented. Edward Pugin himself is also depicted on the left of the painting holding the plans of the church.

Between 1985 and 1989 phase one of restoration work was undertaken and included masonry cleaning and pointing, dry rot eradication, damp proofing, repair to walls, railings and gates, roof repairs, work on the bell tower and restoration of the 23ft long and 10ft wide sanctuary mural. Sacristies standing between the church and friary were demolished in 1963 due to dry rot. The space was used to build a community hall.

Phase two of this restoration commenced in 1990, which involved strengthening the west wall, rebuilding the bell tower and restoration of the rose window. From 2008 to 2010 another major restoration concentrating on the sanctuary was carried out, which included a new roof drainage system and reinstatement of the painted ceiling. The presbytery is a Grade II listed building.

Chaplains and parish priests are listed in Table 5. Research has shown that some of the earlier dates are speculative; where there is a doubt this is shown by a question mark.

Table 5: Chaplains and parish priests of All Saints RC church.

1791–1805	Fr James Haydock
1805–1830	Fr Thomas Sadler
1830–183?	Fr T. Irving
1831–183?	Fr H. Newsham
1832–184?	Fr T. Ball
184?–184?	Fr J. Westhead
184?–184?	Fr J.F. Whittaker
184?–1844	Fr John Hill
1844–1890	Monsignor Canon John Kershaw (first parish priest)
1890–1900	Canon James Hayes
1901–1907	Monsignor Charles Joseph Gadd
1908–1916	Fr William Fowler
1916–1925	Fr Osmond Woods
1925–1925	Fr John Manning
1926–1941	Fr Charles Hanrahan
1941–1958	Fr Thomas Baron
1959–1961	Fr G. Dalston (last parish priest)

The 1901 census shows Charles J. Gadd (62) as head of All Saints chapel and his occupation is described as Roman Catholic Prelate. Charles Diorite (45) is recorded as a boarder with an occupation of Roman Catholic Priest. The 33-year-old Catherine Scott, from Scotland, was housekeeper and Roman Catholic Prelate William Hill (50) is recorded as a visitor.

In 1962 the Orders of Friars Minor Conventual OFM (Conv) were invited by Bishop George Andrew Beck to establish a friary at All Saints.

St Catherine's, Barton-upon-Irwell

The foundation stone of the church of St Catherine was was laid by Lady Laura Ann de Trafford on 22 July 1842. The land on which the church was built was donated by her husband Sir Thomas de Trafford. The church was consecrated on 25 October 1843. The seventeenth-century maps show this church well established (1843–1973) alongside its Roman Catholic neighbour of All Saints. Both fell under the districts of Bromyhurst and Dumplington before becoming Barton-upon-Irwell. The church had a peal of bells, which was scrapped in about 1960. The octagonal spire was 100ft high. Sometime around 1930 the pinnacle of the spire was removed.

The 1901 census shows Thomas H. Davies (41) as a 'Clergyman of Church of England'. His wife Winifred (28) is also recorded as are two domestic servants, Emily Austin (22) from Banbury in Oxford and Lydia Lowe (65) from Cheshire.

The church was demolished in 1973 due to dry rot but the churchyard still remains and Marshall Stevens, founder of the Manchester Ship Canal, is buried here in a plain but impressive granite family vault.

St Catherine's Church and churchyard, Barton. (Author)

Wesleyan chapel, Davyhulme

Manchester was one of the first places in England to hear the preaching of Wesley but the exact dating of Methodism in Davyhulme is uncertain. It appears, however, that Matthew Mayer may have introduced Methodism to the area, establishing public prayer meetings in Dukinfield, Ashton and other places. Wesley himself encouraged Mayer to go about his preaching and for twenty years he carried on his missionary zeal with surprising success. In 1746, John Bennet wrote to Wesley that he had held prayers for a local 'band of wicked, drunken men'.

The New Weslyan church, 1905. (Bob Potts)

It is also significant to note here that Wesley visited Davyhulme on five separate occasions over a period of thirty-two years, the first being on Monday 29 August 1748. There is a record in Wesley's journals where he states 'Friday, April 2nd, 1779 (This was Good Friday). About one I opened the new chapel at Davyhulme.' Indeed, tradition has it that at the opening the congregation was too numerous and that Wesley came outside and preached from the horse block.

It is thought that Wesley used to preach under a large oak in Davyhulme.

The chapel itself was registered for the solemnising of marriages on 4 January 1870, and the first couple to be married there were Peter John Walkden of Flixton and Sarah Ellen, only daughter of James Booth of Flixton. This marriage took place just sixteen days later on 20 January.

The original Wesley church on Moorside Road became too small and costly to renovate. The New Wesleyan church on Brook Road was opened on 1 April 1905. The opening was performed by Miss M. Wilkinson and officiating was Rev. F.L. Wiseman. The postcard above was sent by 'Lilly' to James Chapman in Stalybridge a mere three weeks after the opening with the text 'Thought you would like a view of our new Church.' It seems quite remarkable that commercially available postcards were available so soon after the opening but Lilly was obviously proud of the new building and keen to share the photo with her friend James. This church was demolished in 1982.

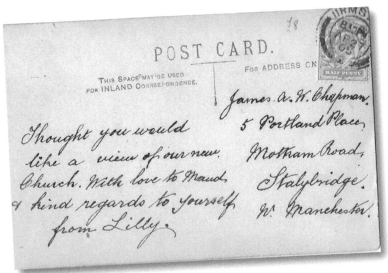

The reverse of the New Weslayan Church postcard. (Bob Potts)

A stone-laying ceremony took place in 1937 to mark the building of a new Sunday school, which was opened in January 1938. Photographs show the magnificence of this Gothic structure, which carried a large organ, wooden pews and choir stalls. In 1946 a celebration was held here; it had seen 200 years of Methodism.

English Martyrs, Urmston

If I have any affinity with a church it is English Martyrs on Roseneath Road in the centre of Urmston. My mother and father were married there on 31 March 1951 and I was born two years and a day later and baptised in the church soon after.

The Catholic Mission in Urmston began when Canon Kershaw, the parish priest of All Saints, Barton, purchased a plot of land in Urmston in 1890. A small building had been erected on this land in 1874, which was used as a high school and also as the Congregational church; indeed the stone tablet over the door carried the inscription 'Urmston High School 1874', popularly known as Weeton's School. This building was later used by the Catholics in 1891 as a church and as a school until 1901 when the new Catholic school opened.

English Martyrs' Roman Catholic church, before the brick structure was builthe tin chapel was dismantled and moved to become St Dunstan's in Moston and then to Droylsden after which it ended up in Nottingham (Bob Potts)

This church was opened on Sunday, 4 October 1891 when Mass was celebrated in Urmston for the first time.

Father Francis Newton, who was a curate at All Saints, was appointed by Bishop Herbert Vaughan to be the first rector of the new Mission. The Congregational church left the premises in May 1880 after their new church was opened on the corner of Wycliffe Road and Flixton Road in 1879.

Lady Annette de Trafford was one of the chief benefactors of the church at All Saints in Barton and she paid for the iron church overseen by Father Beulink, who arrived at English Martyrs in 1893; the iron church was built soon after his arrival. The congregation at this time was some 150 souls. The present brick building was erected in 1914 by Spark the builders around the iron structure, after which the smaller building was dismantled from the inside leaving the new church empty for the fixtures and fittings to be installed. The foundation stone was laid on 24 May 1913 by Bishop John Vaughan and the cost of the church was £2,573 6s 5d, the work being completed in October of the same year. The formal opening took place on Sunday, 25 January 1914.

Numbers 5 and 7 Roseneath Road, adjoining the church, were purchased at a cost of £700 to serve as a presbytery. This is the same presbytery in which the parish priest lives today. On 22 June 1901 the foundation stone for the new school was laid by Bishop Bilsborrow at a cost of £1,250. The contract was given to the same local firm, Spark & Sons Ltd.

The population of Urmston was growing at a steady rate due to the railway and the work on offer in nearby Trafford Park in the last quarter of the nineteenth century. To cater for this increase in population new homes were being built in Stretford and Flixton and many Catholic people were coming to settle in the area. To alleviate the pressure on English Martyrs, a new parish was established in Lostock. On Saturday, 4 June 1938 Bishop Henshaw blessed and laid the foundation stone of the new Mission of St Hugh of Lincoln, situated just outside the Davyhulme–Stretford border.

Further increases in population resulted in a new Mission in Flixton in 1953 to be known as St Monica's and on 30 September 1960 Fr Fitzpatrick was appointed to establish a new parish in Davyhulme. The first Mass of the new parish was celebrated on 2 October 1960 and, on 22 March 1986, a new church of Our Lady of the Rosary was built just next to Davyhulme Circle and officially opened and dedicated by Bishop Kelly. The site for this church was once home to Crofts Bank House. However, this latter church has been amalgamated with English Martyrs under the new title of Our Lady and the English Martyrs.

St Monica's, Flixton

St Monica's was a newly formed parish in 1950. Masses were held in the John Alker Memorial Hall. Foundations for the new church were laid on 16 September 1952 and the first Mass was held in the new church on 1 June 1953. St Monica's celebrated its fiftieth anniversary jubilee on 14 June 2000.

Congregational church, Flixton Road

Built in 1879 and enlarged in 1901, the Congregational church was an impressive stone and red brick building. Originally, the services were held at the Urmston and Flixton Congregational church, sited at the corner of Roseneath Road and Flixton Road (remembered as Weeton's School). The building, built in 1874, was used by the Catholic Mission when the Congregational church moved out in 1880. The building was eventually demolished to accommodate the building of the new Catholic school, English Martyrs. The Congregational church moved to new premises built in 1879 further down Flixton Road. This building became a school when a similar building was erected next door in 1901 on the corner of Wycliffe Road and Flixton Road. This new building was built to be to be the new Congregational church. This building was demolished in 1979; the site is now occupied by Wycliffe Court.

HEALTH AND WELFARE

L ong before the advent of the National Health Service the relief of the poor had been very much the role of the Church. Indeed, as long ago as 1010, through an edict of King Ethelred, it was provided for one third of the tithe to be given to the poor.

In 1536 the parish was held legally responsible for caring for the poor, although some of this responsibility was taken away from the Church in 1597 when the first official Poor Rate was levied. There were also various charities in operation in all three of the townships. Altruistic acts by benefactors were also in evidence, such as John Wood making provision in 1779 in his will for the schooling of poor children. In 1786 William Gregory donated £10 to supply bread to the poor of Urmston. There are many other written accounts paying testament to the philanthropy of the more well-off citizens of the area.

Friendly Societies and Sick Clubs also helped with the relief of the poor. Prior to the Poor Law Act of 1834 powers were vested to enable poor houses and the levy of taxes from the householders of the parish. A stipulation was made, however, that the poor could not leave the parish without permission.

In his 1842 *Report on the Sanitary Conditions of the Labouring Population of Great Britain*, Edwin Chadwick commented that agricultural labourers were among the healthiest of working men. He stated that the average age of death among the working classes of Manchester in 1837 was less than half of the agricultural labourers of Rutland. Fifty years later his views were still valid. In spite of low wages the good health of the agricultural labourer was attributed to fresh air and a country environment. And when it came to industrial accidents, despite the hazards of farm machinery, the agricultural labourer fared better than the national average. Illnesses mainly included respiratory infections and diseases such as bronchitis, pneumonia and tuberculosis. With the elderly, rheumatism was the perennial problem attributed to dietary deficiencies and spending long hours out in the open in all weathers without shelter.

In spite of all, mortality rates were lower in the the villages as compared to the towns. However, in both rural and urban areas stomach disorders such as diarrhoea, dysentery and enteritis were major killers for children, highlighting the need to improve water supplies and to raise the general standard of hygiene.

Falling ill was an expensive business as few could afford to pay the doctor's bill or even join a Friendly Society or Medical Club that would, so they promised, 'provide for the comfortable relief of its members'. The 4s subscription per quarter was an onerous sum of money to find for those who were basically living on the breadline. Charity and the poor laws were the only alternative. Self-help was therefore the first option for those of limited means. For instance, pregnant women who were at their time of confinement would rely on the older women in the community to act as midwife as they would have had the experience of maybe having several children themselves. The standard fee was 2s 6d. Only if complications set in would the doctor be called. For general use, herbal concoctions were used: stewed groundsel for poultices, marshmallow leaves and flowers were made into ointment for boils, lily leaves for cuts, dock leaves for galled feet, green broom for kidneys, dandelion roots for liver troubles and coltsfoot leaves for bronchitis.

For children of the labouring classes – whether in rural or urban areas – the first months of life were critical. Regardless of the statistic that infant mortality in rural areas was about 25 per cent lower than in urban areas, the average mortality rate at the end of the nineteenth century was 138.8 per thousand of male births. This could not be considered satisfactory as one in ten babies would not make it beyond their first birthday.

Many took to opium, as this was virtually the only analgesic available. Indeed, when it came to lulling restless babies to sleep, it was common for opiates to be used; Godfrey's cordial being one such mixture with laudanum being the main ingredient. This, if administered too frequently and too freely, could prove fatal. Also, the poverty of the labouring classes prevented the calling of a doctor to attend to their ill children and, although the Poor Law was a way of applying for medical relief, this for a long time varied the stigma of pauperism. Prescriptions were also somewhat bewildering, with half a pint of brandy being prescribed to women recovering from childbirth. Porter and gin were also common 'remedies'.

The last case of smallpox was in 1978 and it is now eradicated, but back in the nineteenth century this disease, together with typhoid and diphtheria, were the most feared. From 1854 every child was supposed to be vaccinated against

Park Hospital, aerial view.

smallpox but it was not until 1871 that legislation began to be effective after a severe outbreak.

It is an undoubted fact that improved sanitation during the Victorian period was responsible for a significant improvement in the health of the nation. Part of these improvements saw the construction of the sewage works in Davyhulme, which took place in 1894, and on a warm day even now it is impossible not to be aware of this facility due to the less-than-pleasant aromas emanating from the works.

The 1940s brought a radical reform in healthcare and, for the first time, all aspects of the medical service were brought together under one umbrella and made available for free. Prior to this, only those who paid national insurance, and this was mostly men, were covered for medical treatment. Consequently, those who were impecunious would have to forgo treatment.

Park Hospital opened to patients on 17 December 1928, being officially opened by the first Princess Royal (HRH Princess Mary, Viscountess Lascelles) on 1 June 1929. When the Local Government Act of 1929 got rid of the Poor Law unions, ownership of the hospital passed to Lancashire County Council. Park Hospital's distinguishing feature was the verandas at the end of each ward

Park Hospital. (Author)

to provide light and fresh air for the patients, a feature I remember well as a 15-year-old when I was admitted to have my appendix removed.

On 5 July 1948 the Minister for Health, Mr Aneurin Bevan, visited Park Hospital. The date marked the first day of the National Health Service, which had been created as a result of the passing of the National Health Service Act of 1946. The purpose of the act was for the NHS to take over the running of all hospitals from 5 July, the day of his visit, and the hospital became the first in the world to offer free healthcare for all. For the first time hospitals, doctors, nurses, pharmacists, opticians and dentists were brought together under one umbrella organisation that was free for all to access at the point of delivery. The central principles were clear: the health service would be available to all and financed entirely from taxation, which meant that every taxpayer contributed to it. With the introduction of the National Health Service 97 per cent of people registered with a GP and such was the huge response that the system of funding through taxation came under strain. However, the concept of good health for all came to be regarded as a basic human right.

Bevan symbolically received the keys from Lancashire County County and nurses formed a 'guard of honour' outside the hospital to meet him. The

Aneurin Bevan on the day the NHS was born.

National Health Service was born and, from that day forward, the healthcare of the nation changed forever.

Sylvia Diggory (nee Beckingham) became, at the age of 13, the first NHS patient and Park Hospital had the honour of caring for her on that auspicious day. The hospital also witnessed the first baby born under the NHS; 6lb 11oz Sandra Pook. Now called Sandra Howarth, she lives in nearby Eccles and shares her birthday with the NHS.

In 1988 Park Hospital was renamed Trafford General Hospital and is now controlled by Trafford Healthcare NHS Trust, formed in 1994 following a reorganisation of the NHS. In 2008 the hospital had 530 beds, employed 2,100 staff, treated 24,000 in-patients in a year and handled 175,000 outpatient appointments. However, there are now no midwifery services at the hospital and the A&E unit has controversially been downgraded.

Urmston's other hospital was Urmston Cottage Hospital on Greenfield Avenue, which opened in 1900. It was closed as a hospital in 1980 and is now called Serendipity, a residential care home for the elderly.

Eleven

TRANSPORT

Before the advent of the railway the common people were, to all intents and purposes, confined to their village of birth and getting round the area was either on foot or by horse. However, the nineteenth century brought with it many advances in technology, and on Tuesday, 9 December 1902, the *Manchester Evening News* reported that a public meeting had been held the night before, regarding negotiations between the District Council and Manchester Southern Tramways regarding the building of a tram system in Urmston. The resolution of the meeting was that the streets were too narrow to accommodate such a scheme. Again, on 3 April 1903, it was reported in the *Manchester Courier and Lancashire General Advertiser* that the council met and opposed the tramway.

Some council meetings were rather heated on this topic and on 11 January 1905 Dr Clegg proposed to defer the matter of the tramway; a Mr W. Hill JP is reported to have deplored the remark. Mr W. Johnson said that they had been bluffed by Manchester Corporation. Mr Y. Scholfield is said to have retorted 'Don't make your dirty remarks to me.' A scene ensued and the chairman had to insist on order; frequent interruptions were made during the ensuing discussion to appoint a committee to decide whether or not Urmston should have a tramway.

An article published in the *Manchester Guardian* on 30 January 1905 shows that there were negotiations under way for a tramway to run from Stretford Road to Station Road and thence on to Crofts Bank Road but, with the projected cost proving too costly, the proposal was not followed through.

Yet again it was reported in the *Manchester Courier and Lancashire General Advertiser* on 14 February 1906 that Manchester Corporation had decided to drop the Urmston tramways clause in its parliamentary bill. A Mr T.Ogden said that the trams were further off than ever, which was 'a pleasing fact to his mind'.

Another report in the same newspaper only a few days later on 23 February commented that Councillor W. Johnston of the Urmston Ratepayers' Association was strongly opposed to the tramways proposal. It was decided at this meeting that they were not necessary and proposals were approved to initiate a bus service from Barton to Stretford via Urmston. Urmston, therefore, never acquired a tramway but it seems that the decision was not made until after many, many hours of at times fractious council and committee meetings.

Up to 1846 commuters were obliged to walk to the Angel Hotel in Stretford to catch a stagecoach or two-horse omnibus, where there was an hourly service to Manchester. The horse-drawn service was discontinued on the opening of the railway in 1873.

It was announced in 1846 that John Thornton was to operate an omnibus route in the town. It was to run through Flixton, Urmston and Davyhulme with a final pick-up stop at Crofts Bank. From there it would travel to Manchester via Stretford. In 1848, John was fined £5 for running the bus on a Sunday.

By 1869 competition was fierce with the company of Shawcross & Worrall's in opposition to the Stretford Omnibus Company in trying to capture the public for this form of transportation. A company from the Midlands called Ryknield ran a motorised public service operating buses in 1907 throughout the district. It had a temporary licence for twenty-seven days from August to

A charabanc; the driver is the author's grandfather. (Author)

September. The licence renewal was refused due to adverse publicity that the buses were too heavy and would damage the roads, thereby increasing the rates by 2*d* per week.

The first recognised bus service was owned by Harry Smith in about 1901 and was to be found behind the Victoria Hotel in Urmston in what was then known as Victoria Mews, later to become Bold's Garage. The service linked Stretford and Urmston. The horse-drawn vehicle was replaced with a motor bus in February 1914 but during the First World War the War Department requisitioned the vehicle and Mr Smith returned to using the horse-drawn bus.

In 1920 the brothers Harry and James Tetlow began an excursion running from Urmston to Blackpool using a fourteen-seater open coach. This service was taken over by the North Western Road Car Company in 1938, as reported in the press on Friday, 11 February. By January 1921 the Northwich-based Mid-Cheshire Motor-Bus Company had established a depot at the old Tithe Barn in Chassen Road, Flixton. Then, in 1923, the Tetlow brothers formed the Blue Motor Bus Service at their garage on Flixton Road near Abbotsfield House. From here was operated a service which was eventually sold in 1938 to the North West Road Car Company Limited. The company operated services from Flixton Road, Woodsend Road and Irlam Road to Flixton and Urmston railway stations. There was also provided a service from the Nags Head to Stretford via Lostock Road and Derbyshire Lane. 'The company of Messrs H. & J. Tetlow of The Garage, Flixton Road, Flixton' was granted a licence to keep petroleum on the premises on 24 January 1923 by the Rural District Council of Barton-upon-Irwell. The licence is stated to be 'not transferable' and for the year ending 31 December 1923.

North Western ran the local bus service in 1920, operating a route from Flixton Station through to Station Road, Urmston. The Lord Nelson also acted as a terminus for the beginnings of this mode of transport.

James Tetlow died in 1923 and his brother Harry went into partnership with James Collier, although the firm still traded as H. & J. Tetlow. Mid-Cheshire had a fleet of five buses at Flixton with additional services in Urmston, Flixton and Davyhulme. The buses were 36hp Leyland MA 4099 vehicles in brown and yellow livery, later changed to blue; the seating capacity was for thirty passengers with a separate smoking compartment near the door to the rear. In 1924 the Mid-Cheshire was, in turn, taken over by the Stockport-based North Western Road Car Company; its livery was red and cream.

In 1927 Harry Tetlow expanded his business to include a garage where cars and petrol were on sale, and from where he operated a taxi service. This business was run from Lostock Road. The Tetlow bus service was taken over the year later in 1928 by the North Western Road Car Company, which retained the Tetlow bus crews. However, as to the buses themselves, four of the fleet were sent for scrap in 1929 and the rest sold off. This was due to the fact that the bus manufacturers, Tilling Stevens, had a financial investment in the North Western Road Car Company.

After the Second World War North Western provided a service covering the main districts of Urmston, Flixton and Davyhulme to Piccadilly, Manchester. Three buses ran routes covering Davyhulme and on to Woodsend; the numbers were 11, 13 and 23. The 23 terminated at Woodsend.

The author's aunt, Molly Kennedy (nee Johnson) worked for Mee's garage (later taken over by a Greek owner on Lostock Road opposite Tetlow's garage, later to be taken over by David Herd and now an Enterprise car-hire firm). One day, in the early 1950s, Harry Tetlow stopped her outside his garage and offered to double her wages when she was at Mee's, from 5s to 10s per week, to work for him as he had seen how hard she worked on the forecourt at Mee's. She also worked for David Herd when Tetlow's decided to call it a day and retire. By all accounts Harry Tetlow 'was a lovely man to work for'.

Bus services are now run by Stagecoach, Arriva and various other companies.

Railways

The railway system in Great Britain is the oldest in the world; the world's first locomotive-hauled public railway opened in 1825. The early railways were a criss-cross of local lines operated by small private railway companies. Over the course of the nineteenth and early twentieth centuries, these were amalgamated or were bought by competitors until only a handful of larger companies remained. Flixton and Urmston acquired their stations comparatively late on in 1873 compared to other suburbs, with Altrincham's and Sale's opening in 1849. The Cheshire Midland Railway opened a station in Bowdon in 1862. However, Chorlton-cum-Hardy's station had to wait until 1880.

The growth in road transport during the 1920s and 1930s greatly reduced revenue for the rail companies. They accused the government of favouring road haulage through the subsidised construction of roads. The railways entered a slow decline owing to a lack of investment and changes in transport policy and lifestyles. During the Second World War the companies' managements joined together, effectively forming one company. A maintenance backlog developed during the war and the private sector only had two years to deal with this after the war ended. After 1945, for both practical and ideological reasons, the government decided to bring the rail service into the public sector.

In 1948, the 'big four' (the Great Western Railway, the London and North Eastern Railway, the London, Midland and Scottish Railway and the Southern Railway companies) were nationalised to form British Railways (latterly 'British Rail') under the control of the British Transport Commission.

Railway operations were privatised between 1994 and 1997. Ownership of the track and infrastructure passed to Railtrack. Most of the railway track is now managed by Network Rail, which in 2015 had a network of 9,790 miles of standard gauge lines, of which 3,276 miles were electrified. These lines range from single to quadruple or more.

But how did the advent of the railways affect rural townships such as Flixton, Urmston and Davyhulme?

From a social point of view, the railways broke down stereotypes, and cultures became mixed because people from different regions were able to meet. Railways encouraged people to travel further and this meant they could move to different areas to find work. Families were able to take short holidays and day trips. Many sports became regulated because national competitions could be set up for rugby, football and cricket.

From a political perspective, political movements spread around the country because members of organisations such as Chartism and the Anti-Corn Law League could travel around the country to drum up support. Also, political newspapers, pamphlets and newsletters could be delivered quickly by train. And when feelings became inflamed the government could send soldiers by train to stop political unrest and patrol protests.

From the economic angle, railways became a major employer because people were needed to build, run and maintain them. Indeed, from the 1891 census, in addition to occupations that had been present in previous census reports, we now see those of railway engine driver, platelayer, stoker and signal man appearing.

Regional products now became household names around the country and perishable food could be moved quickly, so foods such as vegetables and dairy

Urmston station approach. (Author)

products could now reach the market while they were still fresh. Also, national newspapers could now be delivered.

Langton tells us in his *A History of the Parish of Flixton* that the coming of the railways in 1873 resulted in a great change to the roads of the townships of Flixton and Urmston, both materially and in the lost names of the old roads. In his *A History of Flixton, Urmston & Davyhulme*, Lawson states that modern Urmston dates from the arrival of the railway through the town. Both Flixton and Urmston stations were opened on 2 September 1873 with the trains running into Manchester's Oxford Road Station; Central Station (later GMEX, then Manchester Central Convention Complex) not being opened until 1880. The well-known (according to Lawson) Duke of York public house was demolished to make way for Urmston station. It is somewhat ironic that the station buildings are once again a pub, The Steamhouse, which was opened in 2008.

The original station was Gothic in style and in 1889 a new booking office was constructed on the opposite side of the bridge and a ladies' waiting room built. Lawson also goes on to tell us that, before the railway arrived, the means of travelling to Manchester was by bus; one of which went to Stretford station and one to Manchester, which returned in the evening.

The station footbridge was taken down in 1927 due to the widening of the road bridge and the platform canopies were taken down in 1965. As a child I remember the coal yards at the back of the station but they are no more.

Urmston railway station. (Author)

The Liverpool to Manchester railway runs through the townships now and the three railway stations are Urmston town centre, Chassen Road and Flixton. Urmston, as yet, is not served by Metrolink and the nearest tram stations are in Stretford and Eccles. As the railway line is still in use for trains it is unlikely that the area could accommodate the Metrolink system.

One of the major transport developments in recent years has been the Stretford–Eccles bypass, the M62 motorway. A feature of the motorway is the Barton high-level bridge that spans the Manchester Ship Canal. The opening of the M62 motorway in October 1960 relieved the traffic congestion at the nearby Barton swing bridge on the border between Urmston and Eccles just by the church of Barton All Saints. Consequently, there has been achieved a much quicker movement of heavy traffic from Trafford Park industrial estate. The estate included, in the early 1970s, industries concerned with the production of organic chemicals, plastics, wood wool, core rope, synthetic lubricants for jet aircraft engines and carpets, among other products. Also, at the time, the largest maize wet milling plant in Europe, paint and enamel depots, manufacturing of scaffolding, glass fibre products, asbestos, frozen foods, weed killers, abrasives, electrical equipment, and the largest manufacturer of railway wheels, tyres and axles in the British Commonwealth. It goes without saying that the transport implications for such a major estate, some 1,200 acres and 200 factories at the time, had to be considered with great care to keep such heavy traffic away from the town centres. Just prior to the opening, pedestrians were allowed to walk over the high-level bridge, which I remember doing with my father and grandfather.

For those interested in the technical data, the high-level bridge is 2,425ft long rising to a height of some 100ft above water level over the Manchester Ship Canal with a maximum gradient of 1 in 25 and is on horizontal curves of 2,604ft radius (south) and 2,865ft radius (north). There are eighteen spans; thirteen of 115ft, two of 235 ft and one of 310ft. The 310ft span crosses the Manchester Ship Canal itself and includes a 155ft centre suspended span carried on 77ft 6in-long cantilevers, which continue out from the 175ft anchor spans on each side. Leading up to the canal crossing are six spans on the south side of the canal and eleven on the north. The width of the bridge is 73ft between parapets to accommodate dual 24ft carriageways, 1ft wide marginal strips, a central reserve 9ft wide and two 6ft side verges. This information was correct at the time of opening.

Twelve

LIFE AND DEATH

As early as the fourteenth century there had been established the means for the provision of a decent burial. Guilds or societies provided for contributions to a common fund for the proper interment of its members. These guilds and societies were the forerunners of the sick and funeral societies that Lawson tells us were in abundance at the end of the nineteenth century. All relatives were expected to attend the funeral and also an extensive congregation of friends. Naturally, interments for the higher strata of society were accompanied by much ceremony and extravagance, and a clause would be inserted in the wills of the deceased for all relatives to be present for the reading of the will, where there would be provision for gifts to be made such as mourning rings, gloves and suits of clothing. These were intended as 'gifts of esteem' rather than the bequeathing of items that would necessarily have any practical use.

There was a distinction between a funeral and a burying, as Lawson found out while talking to one old Flixton resident. Lawson reports that he referred to the ceremony as a 'funeral', to which the resident replied, 'Aw didn' say a fun'ral ... buryin' is when yer walk, an' er fun'ral is when yer have carriages an' sich like.'

Lawson also reports that, as a rule, from the evidence of gravestones in the churchyard, the Flixton residents were a long-lived congregation, many folk being in their seventies and eighties when they died. However, only one centenarian has come to light: James Ashton, who died on 10 January 1877 aged 100 years and 8 months.

In Flixton church an interesting custom was practised back in the nineteenth century where a tray of rosemary sprigs would be presented to mourners at funerals, which they would collect on paying their last respects at the house of the deceased. The men would wear them in their buttonholes and take them home to plant in their gardens as a token of a permanent remembrance of the deceased; the women would hold theirs in their hands. Other mourners would throw the rosemary sprigs into the open grave at the interment. It is interesting to observe on walking around the churchyard that to this day rosemary can be seen growing among other plants by the side of the paths.

Rosemary is a herb symbolic of remembrance, as witnessed in Act IV of Shakespeare's *Hamlet*:

> Ophelia: There's rosemary, that's for remembrance: pray, love, remember: and there is pansies, that's for thoughts.
>
> *Hamlet*, Act IV Scene 4
>
> Rosemary is for remembrance,
> between vs daie and night,
> Wishing that I may alwaies haue,
> You present in my sight.
>
> 'A Handful of pleasant delites', Clement Robinson, 1584.

Another custom would be the baking of special cakes made available to the mourners, presented on another tray; they were served with ale, often hot and spiced. The heads of families in the village would visit as a matter of duty and the more visitors attending, the greater distinction would be accorded to the deceased's family.

The quart pot of beer would be passed around and there is one amusing story that tells of a stranger to the area being at a funeral and, when it was his turn

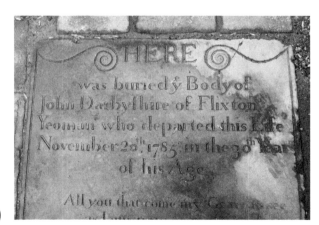

The gravestone of John Darbyshire, Yeoman. (Author)

to sup from the pot, he drained it, much to the consternation of the rest of the party. Langton also tells of it not being uncommon for funerals in Flixton to end up in a free fight.

Often posies of polyanthus, rosemary and ladylove would be placed on the breast of the corpse, possibly a link with the practice of 'burying in sweet flowers'.

It is interesting to note that there are some gravestones that refer to the deceased as 'yeoman' and Langton commented on this, stating that a yeoman was 'a freeholder of land worth 40s per annum, qualified to vote for knights of the shire'. Here are six of them:

Timothy Barlow of Flixton Yeoman who departed this Life February 11th 1776 aged 56.

John Darbyshire of Flixton Yeoman who departed this life November 20th 1785 in the 30th year of his age.

John Owen of Flixton Yeoman who departed this life Feb 1796 aged 93.

Thomas Rogers of Green Lane Flixton Yeoman and Land Surveyor who departed this Life Dec 23rd 1809 aged 73 years.

Richard Warburton of Flixton Yeoman who died January 1st 1818 aged 75 years.

John Collier Yeoman who departed this life April 12th 1850 aged 65 years.

In addition to Langton's brief description I have also found that a yeoman was a member of a social class in late medieval to early modern England. In early recorded uses, a yeoman was an attendant in a noble household. The later sense of the title, however, was 'a commoner who cultivates his own land' as recorded from the fifteenth century. In a military context, the yeoman was the rank of the third order of fighting men, below knights and squires, but above knaves.

In the late fourteenth to eighteenth centuries, yeomen were farmers who owned land (freehold, leasehold or copyhold). Their wealth and the size of their landholding varied; it has been said that 'a Yeoman would not normally have less than 100 acres and in social status is one step down from the Landed Gentry, but above, say, a husbandman'. In fact, Langton comments on the number of yeoman recorded in the churchyard, and he picks out for special mention:

Betty, wife of Philip Darbyshire, of Flixton, yeoman, aged 23; Alice their daughter, one year and nine months; and Jane their daughter, fourteen weeks.

The epitaph of local blacksmith William Oldfield's gravestone is reputed to have been written by Tim Bobbin, who was baptised in Flixton church under his real name of John Collier, and runs as follows.

My anvil & hammer lie declined;
My bellows have quite lost their wind;
My coals are done; my debt is paid,
My vices in the dust are laid.

Other notable graves include Ensign Ewart, who captured a French standard at the Battle of Waterloo. Also William Johnson of Flixton, who fought at the Battle of Boston Bay in June 1813. Alfred Derbyshire is also buried in Flixton churchyard; he died in 1908 and was an actor who performed with Henry Irving.

There are two Grade II listed tombs in Flixton churchyard. One was surmounted by a bronze or brass sundial made in 1772 by Sandiford of Manchester, surrounded by iron railings. Sadly, the metal part of the sundial and inscription were removed by vandals. The other is the tomb of Johannes Jones who, together with his wife Anna, are buried in a large chest tomb. Johannes died in 1751 and his wife in 1755.

At the end of the nineteenth century it was still the custom at Flixton church funerals and buryings to ring the 'capped bell', also known as the Passing or Soul Bell, on the occasion of the passing of a resident of the village.

There are some very fine monuments in Flixton churchyard, including the tombs of Thomas Chadwick and John Stott, both of whom feature elsewhere in this book. However, there are also quite a few pauper's graves, which are commemorated by the simplest of markers: a small stone about 9in or 10in in height bearing just the initials of the deceased and no more, not even a date. And even some of these initials have worn away with time.

The oldest gravestone is one with an inscription dated 1669, with the deceased merely being known by the initials WD, although the churchyard records show burials of earlier dates including that of Leonard Asshawe, who was buried on 6 January circa 1595.

There seems to be more than one person in this grave as the total inscription reads:

[V] P

1727

W D

1669

E B

IAN 24

1687

M B

The photograph (overleaf) shows a P at the top but the stone is broken at the top left and there is what appears to be part of the letter V, which is revealed when the turf is pulled back. This may indicate that a later interment was made in 1727 of someone with the initials VP. This leaves the last initials MB as unexplained. The general consensus among local historians, including Langton, is that the deceased of 1669 is WD and that this is the earliest interment.

Langton states that the old graveyard surrounding the church is 160 yards from east to west and about 60 yards from north to south. Another ancient stone, as mentioned by both Langton and Lawson, is that of John Johnson, schoolmaster, who died in 1684. Langton goes on to add that the most imposing monument is the one to the memory of Ralph Wright Esq. It is described as 'a sort of mausoleum, surrounded by a strong iron railing', and bears the following inscription:

IN MEMORY OF RALPH WRIGHT ESQ., ONE OF HIS
MAJESTY'S JUSTICES OF
THE PEACE FOR THE COUNTIES OF LANCASTER AND CHESTER,
WHO DIED ON THE
16TH DAY OF NOV., 1831, IN THE 80TH YEAR OF HIS AGE.

As regards to burials, Lawson informs us that 'the body was wrapped or wound in woollen only – thus complying with an Act passed in 1679, which prohibited the clothing of corpses in linen, its object to lessen the importation of that fabric, and so to encourage the woollen and paper manufacture of this country'. Failure to comply with this act could result in a fine of £5. One strange entry in the register states:

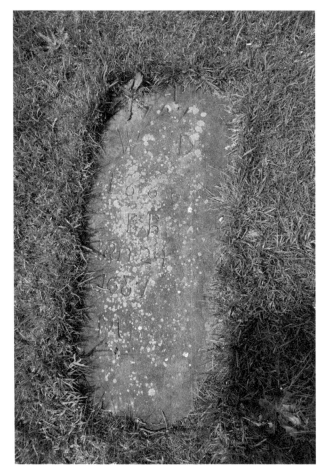

The oldest gravestone in Flixton graveyard, dated 1669. (Author)

A pauper's grave. (Author)

James Parren was not buried in any material contrary to a late Act for Burying in Woollen. – Sworn by Mary Parren, before Justice Peter Egerton. jany. 28th, 1705.

It seems, however, that many could not afford for their loved ones to be wrapped in wool, as aome entries in the parish register show that the deceased was 'buried in sweet flowers only' and 'in sweet flowers and hay only'. Two more such entries in the records for 1705 read:

1705 James Gee of Stretford Buryed in Sweet flowers only Feb 7th
Sworn before Peter Egerton Esq.

1705 Widow Hamson Buryed Jan. 29 in noe materiall contrary to a late act for Burying in Woollen. Sworn before Peter Egerton Esq.

The 1679 act was eventually repealed in 1815.

Langton, however, states that the act in question was passed in 1667 to encourage the manufacture of wool. The clergy were obliged to state in the entry of burials that the law had been obeyed. Custom had it that the parish clerk had to ask the deceased's relatives 'Who makes affidavit?' A relative or friend would then make the necessary oath, after which it was entered in the book. The affidavit would be phrased as follows.

_____ of the Parish of _____ in the county of _____ taketh Oath That _____ of the Parish of _____ lately deceased was not put in, wrapt or wound up, or buried in any shirt, shift, sheet or shroud, made or mingled with Flax, Hemp, Silk, Hair, Gold or Silver, or any other Material, contrary to the late Act of Parliament for Burying in Woollen, but sheep's wool only. Dated the _____ Day of _____ in the _____Year of the Reigns of our Sovereign Lord and Lady William and Mary by the Grace of God King and Queen of England, Scotland, France and Ireland, Defenders of the Faith &c., Anno Dom 1667.

Sealed and subscribed by us who were present   Seal
and Witnesses to the swearing of the above-said affidavit.   Seal

I _____ hereby Certify that the day and year aforesaid, the said _____ came before me and made such affidavit as is above specified, according to a late Act of Parliament, Instituted An Act for burying in Woollen. Witness my Hand the day and year first above written.

Lawson also tells us of another interesting piece of information in that an act of parliament passed in 1783 levied a stamp duty of 3*d* upon the entry of every burial, birth and marriage in every parish in Great Britain under a £5 fine for default. Vicars were to receive 2*s* for their trouble. The act was repealed in 1794 as it placed the clergy in the disagreeable position of tax collectors. It appears that vicars were not in favour of their roles as there were many commissions in the registers.

As a final note, both Lawson and Langton inform us that from July 1873 funerals ceased to be carried out on a Sunday. Today the churchyard is considered full and it is only possible for new interments to be made for members of families who are already buried there.

Urmston cemetery

The end of the nineteenth century saw an increase in population sufficient for plans to be made to increase the amount of ground available for burials, which up to then were carried out in Flixton churchyard.

A meeting was called on 10 October 1887 to discuss the pressing necessity for the additional burial accommodation. Proposals were made to enlarge the Flixton churchyard but this was not carried out and it wasn't until 25 August 1890 that the meeting decided that a burial ground should be provided for the parish.

The Burial Board was formed, consisting of nine people, the vicar and eight ratepayers. In 1892 it was decided at a vestry meeting that a plot of land consisting of 6 acres, 3 roods and 34 perches should be purchased for £2,800 from Mr George Ridehalgh. A further sum of £5,200 was sanctioned for the laying out of the grounds and the erection of necessary buildings, walls and chapels. This is the cemetery that is situated at the end of Queen's Road.

At the time of opening the purchase of a first-class private grave was set at £4 to parishioners and £8 to non-parishioners. The minister's fee was set at 5*s* and 7*s* 6*d* respectively. The digging of the grave was 1*s* per foot in depth and 4 guineas for the erection of a monument, ranging down to 10*s* 6*d* for a more simple headstone. The minister's fee for the funeral was 15*s*. The first interment was on Monday, 14 November 1892 and the deceased was Mr R. James, who had died on 10 November.

During the Second World War, Land Girls worked on the meadows and crops were even cultivated in Urmston cemetery. The Land Girls were one of the more romantic images of the war as overalled women took to the land, their hair tied back with headscarves, sleeves rolled up and entering into 'the spirit that won the war'. The war had taken away many of the men who had made up the agricultural workforce and the women filled in this labour gap. Furthermore, there was an increased demand for domestic food production due to the restrictions of importation. Around 80,000 women were recruited nationwide, earning the respect and adoration of the nation. The intention was for them to work fifty hours a week (forty-eight in winter), for which they were paid 28s plus food and lodging.

The tomb of Marshall Stevens, St Catherine's churchyard. (Author)

St Catherine's graveyard

This graveyard is situated on Old Barton Road, now a cul-de-sac after the road was blocked off just where the cemetery ends. The church has long been demolished but the graveyard remains.

The graveyard is best known for the huge tomb of Marshall Stevens, founder of the Manchester Ship Canal, just a stone's throw from the canal itself almost opposite Barton swing bridge. The mausoleum is an imposing, giant, grey, granite tomb with the following inscription:

FLIXTON WAKES.

W E the undersigned, being the several **ALEHOUSE-KEEPERS** within the several Townships of Flixton and Urmston, impressed with the propriety of *discontinuing the savage and brutal practices* of **BULL BAITING** and **BEAR BAITING,** which have been usually practised at **FLIXTON** and **URMSTON WAKES,** and which appear to us to have originated in, and to be suited only to, the earlier and more barbarous ages, beg respectfully to apprize the Minister of Flixton, and the Magistrates acting for the Division in which we reside, that we have resolved henceforth not only to cease to cause or procure any Bull Baiting or Bear Baiting, or any other brutal or barbarous exercises to be practised at Flixton and Urmston, either at the Wakes or at any other time, but also to discontinue and discourage, to the utmost of our power, the future exercise of all such practices.----Witness our hands the 7th. day of August, 1816.

William Jackson,	Charles Wilson.
James Swift.	Thomas Wilcock,
George Royle,	John Shawcross.
Alice Booth,	

William Millott,⎱ Churchwardens.
Thos. Moston, ⎰

Manchester : printed by C. Wheeler and Son, 7, Pall Mall, King-street.

A handbill distributed by local innkeepers in 1816. (From Langton's *A History of Flixton, Urmston and Davyhulme,* 1898)

MARSHALL STEVENS

SON OF SANDERS & EMMA STEVENS

18TH APRIL 1852 – 12TH AUGUST 1936

WHOSE LIFE'S WORK LIES AROUND THIS SPOT

A FOUNDER OF THE SHIP CANAL

1882–1885

MANAGER MANCHESTER SHIP CANAL CO

1885–1896

DEVELOPED TRAFFORD PARK

1897–1932

MEMBER OF PARLIAMENT FOR ECCLES

1913–1922

Also buried in the tomb are Marshall Stevens's son Major Cored Stevens (died 23 June 1927 aged 37). Another son, Blamey Stevens (died 23 November 1939), is commemorated, although he was buried in Alaska.

Jewish cemetery

At the end of Chapel Street, just off Higher Road, there is the Jewish cemetery built in 1877 on land purchased from the Jackson family. The cemetery was laid out in 1881 and there are some 2,000 graves in all, with a small area dedicated to children's graves. The two sections are for Polish and Spanish/Portuguese Jews. One anomaly is that the two sections are not facing the same way. Traditionally all graves should be arranged with the feet of the deceased pointing towards Jerusalem.

In May 1900 a foundation was laid for a new mortuary and surrounding walls. This resulted in two mortuary facilities, one for English and the other for Polish Jews. Included here is a war memorial dedicated to the fallen of the Second World War. There is no Jewish community in the area but traditionally Jews are not permitted to be buried in the precincts of the synagogue so land is sought elsewhere for burials. The burial register is held at the Manchester New Synagogue.

Fourteen

ENTERTAINMENT, LEISURE, CUSTOMS AND SPORTS

M any village customs nationally were associated with the annual 'wakes' that were originally held in church on the evening of the patron saint's day. In Harland and Wilkinson's *Lancashire Legends and Traditions*, it is said that little pavilions or booths were constructed of boughs where the people would celebrate. However, people being mere human beings, they began to abuse the solemnity of the occasion and introduce drinking into the celebrations. Furthermore, booths were set up where enterprising individuals would sell their wares in the churchyard and even in the church itself until 'the indecency and scandal were so great as to need reformation'.

In 1579 Elizabeth I was so concerned at the situation in Lancashire that she sent down an ecclesiastical commission to rectify the violation of the Sabbath. Langton tells us that the magistrates issued a letter complaining that the Sabbath was profaned by 'wakes, fayres, markets, bayrebaytes, bull bates, Ales, May games, resorting to alehouses in tyme of devyne service, pypinge and dauncinge, hunting and all maner of vnlaw gamynge'.

Consequently, power was given to mayors, bailiffs, constables, churchwardens and other civil officers to suppress these practices. In addition, minstrels, bearwards and other disorderly persons were to be apprehended and brought before the justices of the peace and punished. Furthermore, churchwardens were instructed to present at the sessions those who abstained from attending Sunday service.

Consequently, in 1592 an action was brought against 'Wm. Heywood in Flixton for piping in the house of one James Rile'. It is not clear what instrument was being played, as 'pipe' could refer to most wind instruments including a bagpipe. The charges ran as follows:

Against Wm. Heywood: – a piper plaid in James Rile his howse at evensong time uppon a Holidaie and gave the Sworne man bad words admonished the said Wm. Heywood to publicly confess his fault, in the Parish Church there, and to promis that hereafter he will never commit the like to the offence of any person , – on the 29th inst. and to certify before the Feast of S. Martin next.

Against James Rile : – The said piper plaid in his howse, enjoined by Mr. Richardson the Dean that he suffer not the like hereafter – because he was not at home at the time.

Against the wardens there: – Noe collectors for the poore no levy for William Irlam, one of the wardens, appeared, and was enjoined to provide Collectors according to Statute, and to levy under pain &c.

Against the Curate there: – Gave noe monitions for Choice of Collectors according to Statute. The Curate appeared, and was admonished to publish monition for Choice of Collectors, under pain of the law.

Langton tells us that the gentry felt that this moral discipline was excessive, and that when King James I visited Lancashire the orders were rescinded.

The wakes were celebrated in Flixton on the first Sunday after 11 October and, although they are reported as being occasions of carnivals with the accompanying 'fun, fast and furious frolic and fighting', Langton adds that these exciting practices had, even in the late 1890s, given place to the more sedate 'stalls and hurdy-gurdies'. It is speculated that this may be a reason why public houses are situated near church gates. Indeed, two such public houses are situated very close to St Michael's in Flixton.

The booths erected in Flixton during the wakes celebrations included, according to records, boxing booths, roulette tables, shooting galleries, fat women shows, grinning through a horse collar and climbing a greasy pole. There would also be games, sack racing, fighting and foot racing, and people would come from miles around to witness these events.

Apart from these relatively sober attractions, there was the cruel 'amusement' of burying a goose with only the neck showing. The poor bird's neck would be greased and the object was to ride at full speed past the goose and the competitors would try to grasp it by the neck and pull the unfortunate goose out. A variation would be to hang the goose, again with greased neck, from a pole for the riders to try to take while riding past. Lawson is of the opinion 'that it cannot be denied that in some of the Lancashire sports cruelty to animals was much too prevalent'.

Accompanying the merrymaking would be eating, drinking and fighting. A delicacy consumed at the Flixton wakes was eel pies, locally referred to as snig pies. The local populace would not be able to avail themselves of such entertainment often so the wakes week was of immense importance. Cottages would be made to look their best, inside and out, for the visits by relatives and friends and all the latest gossip would be exchanged.

An advertisement in *The Manchester Mercury* on 22 April 1788 laid out the following enticement:

POSITIVELY THE LAST BENEFIT
FOR THE BENEFIT OF
MR MADDOCKS AND MRS. BANKS
'A laugh & a cry, &.'
After which Shakespeare. King Henry the 4th
Between the play and the farce
THE HUMOURS OF FLIXTON WAKES
in which will be introduced
CUDGEL PLAYING FOR A GOLD LACED HAT
A RACE IN SACKS FOR A HOLLAND SHIRT
(Then a French Duet)
The whole to conclude with a
SUMPTUOUS SNIG PIE FEAST AND GARLAND DANCE
By the lads from Flixton, Urmston and Stretford.

Village sports of a few hundred years ago included such dubious activities as bear baiting, bull baiting, cock fighting and other 'sports' involving animal cruelty. The Nelson, The Roebuck and The Red Lion pubs were well-known venues for accommodating these practices. Nonetheless, it was the landlords themselves who decided that these sports were too cruel and applied to the local justices to have them stopped, even though such a ban would have adversely affected their livelihood.

In his *A History of Flixton, Urmston and Davyhulme*, Lawson states that cock fighting was never a sport in Flixton and goes on to state that it 'seems a phase of amusement reserved for our Eccles neighbours'. He even went on to lament that at the time of writing his book in 1898 the practice had not yet been eradicated in Lancashire. He goes on to describe the practice of throwing sticks or clubs at cocks tied to a stake, but also adds that this was confined to Shrove Tuesday and was a nationwide custom. Men and lads would pay 2*d* for three shies at the cock and this would continue until the cock was killed. In his *Rites and Riots: Folk Customs of Britain and Europe* Bob Pegg tells of the Shrove Tuesday holiday where this cruel practice 'went on until at least the end of the eighteenth century, although it was dangerous (a thirteen-year-old boy was killed in Leeds in 1783) and widely condemned as a barbarous sport'.

This vile practice was eventually made illegal in 1772, as the following notice testifies:

NOTICE NOT TO THROW AT COCKS

By order of the justices of the peace, we the constables of the township of Flixton do hereby give publick notice that that whosoever shall be found guilty of the barbarous and cruel custom of throwing at cocks on Tuesday next or any other day, in any other part of the said Township will be prosecuted with the utmost severity of the law, and that there will be proper persons appointed to give information of the names of any who shall be offending herein:

Given under our hands this third day of February in the Year of our Lord 1772.

JOHN FAULKNER

WILLIAM GERARD   CONSTABLES

Volume 5 of *The History of The County of Lancaster* also mentions that 'throwing at cocks on Shrove Tuesday, pace egging at Easter, and other customs, were practised' in Flixton.

Another practice seems to be that of incarcerating a cockerel into an earthenware pot with its head and tail exposed to view. This would be suspended some 12–14ft above the ground and 2*d* was the charge for four throws. The object was to test the skill of the thrower and he who broke the pot and released the unfortunate bird from its pot prison would have it as a reward.

Bear baiting did take place, usually at the Lord Nelson public house in Urmston; after it ended there they would walk over to Flixton, where it took place in the field behind the churchyard. The owner of the animals would take the bulls and bears to other local wakes. Thankfully this 'barbarous practice' of bear baiting, as Langton refers to it, was stopped in 1816 and bull baiting in 1835.

Langton adds that Mr R. Costerdine, born in Flixton in 1726, mentions in his memoirs that the sports in vogue at the time included hunting, cock fighting and horse racing. The races took place in the fields below the church and were viewed by the people from the churchyard, which they used as a makeshift grandstand. He also mentions that badger baiting, which he refers to as 'a cruel sport', took place in the yards of various Flixton inns. The badger was placed in a box, approximately 2ft square, with a tunnel leading into it through which a dog would be introduced. The aim was for the two unfortunate animals to engage, with the dog trying to pull the badger out of the box.

Both bull and bear baiting were carried on in several parts of the village and 'Schoo' Green' in front of The Roebuck is mentioned as one of the key venues. This is the area once known as Shaightown. A resident who died around 1898 informed Langton, referring to a bear, that 'Hoo wur a big black un, hoo wur.

Badger baiting, a drawing by Henry Aiken *c.* 1824.

Bull baiting, an undated sketch from the early nineteenth century.

It's a shame to tell, but aw helped set a bull-stake at Shaightown ov a Sunday morning'. However, the unfortunate bears often gave as good, if not better, than they got and one account mentions a huge mastiff set on by the bear who immediately hugged the poor dog until his 'ribs cracked and his eyes were starting out of their sockets'.

Bull baiting was a similarly cruel event that involved the bull being tethered to a ring set in stone on a chain about 20 yards long that allowed him enough space to fight. The dog would try to seize the bull by the nose and if the dog could hold on until the bull stood still he was said to have 'pinned the bull' and the contest would be over. However, a wily bull would catch the dog with its horns and toss it in the air, with the possible outcome that the fall would break the dog's back. Villagers would stand by to catch the dog and set him once more upon the hapless bull. The victorious owner would receive a prize, generally provided by the local innkeepers, whose business would have no doubt benefitted from the locals drinking in their inns. Presumably others who had bet on the outcome would have come away richer also.

Other prizes would include legs of mutton for climbing the greasy pole, waistcoats for grinning through horse collars and hats for foot racing. Wakes, Easter and Whit week were the usual times for staging such events. Harland and Wilkinson refer to bull baiting as 'this inhuman practice' in their *Legends and Traditions of Lancashire*.

Another interesting item is the 1618 King James Declaration of Sports, a code of lawful amusements that ministers were obliged to read from the pulpit. This was a declaration issued just for Lancashire in 1617 and then nationally in 1618, and reissued by Charles I in 1633. It listed the sports and recreations that were permitted on Sundays and other holy days. The code obliged:

> That after the end of divine service our good people be not disturbed, letted or discouraged from any lawful recreation, such as dancing, either men or women; archery for men, leaping, vaulting, or any other such harmless recreation, nor from having of May-games, Whitsun-ales, and Morris-dances; and the setting up of May-poles and other sports therewith used: so as the same be had in due and convenient time, without impediment or neglect of divine service: and that women shall have leave to carry rushes to the church for the decorating of it, according to their old custom; but withal we do here account still as prohibited all unlawful games to be used upon Sundays only, as bear and bull-baitings, interludes, and at all times in the meaner sort of people by law prohibited, bowling.

However, so strong was the Puritan opposition to Sunday amusements that King James prudently withdrew his command.

In 1633 Charles I not only directed the re-publication of his father's declaration but insisted upon the reading of it by the clergy. Many of the clergy were punished for refusing to obey the injunction; Lawson tells us that many of them found this code repugnant and after they had read the obligatory passages they would then recite the Ten Commandments, after which one was known to have said, 'Dearly beloved, ye have heard the commandments of God and man, obey which you please.' When Charles was overthrown during the English Civil War, Puritan prohibitions against sports and games on the Sabbath again prevailed until Charles II was restored in 1660.

Fighting also seems to have been a pastime entered into from time to time, with the township of Flixton having the reputation for being particularly pugilistic. Lawson mentions the Uptons, Penningtons, Armitts and Johnsons as being particularly noteworthy for their fighting prowess. It would also seem that these fighters not only attended the Flixton Wakes but also the Eccles Wakes.

There were other customs mentioned by Langton and Lawson, including the gentler practices of singing in the May and the Easter hobby horse. The singing in the May happened towards the end of April, when bands of men would visit the farms of South Lancashire and North Cheshire singing to welcome the advent of the coming month of May. Edwin Waugh, in his *Lancashire Sketches*, refers to men out singing and not returning home at night for several weeks at a time, who 'lived a sort of gipsy life, and were well received wherever they went'.

Lawson tells us that 'of all the customs prevalent in this and the immediate district, none seem to have given greater pleasure to folks than the pleasant one of singing in the May'. He interviewed an old man of between 70 and 80 years of age who told him that the 'singers were peculiarly welcome to all classes of residents in the district, and were well treated both with: "good cheer" and contributions in money; they used chiefly to hail from the Davyhulme side of Flixton'.

The singers would be accompanied by a musician playing the fiddle or clarinet or flute, and they would visit farmhouses and other houses in the district to sing songs peculiar to the time of the year. This custom would begin about the middle of April and lead up to the end of the month and May Day itself; country people used to think that the singing brought good luck.

Two songs were known at this time; the Old and New May songs.

OLD MAY SONG

All in this pleasant evening together come are we
For the summer springs so fresh, green and gay;
We'll tell you of a blossom that buds on every tree –
Drawing near to the merry month of May.

Rise up the master of this house, put on your chains of gold,
For the summer springs so fresh, green and gay;
We hope you're not offended (with) your house we make so bold –
Drawing near to the merry month of May.

Rise up the mistress of this house, with gold along (upon) your breast,
For the summer springs so fresh, green and gay;
And if your body be asleep I hope you soul's at rest –
Drawing near to the merry month of May.

Rise up the children of this house, all in your rich attire,
For the summer springs so fresh, green and gay;
For every hair upon your head shines like the silver wire –
Drawing near to the merry month of May.

God bless this house and harbour, your riches and your store,
For the summer springs so fresh, green and gay;
We hope the Lord will prosper you, both now and evermore –
Drawing near to the merry month of May.

So now we're going to leave you in peace and plenty here,
For the summer springs so fresh, green and gay;
We shall not sing you May again until another year,
For to draw you these cold winters away.

Both Langton and Lawson reprint these verses in their books, but Langton adds that some of the May singers from Patricroft who used to sing in Flixton and the neighbourhood included Lawrence Crompton, James Clewes (of Peggy Mason Street), Ellis Mather and John Fletcher.

The folk custom of the hobby horse is possibly best known in England for the famous example in Padstow, Cornwall, performed towards the end of April where a maypole is set up and decorated by the townspeople with flags and greenery. The horse performs a swaying, dipping dance, after which the music dies and the horse sinks to the ground. The horse then suddenly bounds up, the music revives and the horse dances further down the road to perform the ritual again. The significance of this custom, of course, is a spring fertility performance; a ritual to ensure the prosperity of the crops growing during this period of rebirth and growth leading through spring, summer and to the harvest.

It is interesting to note, however, that Langton refers to 'the hobby horse at Easter' and that it came from Flixton. The hobby horse was a man inside the figure of a horse and usually contained the strongest of the Flixton party of roisterers who would take their entertainment to as far afield as Barton and Eccles. The man in the horse would bound around, opening and closing the mechanical mouth that contained an enormous red flannel tongue. It is said that the shopkeepers in Barton would shut up shop and make themselves scarce during this custom. Langton, however, doesn't go into any further detail concerning the Flixton hobby horse but it may be assumed that the rituals employed were similar to that of the Padstow hobby horse mentioned above.

Another custom mentioned by Lawson and practised during the Easter period was that of 'pace egging', and this is still carried out today by a group who perform the pace egging play at the Saracen's Head in nearby Warburton. The actors in this play are called mummers and pace egg plays are traditional village plays, with a death and rebirth theme, in which St George smites all challengers and the fool, Toss Pot, rejoices. The drama takes the form of a combat between the hero and villain, in which the hero is killed and brought to life, often by a quack doctor who engages in witty banter not only with the other actors but with the audience also.

Lawson comments that St George and the rest of the *dramatis personae*, though they might start with literary English, soon lapsed into rough-and-tumble dialect, 'which it was evident they were more at home in'. Lawson also tells us that the local children, 'adorned with coloured paper caps and carrying wooden swords', would visit houses in the neighbourhood reciting a version of the play and would collect in a basket eggs and cakes donated by the villagers. The Urmston School log book in the 1850s records absenteeism of the poorer children as a result of 'pace egging'.

No photos can be found of the Flixton pace egg play. The plays take place in England during the Easter period – indeed, the word 'pace' comes from the old English word 'pasch', literally meaning 'Easter'. The custom is a tradition that was once widespread throughout England, but is now in the twenty-first century only practised in a few areas, particularly Lancashire and West Yorkshire. One fine revival is still performed at The Ring O' Bells pub in Middleton.

There was a similar custom of the souling play with a similar script to that of the pace egg play. This custom, accompanied by the hobby horse 'Old Hobbs', was held in the first week of November; it was practised in Warburton in the 1800s and discontinued in 1936.

The Warburton souling play was part of the pre-industrial folk culture of Cheshire and is a hero-combat play telling the story of death and revival; the triumph of good over evil. Traditionally performed on consecutive nights from 1 November, it included the characters King George, the Turkish champion, the doctor, the driver, an old woman, a horse and Beelzebub. Katherine Egerton-Warburton, writing in the 1900s, says that 'on 1st November the wilder men of the village used to go about with lanterns at night, one wearing a horse's skull, which they called "Old Warb" and went to the farmers' homes for drink and money'.

The Warburton souling play was revived in 1978 and has continued to the present day. The band of soul players take the play around a variety of venues, during the first weeks of November, including The Church Inn in Flixton and

The Steamhouse in Urmston. Their final play in this itinerary is held at The Saracen's Head in Warburton and all proceeds, usually in the region of £1,500, are donated to charity.

It is tempting to think that the soul players of Warburton and the pace eggers of Flixton knew one another back in the nineteenth century and may have celebrated these customs in each other's pubs. However, this may be wishful thinking as, with transport being restricted at the time, it would have been unlikely that people would have travelled between the villages. It has to be remembered that those taking part in the plays would have been labourers who worked long hours for little remuneration and that the plays would have only been performed once a year.

The same singers who sang in the May would also do the rounds at Christmas, singing carols accompanied by a bassoon and fiddle. Langton tells of other revellers who would jump on the bandwagon and do the rounds simply as begging visits. New Year was also observed with the bells being rung on the stroke of midnight. Many people in the area would visit friends to 'Let in the New Year'. As recently as the 1960s I remember as a child being at family parties where my uncles would leave the house at the rear and re-enter through the front door with bread, coal and a silver coin to ensure we'd not be without food, fuel or money in the coming twelve months. This custom is still carried on today by some folk in the area.

A custom that ceased in the early 1890s was the decorating of the church tower pinnacle with oak boughs. The churchwardens' accounts show numerous entries for bell ringing on this day.

One common custom in the north-west of England was that of the rush-bearing ceremony. The poorer people would have to sit on the flagged or even earthen floor and this would have been somewhat uncomfortable. To alleviate the discomfort there would be rushes cut from the fields and strewn on the floor – as indeed they would be in the parishioners' cottages themselves. This custom is referred to as an 'ancient custom' by Harland and Wilkinson. The rushes would, over time, flatten down and discolour and there would be an annual ceremonial clearing out of the old, brown, limp rushes and a strewing of the new, clean, bright green ones. Thomas Newton, in his 1587 *Herbal to The Bible*, states that 'with sedge and rushes many in the country do use in summer-time to strew their parlours and churches, as well for coolness as for pleasant smell'.

The rush bearing would involve piling a cart high with rushes and decorated with flowers and even the church silver. The cart would then be pulled around the village or town by either the local morris dancers or a shire horse, often calling in at various hostelries for the dancers to refresh themselves. There would be much singing, drinking and merrymaking, and eventually the rushcart would arrive at the church to allow the rushes to be taken and placed in the church. There is mention in Ivor Million's *History of Didsbury* of this rush bearing taking place in nearby Didsbury, but neither Langton nor Lawson makes mention of a similar practice in Flixton. Million tells us that the rush bearing was 'quite common in the villages of Lancashire' and that in Didsbury 'originally it took place on 25th July but after 1752 [due to the Julian calendar being replaced by the Gregorian calendar], it changed to 5th August'. Also, in *A New History of Didsbury*, France and Woodall mention the Didsbury rushcart, adding that churches only introduced pews after the fifteenth century but that 'long after the need for rushes had gone, the ceremony continued to be performed because of the pleasure it gave to participants and spectators'. Significantly no mention is made of rush bearing in Volume 5 of *The History of The County of Lancaster*, in which other customs are mentioned.

Langton does refer to the custom of strewing rushes on the floors of domestic houses for warmth as the floors were 'composed of earth or clay rammed hard'. He goes on to state that reeds were also used for the church, where they would be strewn for the warmth of the congregation, presumably those of the poorer classes who could not afford to pay for a pew. The first mention is in the St Michael's church accounts for 1748 where 5s was paid for reeds. In 1752 it is recorded that reeds cost 8s 6d. Nonetheless, when the floor of the church was flagged the payments for reeds were carried on and the churchwardens' accounts for 1754 include a payment of 10s for two years' supply and in 1757 a payment of 15s. A sum of 10s is also recorded as being paid to James Yates for reeds in the accounts for 1764.

However, although the strewing of rushes in St Michael's is evident, it is probably safe to assume that the traditional north-west custom of rush bearing was not carried out in Flixton as neither Langton nor Lawson have mentioned it, nor is there any mention in Baines.

The Flixton stocks were taken down in 1823 and stood in Flixton village near The Church Inn. The sides of the stocks were thought to be part of the churchyard wall but no evidence has ever been found. The location is commemorated in nearby Stocks House, Stocks Terrace and Stocks View. The now accepted location of the stocks is where the Jubilee Tree was planted in 1887. Although now cut down, a smaller tree stands nearby at the junction of Church Road, Flixton Road and Carrington Road.

There was also a custom where women would stop wedding parties by drawing a rope across the road. A small sum of money would be paid by the wedding party before they were allowed to proceed.

Women were the unfortunate victims of a severe punishment known as the 'scold's bridle'. This rather severe item was kept in the Flixton poorhouse and consisted of an open iron helmet with a piece of iron projecting inwards into the mouth of the wearer. The whole was then padlocked, thereby inhibiting the victim from speaking. This dreadful and degrading contraption was used as a punishment for scolding women.

With only a small police force it was often left to the community to take a hand in the maintenance of law and order, and to remind those who did not come up to acceptable standards of morals and decency and to mete out punishment where it was considered appropriate. Village communities were small and it was hard to keep secret any activities that would give rise to unacceptability.

Hogarth's depiction of rough music during a skimmington ride, in one of his etchings.

Riding the stang, or the skimmington ride, was a custom aimed at those who were found guilty of unfaithfulness. It also included women who hen-pecked their husbands, as well as the husband who allowed himself to be so ridiculed and men who beat their wives. The unfortunate victim would be carried around the village on a ladder accompanied by 'tin-can music'. This 'music' would include the playing of cow's horns and the banging of frying pans, warming-pans, kettles and other implements that would make a loud and raucous sound when beaten. In Flora Thompson's *Larkrise to Candleford*, effigies of an adulterous couple were carried on poles by torchlight to their houses to the accompaniment of the banging of pots, pans and coal shovels with the addition of cat-calls, hoots and jeers. A similar scene is also included in Thomas Hardy's *The Mayor of Casterbridge*. This custom dates back to the Middle Ages and was common across Europe. Bob Pegg, in his *Rites and Riots: Folk Customs of Britain and Europe*, tells us that riding the stang was 'used more particularly in instances where the pusillanimous husband has suffered himself to be beaten by his virago of a partner'.

In *Folk Lore of East Yorkshire*, published in 1890, John Nicholson describes riding the stang as:

> To excite public opinion against a wife-beater, it is customary to 'ride the stang' for him. A 'see' [ladder] is procured and a noisy procession perambulates the streets, singing and shouting, and making night hideous with the braying of horns, clashing of iron pans, screaming of whistles, and banging of drums. This must be done on three successive nights to make it legal, or the 'riders' believe they could be summoned for breaking the peace.

Harland and Wilkinson, in their *Legends and Traditions of Lancashire* of 1873, refer to the custom as stang riding and explain that two poles were procured with a plank of wood connecting the poles to serve as a seat. Those punished were men or women who had been unfaithful; they would be caught and tied to the frame. They were then paraded around by four men holding the improvised seat, attended by crowds who would 'make all the discordant noises they can on pots, pans, tea-trays etc as they pass along the road'. They would then stop alongside various houses and proclaim the names of the parties and the time and place where the infidelity had taken place.

The goal was to enforce social standards and to rid the community of socially unacceptable relationships that threatened the stability of the village or town.

The practice was also a censure against socially unacceptable marriages – for example, the marriage of widows before the end of the customary social period of formal mourning – or to demonstrate disapproval, most commonly of 'unnatural' marriages and remarriages, such as a union between an older widower and a much younger woman. The practice was obviously a nationwide custom. Langton reported that many Flixton residents remembered it well and those detected in acts of unfaithfulness would be carried round the village on a ladder to the accompaniment of 'tin-can music'.

As these pastimes died out, new ones, such as hockey, golf, tennis, bowling, quoits, bicycling, and chess, among others, took their place in the form of social clubs, temperance societies and literary and debating societies. In 1846 the Urmston cricket and lawn tennis clubs were formed. The cricket club met near Humphrey Lane and, by all accounts, were a strong team who frequently beat the team from Sale. The club moved to Newcroft field and then again in 1850 to a field called The Gales on the north side of Gammershaw Lane, now Stretford Road. The club was dissolved in 1864 and proceeds from the sale of equipment, some £30 to £40, was given to Mr John Tomlinson Hibbert of Urmston Grange to buy books for Urmston library.

In 1885 The lacrosse club was formed; The rifle club followed in 1899. *The Lancashire Evening Post* reported on 18 July 1910 that 'Urmston Rifle Club defeated Leyland Rifle Club by 128 points at Urmston. Afterwards the visitors were entertained to tea'. In 1903 a men's club was formed, open to all male church-goers over the age of 18, and activities included gymnastics, dominoes, draughts, chess and ping-pong. The church withdrew its support and sponsorship in 1907 after differences of opinions between members of the club and the church council.

Towns the length and breadth of the country celebrated the end of the First World War and parades were held in the streets on 19 July 1919. After a thanksgiving service, the Victory parade, as it was called, set off down Flixton Road, Brook Road, Moorside Road, Irlam Road, Flixton Road and round the Jubilee Tree. The public were invited to decorate the processional route and wave flags.

There is also a memorial on Crofts Bank Road, on the site once occupied by the house known as Arrandale, behind which is Golden Hill Park.

The 1958 *Urmston Official Guide* tells us that 'mention must be made of the Urmston show – the great annual family show and one of the most attractive ideas born of Urmston'. The feature goes on to tell that the history of the show can be traced to pre-war days when a carnival was held annually to raise money

Urmston carnival, Abbotsfield Park, 1928. (Bob Potts)

for the local cottage hospital. The carnival also came to be associated with the annual horticultural show promoted by the Urmston and District Allotments Association. Sadly the carnival was suspended during the war years and never revived in its old form due to the advent of state-controlled hospitals.

The annual horticultural show carried on and increased in size with regular entries in newspapers such as the *Manchester Courier and Lancashire General Advertiser*, which on Monday, 18 August 1913 reported that there were in excess of 1,000 entries including poultry and pigeons. It was also noted that 'sweet peas were a noticeable class' and that 'herbaceous plants and vegetables [were also] strong features of a good all-round exhibition'. In the 1913 show there was also a separate provision for a children's plot and children's sports, which included morris dancing, a marathon race and a demonstration by the Boy Scouts.

Then, on August Bank Holiday Monday, 1947, a new, more ambitious event was born: the Urmston Show.

The new version of the event is now called the Flixton, Urmston and Davyhulme carnival; it starts with a parade leaving The Church Inn, Church Road, travelling through the town centre, down Moorside Road and finishing on Woodsend Field. The 2015 event included a number of information

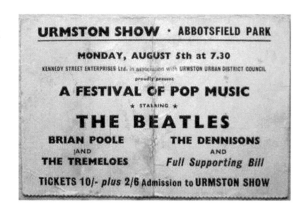

The Beatles. A ticket for the 1963 Urmston show at Abbotsfield Park.

URMSTON SHOW · ABBOTSFIELD PARK

MONDAY, AUGUST 5th at 7.30

KENNEDY STREET ENTERPRISES Ltd. in association with URMSTON URBAN DISTRICT COUNCIL

proudly present

A FESTIVAL OF POP MUSIC

★ STARRING ★

THE BEATLES

BRIAN POOLE | **THE DENNISONS**
|AND | AND
THE TREMELOES | *Full Supporting Bill*

TICKETS 10/- *plus* **2/6** Admission to **URMSTON SHOW**

stalls, charity and trade stalls with a display arena at which performed Flixton dance school, Flixton brass band, The Jayne Jarvis dance school and Angela's dance school.

The photograph of the 1928 Urmston carnival shows the young girl who was chosen as the carnival queen. Lime Avenue is in the background. This honour is still conferred today at the current carnivals.

One claim to fame for Urmston is the appearance of the Beatles at the Urmston show in 1963. The council booked the Fab Four for the show held at Abbotsfield Park on Chassen Road, with Brian Poole and The Tremeloes as second on the bill. The band were not well known at the time of the booking but had risen in popularity by the time of the show and compere David Hamilton is on record as saying that 'the boys were smuggled in in a van ... screaming girls rushed the stage to get hold of their idols ... it was certainly a hard day's night!'

Another high-profile group of the day appeared at the Flixton Show on Saturday, 19 September 1970 on Woodsend Fields on Woodsend Road. This was The Move, featuring Roy Wood, Jeff Lynne, Bev Bevan and Rick Price. Mungo Jerry were also on the bill and the compere was Radio 1 DJ Dave Eager.

Parks

Urmston Council pursued a policy of acquiring lands to provide amenities for the local residents and to that end, during the 1920s and 1930s, lands were bought and developed into Davyhulme Park and Golden Hill Park, both of which were built during the 1920s and appear on the OS maps in 1928.

My own memories regarding entertainment are gleaned from the late 1950s into the 1960s. This was the era when children were allowed to play in the street, stepping back on to the pavement when the occasional car drove past before resuming the game. It wasn't unknown for us to spend virtually the whole day at weekends or during school holidays at the local park, in my case Davyhulme Park, which was on the corner of Canterbury Road and Crofts Bank Road.

We'd sometimes take sandwiches and a drink to see us through lunchtime and return home late afternoon in time for tea. These were the days of make-believe where we'd act out scenarios around the park; taking in such features as the arch, the rose bowl, the lily ponds, the paddling pool, the bandstand and the concrete map of Britain. Opposite the concrete map, on the other side of the path, surrounded by water was a fountain and just past the arch was a concrete bird bath.

The arch at the entrance to the park was wonderful to clamber over as a child, and I did this often, but modern health and safety regulations would not allow such a structure to survive in today's cautious times. There was a rather grumpy old park keeper referred to as Parky, whose only jobs seemed to be raking up leaves and chasing cheeky boys.

The paddling pool was a focal point for children, especially during the summer months. I remember having a toy battery-driven motor boat that I loved to set loose on the water. One danger was broken glass on the bottom of the pool so it was inadvisable not to have some form of footwear, such as an old

Davyhulme
Park.

The author in Davyhulme Park paddling pool, c. 1958. (James Billington)

pair of pumps, while paddling. The park looked lovely back in the 1950s and 1960s. The gardens were magical when in full summer bloom with the beautiful arch leading from the gardens to the bandstand area, both structures sadly now demolished. The bandstand was somewhat unusual in that it didn't follow the traditional drum-shaped base with an iron canopy; rather it was in the shape of a concrete shell-like arch. There are still the two lily ponds, often the receptacles of rubbish, but these days somewhat tidier.

Sadly the paddling pool has been filled in, the castle, rose bowl, bandstand and arch pulled down, the bird bath taken away and the four tennis courts reduced to just two. It seems somewhat ironic that the plaque on the new brick entrance to the park is 'to commemorate the improvements to Davyhulme Park'. Many would argue at the choice of wording. The plaque was unveiled on 18 May 1992 by the Mayor of Trafford Cllr Mrs Lydia Burton.

Abbotsfield Park is a park in Urmston and, because of its location, on Chassen Road, it is also known as Chassen Park. This was once farmland known as Abbots Pit Fields, hence the name. The bowling green is sunken into the ground as the area was dug out during the war to fill sandbags, leaving a hollow. There is a thriving model railway that still runs regularly on the park, and also a children's playground and fields, amounting to a very pleasant recreational space. A May Day steam event was once held on the park, with traction engines and other machines from the past, but, since 2011, this has been discontinued.

A smaller park called Golden Hill Park, named after the field Golden Hill in the tithe map, is situated behind Sainsbury's supermarket and bordered by Crofts Bank Road and Moorside Road. There are playing fields, ornamental gardens, flower beds and a bowling club. There is also a small single-storey building that was once a library; it is now a childcare centre offering breakfast, after-school and holiday clubs. The park also includes a large granite cross commemorating the dead of two world wars.

Two other parks can be found on Broadway in Davyhulme and near Flixton House, Flixton Road, Flixton.

Cinemas

The first decade of the twentieth century was the decade when the silver screen increased in popularity.

The Picture Palace.
1(Alan Crossland)

The Empress Cinema. (Alan Crossland)

The **Urmston Picture Palace** was opened on 12 December 1912 and was situated opposite the market on the corner of Railway Road and Greenfield Road. The architect, Percy Hothersall, came from Prestwich. The Palace Cinema, as it was later known, had a proscenium 35ft wide, a stage 10ft deep, two dressing rooms and 500 seats for patrons. The Palace Cinema closed in the late 1950s and was converted into a factory and later occupied by Peter Nyssen Bulbs, a family business that started in 1958. This too was closed sometime after 1998. The building has been demolished and the land is now occupied by Elstree Court. Peter Nyssen Bulbs now occupies a much smaller premises at 124 Flixton Road.

The Empress opened in 1921 and was situated opposite where the old post office building stands on Higher Road. Seating was provided for 900 and the decor consisted of flats and cut-outs erected on each side of the screen that depicted Italian scenes, enlivening the plainness of the auditorium.

There was no plaster ceiling, just the roof trusses showing. In 1934 it was redesigned into an art deco style cinema by architects Drury & Gomersall. A balcony was added and the seating capacity was increased to 1,228. A new proscenium was also added that was 35ft wide. It reopened as The Empress

The Curzon Cinema.

Cinema on 5 August 1935 with Will Hay in 'Radio Parade of 1935'. In the reopening programme the manager, Ernest Hough, welcomed new patrons, saying that 'the staff have been trained to give the utmost courtesy and attention to every patron' and that the modernised cinema 'would be capable of accommodating a steadily increasing patronage'.

The Empress was demolished in 1962, and took two years to clear to make way for phase two of the Urmston town centre redevelopment, which included Victoria Parade and The New Victoria public house.

Due to the availability and popularity of television sets, the decline of the cinema seemed inevitable.

Interestingly, Will Hay lived in Salford but appeared as a stand-up comic in Urmston when in his teens. This was at a venue called **The Pavilion** at Station Road. The Pavilion, as stated in *Slater's 1910 Street Directory*, was situated between 20 and 22 Station Road. Research shows that this was more likely an access point to the area behind, which is now occupied by the houses near Royal Avenue. Indeed, the OS map of 1912 clearly shows an unadopted road, which was later built in 1937 as Royal Avenue. Two other access points to The

Pavilion were behind Mayo's (where Woolworth's was eventually built) and Church Road. Furthermore, the 1912 OS map does not show any structure on the land behind the police station stretching up to Mayo's, which is somewhat irksome to the researcher.

The grand opening of the Urmston Pierrot Company at the venue was on Saturday, 27 May 1905, as advertised in *The Western Telegraph* on 26 May. The general manager, John Matthews, was described as booking 'high class artistes, a refined entertainment' in the music hall tradition. The very same day the company were advertising in *The Era* in the wanted section for 'artistes for Pierrots'. Indeed, Will Hay himself was employed by the company as MC and stand-up comedian. The heyday of the Urmston Pierrot Company was between 1905 and 1910. One reporter on *The Western Telegraph* remarked that it was the only regular place of entertainment in Urmston. There is no mention of it thereafter.

An intriguing advert has also come to light, unattributed to a date or periodical. However, it quite clearly states that there would be a special visit (circa 1910?) commencing 2 April and until further notice of the 'Travelling Picturedrome'. The advert describes the structure as heated by steam and lighted by electricity with wooden floor and tip-up chairs. 'This building is NOT a show, but the most up-to-date structure in existence', the advert declares. Prices were 2*d*, 4*d* and 6*d*, with shows twice nightly at 6:45 and 8:45.

On Thursday, 24 May 1910, however, there was an entry in *The Stage* which ran: 'For Sale, Urmston Pavilion near Manchester. Large grounds, splendid stage, dressing rooms, office, pay box, etc. 7th season. Cheap rent. What offers? Write Arthur Guildford, 358 Stretford Road, Manchester.' Not only that but just over a month later, on 30 June, the proprietors of Urmston Pavilion, who are described as 'Urmston Entertainment Co.' were seen as advertising for 'artistes, all lines' requesting 'photo, references, lowest terms to Walter Bellian, business manager'.

The Stretford Telegraph, furthermore, reported on 14 October 1910 that the venue was to be reopened as a cinematograph pavilion the following day, to be called The Picture Pavilion. *The Stretford Telegraph* went on to report that the lessee, Mr Adrim, announced his intention 'to show the best of films of which an exceedingly fine set have been secured'. It had a chequered existence because the public demand for films exceeded the supply. A local resident, Miss Marshall, recalled going to The Pavilion, where 1*d* was the admission price and a further 1*d* would buy fish and chips.

Mr E. Adrim, who took over soon after on 20 January 1911, carried out structural improvements to the building including a gallery. He renamed the venue The Bijou Hippodrome for the showing of films and vaudeville acts. What is even more remarkable is that the same newspaper reported that plans were afoot to build a 1,000-seat cinema on the same land. The scheme was abandoned when an alternative site was found on Railway Road, where the 500-seater cinema called The Picture Palace was eventually built and opened on 12 December 1912. It was owned by The Urmston Palace Company.

The Curzon opened in 1934, although some sources show it erroneously as opening in 1931/32. A veteran Flixton resident remembers the cinema opening the year after Urmston Baths opened in 1933. It is the only building of the three still standing today, although it is no longer used as a cinema. Picture-goers now have to travel to one of the nearby cinema complexes, such as the one at the Trafford Centre, or travel in to Manchester city centre. The Curzon was built by Ernest Nash-Eaton, once resident at Highfield House, who was responsible for a dozen cinemas around Manchester for the period. The stage area was 45ft wide and 20ft deep and had three dressing rooms available for artists when there were live performances showing. It closed on 5 September 2008 and Flixton Academy of Performing Arts now occupies the building.

There was time when all three cinemas were doing a roaring trade, especially during the war years. An advert in the *Manchester Evening News* on 25 November 1940 announced The Empress as showing Fred Astaire and Eleanor Powell in *Broadway Melody of 1940*, while The Palace was screening *Women Without Names* and *The Farmer's Daughter*. The Palace's telephone number is stated to be URM 2236.

On 21 August 1944 the Manchester Evening News advertised the Curzon showing *Standing Room Only*, while The Empress was screening *ABC*, the Clark Gable film. Or you could watch *You're A Lucky Fellow Mr Smith* at The Palace. Pathé news bulletins would regularly show newsreels of the progress that the Allies were making during the war campaign.

However, not everybody lauded the coming of the cinemas. They were accused of encouraging imitative crimes due to the sensational films shown, thereby tempting youngsters to steal and acquire the few pence needed to get in. Charles Russell was Chief Inspector of Reformatory and Industrial Schools in 1917. In a lecture, 'The Problem of Juvenile Crime', which he gave the same year, he warned that watching films not only caused eye strain but 'undue excitement' among children and went on to say that 'the distorted and unreal, Americanised (in the worse sense) view of life presented must have a deteriorating effect, and lead, at the best, to the formation of false ideals'.

Nonetheless, Cyril Burt, a researcher into juvenile delinquent behaviour, was of the opinion that the cinema actually reduced hooliganism, withdrawing young men from the pubs and supplying girls with a safer substitute for lounging with their friends in the alleys and parks. Not long after The Urmston Picture Palace opened on 12 December 1912, Mr Fletcher, headmaster of the elite Higher Grade School on Ross Grove, Urmston, wrote to *The Western Telegraph* that he was of the opinion that films were having a bad effect on children and setting a bad example.

The entire takings on the opening night were donated to the Urmston Cottage Hospital. Ironically, Mr Fletcher was on the hospital committee.

Case Study 3: Ernest Leonard Leeming

1889–1964

Ernest Leonard Leeming MSc (Tech.), Assoc. M.Inst.C.E., M.I.Mun.E., was born in Manchester in 1889. *The Manchester Courier and Lancashire General Advertiser*

The opening ceremony of the cenotaph at Davyhulme Circle, 20 July 1929. The author's grandmother can be seen in the white dress just to the right of the clock tower. Ernest Leeming is behind the girl presenting the flowers. (Author)

reported on Monday, August 8 1904 that he had been granted a three-year scholarship worth £60 per annum to study at Manchester University. He graduated from Manchester University in 1907 when only 18 years of age; he became a civil engineer in 1911 and was, after a spell with Barton-upon-Irwell, the Urmston Urban District town engineer from 1933 until 1954. He died in 1964.

A war memorial was erected at Davyhulme Circle in 1924, in what was then Bethell's farmyard, and this now holds the names of the dead of both world wars in addition to more recent conflicts. The photo of Davyhulme Circle (previous) shows the formal opening of the cenotaph on 20 July 1929. Bethell's Farm was demolished to make way for the Circle. The memorial cenotaph had been erected in the farmyard shortly after the end of the First World War some years before the construction of the Circle.

The tree on the left in the photo was struck by lightning around the early 1940s. The gentleman on the right is Councillor C. Forsyth JP, chairman of Davyhulme parish council; in the centre foreground is his wife Mrs T. Forsyth, and the man third from the left behind the girl presenting the flowers is Ernest Leeming, surveyor to Barton-upon-Irwell Rural District Council.

Leeming's favourite construction material was concrete – he was known as 'the concrete king' – and even a cursory observation of the paths and low walls circumventing the cenotaph demonstrates this. The memorial, made of ashlar sandstone, was originally erected to commemorate twenty-three men killed during the First World War. After the Second World War a further six names were added. The cenotaph includes a brass clock dial glazed in opal on each of the four sides, the mechanism consisting of a Graham deadbeat escapement and a nickel steel pendulum. Below the dials is a band that includes the inscription running counter-clockwise 'In memory of those who fell in the Great War 1914–1918'.

The cenotaph itself is a tall square tower incorporating low buttresses. The west face is inscribed with the legend 'Roll of Honour' with the names of the twenty-three men killed in the First World War. Below is the inscription 'Tell England ye who pass this monument,/ we died for her and now we rest content.' A later inscription follows underneath: 'Also those who gave their lives in the Second World War 1939–1945', followed by the names of the six. A lower space on the base has been added with the inscription 'Also those who gave their lives in subsequent wars'. Sadly, one name was added in 2006: that of Gary Paul Quilliam. The memorial was rebuilt in 1965 and is listed as Grade II.

A portrait of Ernest L. Leeming. (John Howe)

Davyhulme Circle, 2017. (Author)

The Circle was overseen by Leeming, who was a civil engineer; in the 1964 edition of his 1924 book *Road Engineering* he included a whole chapter on traffic circles and roundabouts. Here he states that the advantages of such roundabouts are the provision of a one-way traffic movement whereby a considerable volume of traffic can be kept moving in safety. Also, that right-hand turning is made easier and the passage of traffic is quicker than by the use of traffic lights. An aerial view of the circle is included in his book and it is tempting to speculate that, as a keen aviator himself, he may have been at the controls of the plane when this photograph was taken.

Leeming describes the circle at Davyhulme as a 'turbine type rotary'. The dimensions are as follows; diameter of circle 200ft; width of carriageway around the circle 40ft; width of the carriageway at the directional islands 30ft, area of the whole circle including footpaths etc., 2.5 acres. He even stated that the height of the soil, turf or shrubbery should not exceed 3ft 6in to prevent 'dazzle from opposing traffic, but [allowing] visibility for all drivers across the circle itself'. Leeming was also at pains to point out that pedestrians should not cross the central island and that 'crossings at the junction of the radial roads should be provided'. These are provided for by what he termed as 'directional islands', which he clarifies as 'refuges for pedestrians'. These features described by Leeming are admirably in evidence at Davyhulme Circle.

It is interesting to note that there were originally benches provided for pedestrians on the island itself but these were removed after the Manchester riots in 2011 when there was the threat from hooligans to use them as battering rams to smash through shop windows on the circle.

Leeming went on to mention that he saw some defects with the layout of the circle such as the turning on to Barton Road being insufficiently superelevated, that the road around the circle was likewise insufficiently superelevated and that the footpaths across and around the circle were undesirable. Superelevation is the civil engineering practice of banking the road at the sides to reduce road and tyre wear.

The advantages to the Circle he mentioned are that the carriageway is 40ft, which allows for parking in the outside lane, which today can be seen in the section between Lostock Road and Crofts Bank Road; also that a car park could be provided – this can still be enjoyed by motorists in the section outside The Nag's Head public house.

Leeming was also of the opinion that there had been objections to concrete paving being white or dull grey in appearance so he experimented with a variety of mixtures and textures of concrete, including the use of aggregates, using two colours, green and yellow, and these experimental panels can still be seen in front of the barber's shop on the railway bridge at the crossroads of Crofts Bank Road and Higher Road. They were laid in such a public place so as to monitor the wear and tear due to the constant traffic of pedestrians. The appendix to his book lists a variety of concrete mixtures.

He also advocated 'warmer' tones by using a coloured aggregate such as red or pink granite or gravel with sand and rapid-hardening 'Colorcrite' cement. These pink tones can still be seen in the pedestrian pathways on Davyhulme Circle and also on the cycle tracks that run the length of Lostock Road and which are continued for some distance under the motorway on the Stretford side. In fact, Leeming was very conscious of the necessity, where possible, of segregating cyclists from the roads, and he devotes a whole chapter in his book *Road Engineering* to his proposals for making the life of the cyclist safer. Another of his contributions to the area was the reinforced concrete road signs, some of which can still be seen.

Leeming stated that 'it is the duty of every Local Authority to provide for every street name-plates in a conspicuous position; frequently these are fixed

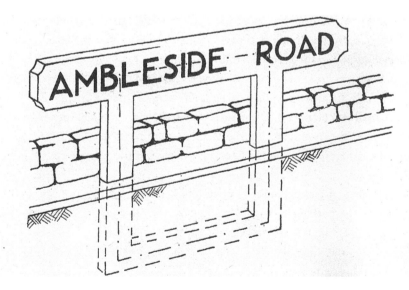

A diagram from Leeming's Road Engineering, showing the structure of road signage. From *Leeming's Road Engineering*, Third Edition (1952)

A Davyhulme Circle sign. (Author)

on buildings at a high level, and this is not suitable for busy town streets'. He goes on to explain that 'a lower level of sign will enable the motorist to observe it by head-lights in periods of darkness'.

The letters are sunk into the concrete and mounted on a reinforced concrete frame that cannot easily be lifted out of the ground. A diagram of the sign can be seen above and how it is secured under the pavement. As can be observed, the structure is embedded below ground with the vertical posts connected by a concrete bar. They were installed from the 1920s onwards but many have been taken up over time and replaced with white metal panels with black lettering. Road signs had hitherto been placed high on walls and some still exist, such as Parsonage Road and the stone sign on Lily Street, now Grosvenor Road.

The concrete pebble-dashed benches that were widespread in the area are also possibly of his design. There are still a few surviving examples; on Moorside Road next to Golden Hill Park, on Church Road just a few hundred yards up from the old police station, Davyhulme Road near the large urn, at the junction of Rathan Road and Hayeswater Road, two on Flixton Road at the side of Ambleside playing fields, at the Church Road and Snowden Avenue junction and on Cornhill Road, to name just eight. Leeming stated that these seats should, in some areas, 'be anchored in the ground to prevent disturbance by mischievous persons'. Incidentally, similar benches can still be seen in neighbouring Sale and Stretford.

Leeming's vision for the roads and streets of the area included the planting of trees, which he aimed at being one tree for every inhabitant; indeed, he advocated that 'no modern road should be without trees'. He proposed that the Ministry of Transport should create a special mobile department of experts with lifting equipment to move large trees where they conflicted with road and planning needs and be replanted elsewhere in the area.

In his book he stated that 'we cannot afford to go on losing our beautiful trees and producing barren-looking new highways when there is a remedy at hand'. His idea was to avoid monotony by planting saplings of several varieties, which he suggested should be limes, planes, horse chestnut, larch, and copper beech as well as flowering trees and shrubs. He added his opinion that silver birch 'add beauty to a road and are especially useful on the outside of a curve'.

He also advocated concrete flower baskets and hanging flower baskets suspended from lamp standards to decorate the streets.

In his book *Road Engineering,* Leeming was at pains to point out that 'one of the greatest fascinations in new town planning is the opportunity to introduce landscape features. It will require imagination and patience, since it may be several years before the real beauty shows itself.' He also commented that one of the aspects to town planning that had come in for criticism was the design that incorporated parallel lines, centre margins, double carriageways, kerbs, cycle tracks and footways as a matter of mere utility. He therefore advocated designing the layout in a more imaginative way using bends and curves to break up the regimentality of modern town planning. As he said, 'an undulating country helps to remove the monotony of a straight road'. The town planners of Milton Keynes would have done well to have consulted Ernest Leeming!

Leeming was also concerned about the wear and tear to roads in the area. *The Yorkshire Evening Post*, on 25 November 1925, reported that Leeming proposed a greater tax on road users who used vehicles with solid tyres over vehicles with pneumatic tyres. Leeming declared that it was 'deplorable that pneumatic-tyred vehicles should be paying at the present rates for the damage caused almost entirely by solid-tyred vehicles'. He also went on to say that road damage was also attributable to back-axle drive vehicles.

Leeming suggested many initiatives that were rejected for various reasons. He prepared a proposal for the electrification of the Greater Manchester railways in 1930; in 1935 he proposed a flying arena on the Meadows with an aerial taxi service to Speke and thence to connect to Blackpool. The plan was rejected by the council, as was his proposal for a water taxi service on the Manchester

Ship Canal in 1935. The water buses would have left the canal at each set of locks and re-joined the canal after circumventing the lock.

Interestingly, this service did eventually become a reality. Following negotiations between the Bridgewater Canal Company Limited (BCCL) and Manchester Water Taxis it was announced in 2016 that a licence had been awarded to operate two boats on the canal. Under the terms of the licence, Manchester Water Taxis would run a service to the Intu Trafford Centre via Old Trafford and Hotel Football as well as a service to Sale both terminating at Dukes 92, Castlefield. The water taxis were to be called 'Waxis'. Manchester Water Taxis was founded in February 2009 by entrepreneur Steven Cadwell, who had initially planned to launch on the Manchester Ship Canal providing public transport services between the city centre and MediaCityUK. It should not be forgotten, however, that the idea was Ernest Leeming's from over eighty years ago.

Another of Leeming's ideas was to place 'welcome' signs around Urmston, which he did but the Ministry of Transport felt that these would be a distraction to drivers and they were taken down. These welcome signs are now ubiquitous around the country, including, of course, in Urmston. Yet another idea rejected was a 1936 proposal for a bridge to be built over the Manchester Ship Canal in Trafford Park on the opposite side to Barton Bridge.

The exterior of Urmston Baths. (Bob Potts)

In 1945 Leeming made a suggestion for the new estate on Broadway in Davyhulme. This involved the supply of 'socialised gas' where there would be one central unit rather than individual meters in each house. The idea was for the total gas consumption to be calculated on an annual basis and the cost divided equally among the households and added to the individual rents. The logic was that the payment of gas should be similar to that of the water supply, which was identical for each household.

A year later Leeming proposed the Woodsend Estate heating project, where a clustering of the homes would, he suggested, make heating homes more efficient. This proposal reached fruition in 1951 and the boiler house is located on Cheriton Road and piped throughout to radiators and tanks in each home. Many of his ideas were inspirational but occasionally they could verge on the bizarre, such as his idea to ask the railway companies to place wooden decking on railway bridges when trains were not in service so that they could accommodate road traffic. The idea was also for the companies to collect toll charges to aid running costs. One project that was, however, accepted was the design for the public swimming baths built in 1933 on Bowfell Circle; this was an impressive glass-domed building, and Leeming was the engineer and architect of the project.

The baths were a combined effort between Urmston Urban District Council and the parish councils of Flixton and Davyhulme; they were formally opened on 31 March 1933 by Councillor Lt Col S. Stott JP. The construction was by

The interior of Urmston Baths.

Brew Bros. of Cadishead and the steelwork supplied by Edward Wood and Co. from Manchester. The baths were under the management of the new Urmston Council from the beginning and the newly constituted Urban District Council actually fulfilled those plans with the aid of an unemployment grant. The £31,000 project resulted in a simple but dignified and imposing building with artificial stone façade and a superstructure of rustic bricks set in white cement.

As you climbed the steps and entered the building you were greeted by the sounds of chatter and splashing and the occasional clang of the metal lockers shutting down below in the changing rooms. A shallow section of disinfected water had to be walked through to gain access to a room with warm baths that were bliss to lie in on cold days but often full of cloudy water after frequent use. The pool itself was an impressive site; rectangular in shape with rounded shallow sections at the sides, 2ft 9in deep, accessed by steps for children to play or to learn to swim away from the deeper parts of the pool. Indeed, it was in these shallow sections that the author learned to swim on school visits from Whitelake with his teacher Mrs Webber. As the *Urmston Official Guide Book* from 1958 states, 'the pool itself is unusual, departing from the conventional rectangular shape by having a circular expansion in the centre. This provides ample room for those learning to swim and leaves the main channel clear for accomplished performers.'

The pool, of competition length, was 109ft long by 36ft wide. The deep end was at the end where the diving boards were situated and the diving pool was 9ft deep. The opposite end was 4ft deep and behind this end of the pool was an upper-level spectators' seated area, underneath which was a gymnasium. The depth at the centre was 4ft 8in. The capacity of the pool was 180,000 gallons and the water constantly circulated through filters and aerated.

The glazed dome reached a height of 50ft above the water and an additional feature was underwater floodlighting and glass ports for underwater viewing. *The Official Urmston Guide* of 1971 mentions that the pool could accommodate 180 bathers and 200 spectators. The handrails were of stainless steel and steps into the pool were at strategic points. The walkways round the pool were made of non-slip mosaics set in terrazzo coping. At the diving board end there were two fixed diving boards surmounted by a long springboard.

After drying off, bathers could go to the cafe that overlooked the pool at the diving-board end and watch the swimmers while sipping hot Bovril. The cafe was on the upper level situated over the boiler room and laundry. In addition to the main pool were slipper baths, footbaths and showers.

An added facility was that the pool could be covered over for dancing events; the pop group The Hollies performed there supported by local band The Astrals on 5 November 1963 at a concert billed as a Guy Fawkes concert. The Rolling Stones were the attraction on Friday, 29 November 1963. The dance floor can clearly be seen in the demolition photo (opposite). The baths were opened for business on 31 March 1933 and closed for demolition on 28 June 1987; a lifespan of a mere fifty-four years. Reasons for the demolition included speculation that it was too expensive to maintain the building, especially as the filtering system needed to be updated to meet with health and safety standards, and also concerns that the glass dome was beginning to disintegrate and the steel structure was rusting away.

One final interesting fact is that during the Second World War, the Dunlop Rubber Co. Ltd used the pool for experiments connected with work on inflated aircraft dinghies that they were manufacturing.

The land is now occupied by a housing development called Charleston Square. Perhaps a more fitting title would have been Leeming Square to honour a man whose mark has been indelibly stamped on the area. The plaque

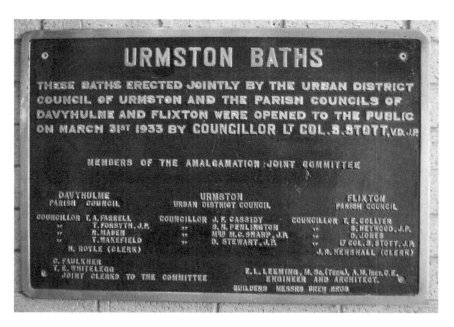

The plaque commemorating the opening of the baths in 1933 greeted bathers when they entered the foyer; it has now been relocated to the new leisure centre. (Author)

The demolition of Urmston Baths. Notice the hard flooring, which covered the pool for events such as concerts and boxing matches. (Rosemary Sumira)

commemorating the opening of the baths has been relocated and is now mounted on a wall in the reception area of the Bowfell Leisure Centre.

There is no doubt that Ernest Leeming was a visionary and his mark has been left indelibly on Urmston. He was forced into retirement at the age of 65, rejecting the council's opinion that his work was done. He requested an extension to carry on his work with the engineering department but his plea fell on deaf ears. Quite simply, his ideas were way ahead of their time and his employers just couldn't appreciate his vision and innovative ideas.

Significantly, the Ministry of Transport rejected his proposal for a motorway network in England to connect the major cities. It must have been very satisfying for him to see the construction of the M1 before he died. He also predicted the construction of the Channel Tunnel but did not live to see it opened in 1994.

Even in his retirement Leeming was still active. In 1963–4, when the extension of the M6 from Carnforth to Carlisle was being planned, he conducted a campaign for it to be routed via West Cumbria rather than Shap and Penrith, and for it to cross Morecambe Bay on a barrage. He would doubtless have continued the campaign longer, but for the fact that he died at the end of 1964.

The barrage would have run from Hest Bank near Morecambe to Bardsea near Ulverston. It would also have served for fresh water storage, and maybe hydro-power too. The northern part of the Lancaster bypass would have become a spur.

Leeming was a keen aviator. In the Royal Aero Club's publication, *Flight*, of 18 May 1939 under the news and official notices for the week ending 13 May, Leeming's name appears in the Aviator's Certificates list. His certificate has number 18029, his club is shown as the Northern Aviation Club and the entry is dated 3 May 1939.

Leeming's visions were not just confined to the Urmston area, as we have seen. Another of his proposals, reported on 16 November 1950 in *The Lincolnshire Echo*, was his 1944 idea that British cities should sponsor the building of new twin towns in Rhodesia. This was a project to attract more white emigrants into Southern Rhodesia to accommodate the overspill population of Britain's large cities.

As early as 1936, as reported in *The Aberdeen Press and Journal*, Leeming forwarded the idea of a memorial to the late king for a great highway from London to Glasgow with no speed limit. The estimated construction time would have been five years at a cost of £40 million. Flyover junctions were planned at important intersections. On 24 May 1945 *The Evening Dispatch* reported that Leeming had proposed a scheme for a new 'backbone' for Great Britain in the form of a 400-mile super motor road to be known as 'The Churchill Highway'. It was also proposed that German POWs would provide the labour.

Leeming lived at Kelmscott, 44 Cornhill Road in Urmston, just around the corner from the swimming baths. The house is no longer there and Kelmscott Lodge, a housing complex, now occupies the site.

Fifteen

URMSTON AT WAR, 1939–45

T he Luftwaffe air raids over Manchester during the Second World War were targeted mainly at shipping, rail communications and Trafford Park, where tanks were being manufactured at Metro-Vicks. The Manchester Ship Canal Company was well aware of its particular vulnerability, and set up a full-scale internal Air Raid Precation (ARP) service before the outbreak of the war on 3 September 1939. This was manned by volunteers from all sections of its staff.

However, thousands of bombs fell wide of the mark, causing many injuries and deaths in Manchester and Salford. Urmston Urban District was a vital frontline sector in the defence of Trafford Park. Mobile light anti-aircraft guns from the ordnance at Flixton Drill Hall fired morale-boosting salvoes at enemy aircraft supported by searchlight crews, barrage balloons teams and static heavy guns that were grouped in Davyhulme and nearby Stretford.

During raids civilians opted for cover in Anderson shelters, light steel shelters erected in the gardens of civilians with children and an income of under £250 a year, or under Morrison shelters, which were steel tables in the houses. Those who did not qualify could purchase their own Anderson shelter. Many, my grandmother included, often remained indoors and carried on with their household activities in stubborn defiance of the enemy; also, many stayed to safeguard their property and possessions.

The Luftwaffe left in its wake horrendous scenes of death and destruction but, by chance, Urmston's casualties were far fewer than neighbouring Stretford's. The injured were taken to Flixton's Abbotsfield Hospital (now the Conservative club) and also hospitals in Manchester and Salford. Also active during the raids were the fire brigade, medics, ARP wardens, the Home Guard and the Women's Voluntary Service.

The main raids were on 22, 23 and 24 December 1940. Among the dead during these Christmas raids were John (47) and Emily Cross (46) of 8 Hilrose

Avenue in Urmston; David Roberts (48) of 33 Winifred Road, Urmston; Milly Davies (50) and her mother Annie Davison of nearby 12 Hilrose Avenue; and William Morgan Smith (29) of Gladstone Road, Urmston. The injured included Lily Brophy of 31 Humphrey Park; Henry Archibald of 11 Kirkstall Avenue, Davyhulme; Edwin Burrill of 48 Westbourne Road, Urmston; Albert Hopkinson of 33 Newstead Road, Davyhulme; James Rogers of 75 Moss Vale Road, Urmston; Cyril Todd of 11 Humphrey Court, Urmston; and Alan Knight of Carlton Crescent, Urmston. Other raids took place, including that of 11 March 1941, during which William Clarke (37) of 150 Firwood Road, Urmston, was killed at home. On 10 October 1940 a raid injured Edith Mason of 5 Snowden Avenue and Irene Cross (46) of 8 Hilose Avenue.

On 11 March 1941 Theresa Winifred Luckman, the youngest Blitz casualty in the area at the age of 8, of 206 Canterbury Road, Davyhulme, was killed in a bomb blast at her home. Catherine Shipley (81) and her daughter Ann were killed at the same address. The relationship of the Shipleys to the Luckmans is unknown but they were most probably related as all three are interred in the same grave in Urmston cemetery.

Nurse Winifred Spencer (left) and colleague who tended the injured at Abbotsfield Hospital, 1943. (Bob Potts)

Also killed was Basil B. Etheridge of 26 Norreys Road, Flixton, who died of his injuries on 7 August 1943 in Abbotsfield Hospital after firefighting in Trafford Park three days earlier. Arthur Holt (35) of 5 Lodge Avenue died on 29 October 1940 due to his injuries while firefighting in Weaste some four weeks earlier on 5 October. In all, there were twenty civilian casualties over the war period, including twelve dead and eight injured. Compared with Stretford, the casualties in the Urmston, Flixton and Davyhulme area were very light indeed.

In his memoirs, *Reminiscenses of a Flixton Boyhood*, Bob Potts tells of some Anderson shelters being used as sheds after the war and one resident of The Grove, Flixton, who used his as a chicken coop. The 4-year-old Bob and his friend Leslie Morris used his parents' Morrison shelter in the family's front room in The Grove as a den after the Christmas Blitz of 1940. Bob also witnessed a barrage balloon coming down in flames one dark and stormy night in 1941 near Flixton House. It had been hit by lightning. It was during the 1940 Blitz the three bunker-type air-raid shelters on the school field, adjacent to The Grove, were put to their fullest use. The cellars of St Michael's school were utilised as shelters.

There was also a brick air-raid shelter in Chassen Park that was used as a club house for players on the bowling green. An underground air-raid shelter survived up until the 1980s on the land now occupied by Parker's Garden Centre on Carrington Road, Flixton. Also of great interest is a shelter that still survives fully intact underground in Urmston. It is situated on Flixton Road next to Urmston railway station, opposite the entrance to Eden Square. It is covered over and no access is allowed to the public for the time being.

Case Study 4

THE TOWN CENTRE
REDEVELOPMENT IN 1970

My recollection as a child of the shops in Urmston is very different to the appearance of today's retail outlets. I still vaguely remember the old Victoria public house that was demolished and is now occupied by part of what was known as phase two of the buildings that were constructed during the 1970 redevelopment programme; a development that included a new but soulless Victoria public house, which now lies vacant.

I remember Woolworth's on Croft's Bank Road with the old, dark, polished, wooden hollow square display units where the shop assistants would stand and serve from inside the hollow space. There were no supermarkets as now; meat was bought from Cuthbert's, fruit and vegetables from Silcock's, both on Crofts Bank Road, and dairy products and cold meats from the Maypole opposite Woolworth's. Bread would be bought fresh from the bakery. The post office was still a viable concern in its beautiful building on Higher Road and Terry's was selling remaindered goods cheaply such as furniture, tools, clothing, etc. at the end of Station Road. The building's original purpose was as a temperance and snooker hall and it is almost identical in architectural design to the building that is now a Wetherspoon's pub in nearby Chorlton-cum-Hardy. The building was also a roller skating rink and then Vernon's supermarket for a while. At the time of writing the building was occupied by the Istanbul Grill.

Rose's chemist was not only a traditional drug dispensers serving the doctor's surgery on the corner of Station Road and Gloucester Road but also a shop where my father would buy a camera and other photographic supplies. Les Kasmati, a director of the board at Rose's, was also a member of the same camera club that my father attended and would suggest photographic items that might interest him. A nice personal touch.

Shannon's, just across the road from the chemist, was where I bought many classical LPs, and nearby was Eddie McGrath's where my first bike was bought. Another shop was the wool shop where my mother bought many a skein of wool to wind into balls herself, and the shoe shop that stocked Start-Right shoes – I still have my first pair, which were Jumping Jacks. The TSB, where my mother opened an account for me as a child, is one of the few places I remember that was still operating in its original function in 2017, as well as Smethill's the undertakers, though this had previously been Ridings the furnishers. It is now still a funeral directors' operated by the Co-operative.

My childhood doctors' surgery, Gloucester House, on the corner of Station Road and Gloucester Road, a beautiful half-timbered black and white building is, likewise, still operating as a surgery. The gas and electricity showrooms also are now a thing of the past but Urmston's were on Flixton Road opposite the entrance to Roseneath Road and built in the 1930s on land that was once Moss Farm. The gas showroom was designed in the art deco style and the building is now a pub and night club. The electricity showroom is, likewise, a pub occupied by The Tim Bobbin of Wetherspoons.

1970: A new shopping experience

Between 1970 and 1972, during my late teens, I was studying for my A-levels at De La Salle College in Weaste, Salford. For my art studies I had to do three papers: a painting, an objective drawing and an architectural thesis. For my thesis I chose to write a paper on the town centre redevelopment of my home town. In preparation for my research I interviewed Mr Ashcroft at the developers, Metropolitan Estate and Property Corporation Ltd, Mr Jackson of Urmston Council, Mr Jones from the architect's office at Leach, Rhodes and Walker and Mr Eccles of Urmston library, who supplied maps and other information. The quantity surveyors for the redevelopment were Tozier, Gallagher and Partners and the letting agents for the units were Dunlop Heywood and Co.

Until the end of the Second World War the town centres of Britain had changed little in the previous 100 years. The need, and the opportunity, for large-scale redevelopment of some town centres was the result of bomb damage and those towns and cities that had suffered the most were, naturally, the first to benefit from such a programme of rebuilding and redevelopment.

Also, a post-war increase in consumer spending led to more demands for shopping space and, with that, a demand for larger shops and office spaces also. However, the huge increase in motor car ownership also presented an added dimension to the problem. There was certainly a conflict between the desire for vehicular access to town and city centres while retaining a civilised environment free of noise, fumes and physical danger.

Between 1947 and 1967 twenty-one new towns had sprung up in Britain, including the ring of new towns around London such as Hemel Hempstead, Basildon, Harlow, Stevenage, Hatfield, Welwyn, Harlow, Crawley and Bracknell, as well as elsewhere in Great Britain including Cumbernauld, Newton Aycliffe and Peterlee. In addition to these new towns, developed through the machinery of the New Towns Act of 1946, there was started a programme of major town expansion, many being of the same large-scale dimensions as the new towns. However, the speed of the advancement of the motor age took many planners by surprise. Henry Wells, the former chairman of the Hemel Hempstead Development Corporation, admitted that 'if the Hemel Hempstead Development Corporation had known that the motor car age was upon them, they would have produced a very different sort of town', admitting that the provision of more garaging would have been made. This lack of foresight was not always the fault of town planners, architects and engineers, as many had striven to provide an up-to-date road system separating the pedestrian from motor traffic. It was, rather, a penny-pinching ministry who had provided for only one garage for every four houses, a provision that Henry Wells admitted in 1963 was 'totally, hopelessly wrong'. Furthermore, during the first fourteen years of the new town building programme, the number of motor vehicles was rapidly increasing in Britain yet the effects of this increase were only belatedly being recognised by the powers that had the wherewithal to do anything about it.

The coming of this motor car age was a significant factor in the nationwide decision to plan for traffic-free, pedestrianised shopping malls in our towns and cities. As Tetlow and Goss stated in their book *Homes, Towns and Traffic* in 1965, 'we have, in fact, to reconcile two conflicting needs – accommodation and circulation – the need to stay in one place for periods of work, rest and sleep, and the need to move about from home to work, to school, and shop'.

In the late 1960s, as with similar towns the length and breadth of the country, Urmston was feeling certain pressures that necessitated the local authorities taking a long hard look at the town centre infrastructure. The concept had initially been considered in the early 1960s but work was delayed due to economic pressures.

In 1970 Urmston's steadily growing population had reached the 43,000 mark, with over 15,000 dwelling houses to cater for them. The industrial estates nearby, one being Trafford Park, had had a hand in this population rise, offering employment to the residents of the town. Then as now, many of Urmston's residents worked outside the area. Since the 1971 census, however, the population has shown a slight decrease to the level of 41,825 at the 2011 census.

Convenient bus and rail facilities were a further factor in attracting residents to the town.

However, while the considerable growth of housing over the previous thirty years had, to a large extent, satisfied the needs of the growth in population, the shopping facilities had not kept pace with these developments. As a result, the shopping centre in Urmston was inadequate for the needs of

Station Road, showing Mayo's. (Author)

A crowded Crofts Bank Road, *c.* 1911. (Author)

Flixton Road. (Author)

Cuthbert's butchers in 1913, with delivery boy Jack Smethills. (Cuthbert Collection)

Temperence Hall in 1914; it would later experience many functional changes, becoming a rollerskating rink, shop and restaurant.

The police station on the corner of Station Road and Church Road. (Author)

the people, especially with trade being lost to surrounding areas; the photographs accompanying this chapter illustrate the need for some centralisation of the shopping centre, notwithstanding the romantic depictions by these opportunistic photographers.

Car ownership was increasing, with forecasts for ownership to treble by 1980 and more and more shoppers were willing to travel out of the town to do their weekly shopping, to the great disadvantage of local retailers. Furthermore, this was in an age when daily shopping for the household essentials was the norm. Nowadays, of course, it is more usual to make one weekly excursion to one of the big supermarkets. Not only were more shops needed but also a greater choice and variety of goods on offer and in more centralised shops. Hence the need for a central shopping area with convenient parking.

Many of the existing shops were old and in structurally poor condition, being built of heavy masonry. Furthermore, much of the space above these shops was wasted and with narrow frontages. Added to this, the shopper had to walk considerable distances between shops, often on a daily basis, due to the straggling and widespread layout of the shopping area, which presented a conflict between traffic and the pedestrian.

In planning the redevelopment, the size and population of the town had to be considered before making an assessment of the people's needs as well as the competition between Urmston and the neighbouring towns, which were threatening the trade of its shopkeepers. The final plan would have to offer a greater variety of goods and the siting had to consolidate the existing sprawling layout, making a compact shopping centre with minimal walking distances. Traffic would have to be excluded from the shopping area, with shoppers being able to drive up to ample parking facilities or arriving by bus immediately adjacent to the centre. Service vehicles would also have to be able to deliver to the rear of the shops in pre-designed service areas to avoid the dangers to the public and other traffic of unloading at the kerbside.

Station Road in the 1960s. (Urmston Official Guide 1971)

The interior of the library, with Italianate paintings. (James Billington)

And so the idea of a new shopping centre was born. The visibility of the shopping area was restricted from the main roads surrounding the development. From Flixton Road only the large unit occupied by the Eccles and District Co-operative store was visible and, on the Crofts Bank Road side, a limited area occupied by houses converted into local authority offices.

Care was also needed to integrate existing buildings into the scheme wherever possible and, in addition, the local council offices, a public house (Yates's Wine Lodge), the public library and the Conservative club were incorporated.

In an attempt to confront the conflict between traffic and the environment, the resulting shopping precinct was situated in an area free from noise, fumes, vibration and physical danger, all very real concerns in the traditional shopping facilities before the advent of the 'shopping precinct'. A residential road, Winifred Road, was cleared of its houses and became one of the malls

Moorfield Walk prior to the shopping centre being opened, 1970. Late Winifred Road. (James Billlington)

known as Moorside Walk, named after one of the houses on Crofts Bank Road near to where the war memorial is situated on the edge of Golden Hill Park. Moorside House was demolished as part of the clearances to make way for the shopping precinct. Winifred Road was flattened in 1965 and the residents rehoused.

Although, even to this day, this problem of the conflict between traffic and the environment hasn't been entirely solved for all the shoppers in Urmston, the redevelopment did, and still does, to some extent tackle some of these issues. The current malls allow for exclusive pedestrian use, doing away with the shopper having to cross the traffic flow.

The construction of both phases of the shopping area did not, of course, result in the demolition of the other shops within the centre of Urmston so the 'solution' of the traffic versus shoppers conflict was only partially addressed. It must also be realised that the centre of a town is not primarily a place where people and goods travel to and from but a place in which people work, shop, meet their friends, visit doctors' and dentists' surgeries, restaurants, theatres, libraries, banks, swimming baths, concerts, etc. The ability of the pedestrian to move about the town centre unhindered is not a luxury to be underestimated. This is the reason for the traffic-free malls introduced into town centres in the late 1960s. The centre of nearby Stretford was, unlike Urmston and Chorlton-cum-Hardy (two nearby town centres whose identity was, to a certain extent, preserved in spite of pedestrianised shopping malls) completely destroyed to build the Arndale Centre. Few shops survived the Stretford redevelopment.

The Urmston redevelopment was designed not only to provide a safer and more traffic-free town centre but to attract customers from neighbouring areas such as Partington, with its 1970 population of 8,000 (referred to, at the time, as part of the Manchester overspill) as well as Flixton and Davyhulme.

The new shopping centre, finally completed and open to the public in 1970, just 1 mile from the newly constructed M63, in itself a measure that took much traffic away from the town centre, was designed to cater for a 55,000 shopping population. The aim was not only to provide a safe and attractive shopping area for the locals but also to recapture trade lost to surrounding areas.

Table 6 gives the details of the shop areas that, at the time of my research in 1970 just prior to opening, was over half let. There were also 20,000 sq ft of offices (let to the Urban District Council and the Co-operative Insurance Society), the new Urmston library, a Conservative club, three car parks, traffic-free concourses and a public house, Yates's Wine Lodge. It may be of interest to the reader to learn that the shop units were left as mere shells with walls, ceilings and floors left ready to receive the tenant's own plaster and decoration. Tenants were expected to install their own shop fronts and fascias, the designs of which had to meet with the landlord's and architect's approval. Gas, electricity and water were supplied to the units for connection by the tenants.

Table 6: Schedule of accommodation and rents as at 1970.

Shop no.	Frontage	Depth	Area in sq ft, ground floor	Area in sq ft, 1st floor	Rent p.a.
1	60' 10"	53' 9"	3,247	4,053	£3,750
2	17' 6"	42' 8"	747	740	£1,000
3	17' 6"	42' 8"	747	740	£1,000
4	17' 6"	42' 8"	747	740	£1,000
5	17' 6"	42' 8"	747	740	£1,000
6	17' 6"	42' 8"	747	740	£1,275
7	17' 6"	60' 10"	1,065	740	£1,275
8	17' 6"	60' 10"	1,065	740	£1,275
9	17' 6"	60' 10"	1,065	740	£1,275
10	17' 6"	60' 10"	1,065	740	£1,275

Shop no.	Frontage	Depth	Area in sq ft, ground floor	Area in sq ft, 1st floor	Rent p.a.
11	17' 6"	60' 10"	1,065	740	£1,275
12	17' 6"	60' 10"	1,065	516	£1,225
13	17' 6"	60' 10"	1,065	516	£1,225
14	17' 6"	60' 10"	1,065	_	£1,100
15	17' 6"	60' 10"	1,065	_	£1,100
16	17' 6"	60' 10"	1,065	_	£1,100
17	17' 6"	60' 10"	1,065	_	£1,100
18	17' 6"	60' 10"	1,065	_	£1,100
19	Redmans	supermarket	12,968	_	*
20	Co-operative	supermarket	13,540	12,550	*
21	18' 4"	71' 8"	1,182	760	£1,500
22	17' 6"	60' 10"	1,065	740	£1,275
23	17' 6"	60' 10"	1,065	740	£1,275
24	17' 6"	60' 10"	1,065	740	£1,275
25	17' 6"	60' 10"	1,065	740	£1,275
26	17' 6"	60' 10"	1,065	740	£1,275
27	17' 6"	60' 10"	1,065	740	£1,275
28	17' 6"	60' 10"	1,065	740	£1,275
29	17' 6"	60' 10"	1,065	740	£1,275
30	17' 6"	60' 10"	1,065	740	£1,275
31	17' 6"	60' 10"	1,065	740	£1,275
32	17' 6"	60' 10"	1,065	740	£1,275
33	17' 6"	83' 3"	1,457	_	£1,500
34	17' 6"	83' 3"	1,457	_	£1,600
35	17' 6"	83' 3"	1,457	_	£1,700
36	23' 4"	53' 0"	1,133	_	£1,250
37	17' 6"	53' 0"	927	_	£1,000
38	17' 6"	53' 0"	927	_	£1,000
A	17' 6"	35' 9"	625	_	£750
B	17' 6"	35' 9"	625	_	£750
C	17' 6"	35' 9"	625	_	£750
D	17' 6"	35' 9"	625	_	£750
E	17' 6"	35' 9"	625	_	£750

Table 7: Other accommodation.

First floor public house (Yates's Wine Lodge)	4,380 square feet
Ground and first floor office of U.U.D.C.	18,000 square feet
First floor offices	2,671 square feet
First floor Conservative club	4,980 square feet
Library	7,650 square feet

The traffic-free concourse and service roads were adopted by the local authority, subject to a small service charge to cover the cost of maintenance, cleaning
and lighting of the service areas. Incidentally, the development was carried out
at no cost whatsoever to the local authority as the developers prepared the
scheme in partnership with Urmston District Council. It was estimated, at the
time, that the local rates would benefit from the new added income.

The actual plan of the centre revolved around a public square, now called
Eden Square, approached by two pedestrian concourses leading from Flixton
Road and Crofts Bank Road. Within this square, at the end of Moorfield Walk,
were erected three large modern fibreglass seal sculptures finished in bronze. I
remember interviewing the sculptor in her home and she told me that her aim
was 'to create forms with rock-like qualities and built up in thicknesses of glass
fibre and resin to escape from the panel-like construction often characteristic
of work in this medium'. They were a focal point not only for those interested
in a visual impact in the square but also, sadly, for young children who used
the seals as a climbing frame, their sloping curves proving ideal as a slide. They
obviously gave much pleasure to children but my last memories of them were
that parts of the bronze had worn away with the constant attention from the
children and holes had appeared exposing the fibreglass underneath. Within
the precinct gardens were set trees and other landscaping features, including
kiosks, advertising stands and benches.

As can be seen from the accommodation schedule in Table 6, in addition
to the shop units, provision was also made for a supermarket (Redmans), the
Co-operative, a public house (Yates's Wine Lodge), a Conservative club, office
space and a modern library with contrasting classical paintings on the walls.
The shop units were designed to cater for all types of retail use and could be
divided or combined as required, and wide canopies were provided to shelter
shoppers during inclement weather. Originally the plan was to provide for fifty

shops, but this was reduced to thirty-eight as the council felt that the higher number would be too many for the size of the potential custom.

One of Urmston's most attractive features has been the fine array of trees lining many of the roads in the town and they have been well tended over the years. The new pedestrianised concourses and square provided for trees to be incorporated into the scheme and this feature echoed this tradition; sadly not repeated in the recent development.

The actual construction of the buildings in the scheme was simple. Except for the council offices and the library, all the buildings were built on pile foundations due to the soft earth foundations below. Steel-reinforced concrete piles were consequently sunk in the rock below to support the stanchions. The frames of the building were made of reinforced concrete on the site, with reinforced beams and blocks filling in the floor areas. Prefabricated concrete panels were used for the walls, with the ceilings and walls left for screed and plaster.

The design developed using a flexible arrangement of concrete and glazed panels at first-storey level provided with a projection to form a canopy. Care was taken to integrate existing buildings where possible and, in addition, the local council offices, library and Conservative club to provide for a well-disciplined design theme; a vision not shared by all at the time. The roofs of all buildings were constructed as flat surfaces with slight falls to allow for drainage, and the pedestrian concourses were similarly laid to fall down to a central drainage system along the centre of the concourses. This central drainage system was disguised by trees, benches and flower beds.

One surveyor of the scheme had proposed a large hotel, town hall, major bus terminal, restaurant and one-way systems; a further step in Urmston's complete redevelopment process. These were not carried out; rather, the development lasted less than forty years and has now been replaced with another redevelopment scheme. The library, built during the 1970s redevelopment, was leaking and, along with other buildings in the complex, had just reached the end of its useful life and needed to be demolished to make way for the current complex. The new development started in 2009.

The new Eden Square complex, at the time of writing, contains Sainsbury's, Aldi, Quality Save and Iceland supermarkets in addition to Poundland, William Hill, two coffee shops, a restaurant, an estate agent, a greetings card shop, a charity shop, and the new library on the first floor above Sainsbury's. The malls are somewhat bare, with basic seating in and around what can only be described as a soulless central square. There are no trees there now.

Although the redevelopment of the early 1970s had an impact on local family-run businesses, the local Sainsbury's supermarket took much of the trade away from the smaller businesses of the town and the cessation of the long-established Cuthbert's the butchers in 2004 after many decades of trading is a good example of this. The upside, it has to be said, is that Sainsburys has given welcome and much-needed employment in the area. The Urmston branch of the Nat West bank has expanded into what was once Cuthbert's.

Butchers, bakers and greengrocers are sadly depleted as the staple commodities of meat, bread, fruit, veg and milk are readily available in Sainsbury's and other local supermarkets. Also, changes in social habits have resulted in much-depleted services by the likes of the once ubiquitous milkmen and coalmen. Again, milk is readily available in supermarkets and today's centrally heated homes have all but negated the need for coal, although the nostalgia boom for open fires has, to some extent, revived the role of the coal man.

Many remember the pop lorry, a service that delivered Corona lemonade, orangeade, cream soda, limeade and dandelion and burdock direct to the home. A deposit on the empty bottles was refundable when next the lorry visited the street.

Other clusters of shops are situated round the area. Urmston's shopping habits have, however, been more greatly affected by the construction of the mammoth retail outlet known as the Trafford Centre, which was opened for business on 10 September 1998. The land had been sold by the then owners, the Manchester Ship Canal Company, to Peel Holdings in 1986 and the planning process was one of the longest and most expansive in the history of the United Kingdom. Concerns were aired surrounding the effect the shopping centre might have on retailers in the smaller towns and villages in the Greater Manchester conurbation and potential traffic problems caused by the centre's proximity to the M60 motorway. Ultimately the matter was decided by the House of Lords in 1996, which voted in favour of the development. Construction took twenty-seven months at a cost of £600 million – approximately £1 billion at 2016 prices. Two further extensions have since opened, Barton Square and the Great Hall in 2008, at a combined cost of over £100 million. The centre attracts over 35 million visitors annually. There are over 11,500 car parking spaces. Future plans are to create a direct tram link from the Trafford Centre to Manchester city centre via Pomona.

The Urmston town centre shops look much like they have looked over the last fifty years, although the nature of the businesses have, to some extent, changed. The energy showrooms are no more but the buildings live on with the art deco design still retained on the old gas showroom on what is now The Britannia. The electricity showroom is now the Wetherspoon's pub called The Tim Bobbin.

Incidentally, Tim Bobbin was the alter ego of John Collier, a celebrated writer and satirical poet of Lancashire dialect verse and prose who was born in Urmston on 18 December 1708. Collier styled himself as the Lancashire Hogarth. He died on 14 July 1786 in Milnrow. His first and best-known work is *Tummas and Meary*, published in 1746, in which he characterised the Lancashire people of the day. He is buried in the churchyard of Rochdale parish church, St Chad's. He wrote his own epitaph twenty minutes before he died, 'Jack of all trades ... left to lie i'th dark', which is inscribed upon his gravestone. He had also written a number of other humorous epitaphs for graves, a number of which can still be seen in St Chad's churchyard.

Indeed, although some of the old landmarks of bygone days are still evident in the area, such as St Michael's, St Clement's, St Mary's, All Saints, the Temperance Hall, many of Spark's beautiful houses, some of the old pubs and the parks, many things have changed and not all for the better. But the people of Urmston, Flixton and Davyhulme are a resilient lot and a glance at the Facebook pages devoted to interest in the area certainly points to not only a fondness for days gone by but also a pride and optimism in the many cafes, bars and other amenities that are springing up.

POSTSCRIPT

I have made every effort to ensure that my research has been thorough but it may be that there are some errors and inaccuracies, for which I apologise. Feel free to notify me of these or any other comments via the publisher.

Furthermore, in a book of this size, it is inevitable that some details have been omitted. For instance, I have not been able to cover every church in the area in detail nor every one of the various public parks that offer invaluable amenities for all ages of the population. If something that would have been of interest to you has been missed out then I can only apologise. Restrictions on space has made this inevitable but I hope that this story of my home town, which includes much hitherto unpublished information, stories, photographs and maps, proves an entertaining and informative read.

ACKNOWLEDGEMENTS

Thanks must be given to the following for their assistance in the research and writing of this book: first of all, posthumous thanks to David Herbert Langton and Richard Lawson for their wonderful books written in 1898 and invaluable source material for the history of the three townships up to the turn of the century. Thanks must also go to Rev. Karen Marshall, vicar, and Derek Prince, churchwarden at St Clement's church, Urmston for friendship and support and the loan of the photograph of Rev. Elijah Harwood Cooke. I had Derek up on a ladder one day to read out the inscriptions on the west wall stained-glass window while I stood, notepad in hand, to transcribe his words.

My gratitude also to Jen Durber at Flixton parish church; Elsie and Frank Firth at St Mary the Virgin, Davyhulme; the staff in the local history section of Manchester Central Reference Library, especially George Dawes and Janet Parkes who have spent many hours researching with me; my father James Billington for photographs of the town centre redevelopment of 1970 and others from my childhood; Mr Eccles of Urmston County Library for the supply of maps and other information; Mr Jones at Leach, Rhodes and Walker (Architects); Mr Ashcroft at Metropolitan Estate and Property Corporation Ltd (MEPC); Mr Jackson from the Urmston Urban District Council; William Simpson for his co-operation and making available material about his company Simpson Ready Foods; Andrew Ridgeway, Dave Wilcox and Mark Stagg for assistance with the edit formatting; Rob Phillips for computer transfers; Jennie Brooks, Alan Crossland, Bob Potts and David Gilligan for proofreading; and Andrew Simpson for his invaluable help in the early stages of this work by pointing me in the right direction to carry out my research. Thanks also to Norman Booth for granting his permission to use his watercolour painting of the speculative image of the Egerton coat of arms, which now resides at St Clement's church in Urmston.

Many thanks also to John Howe for the photograph of Ernest Leeming, and to Peter Spencer for the photo of the nurses in the Secod World War chapter. I am also indebted to James Crowley for allowing me access to his MA dissertation on the history of All Saints, Barton-upon-Irwell. Many thanks also to Don Fry for allowing me to visit his home at Newcroft House and giving me access to his notes on the property.

Special thanks must go to Alan Crossland for his support and tremendous generosity in sharing much valuable information and many photographs and other resources, especially his research material on Humphrey Park and old houses in the area; similarly to Bob Potts for making available his extensive postcard collection, photos of Urmston, Flixton and Davyhulme and his extensive writings and research materials. Bob must also be credited as co-author of the chapter 'Urmston at war, 1939–45'.

And a final thanks to The History Press, who have put their faith in me and my book.

BIBLIOGRAPHY

41 Years On (1974).

Baines, Edward, *The History of Lancashire* (1868).

Barlow, Nigel P., *Around Manchester* (2016).

Beeton, Isabella Mary, *Mrs Beeton's Book of Household Management* (1861).

Blundell, Fr Brendan (ed.), *All Saints Church Barton-upon-Irwell Restoration 1985–1991* (1991).

Cliff, Karen and Vikki Masterson, *Urmston, Flixton and Davyhulme* (2000).

Cliff, Karen and Vikki Masterson, *Warburton, Partington and Carrington* (2002).

Crossland, Alan, *Looking Back at Urmston* (1983).

Dickens, Steven, *Flixton, Urmston & Davyhulme Through Time* (2013).

Edwards, A. Trystan, *Towards Tomorrow's Architecture* (1968).

Freeborn, J.C.K., *A History of Flixton Parish* (1969).

Gruen, Victor, *The Heart of Our Cities* (1965).

France, E. and T.F.Woodall, *A New History of Didsbury* (1976).

Hammond, J.L. and Barbara Hammond, *The Village Labourer 1760–1832* (1911).

Harford, Ian, *Manchester and its Ship Canal Movement* (1994).

Harland, J. and T.T. Wilkinson, *Lancashire Legends, Traditions, Pageants, Sports Etc* (1873).

Harland, J. and T.T. Wilkinson (eds), *Ballads and Songs of Lancashire collected* (1882).

History of the County of Lancaster, Volume 5, The Victoria History of the Counties of England (1906–1914).

Horn, Pamela, *The Victorian Country Child* (1975; 1990).

Horn, Pamela, *The Rise and Fall of the Victorian Servant* (1975).

Horn, Pamela, *Labouring Life in the Victorian Countryside* (1976).

Horn, Pamela, *The Victorian Town Child* (1997).

Horn, Pamela, *Pleasures and Pastimes in Victorian Britain* (1999).

Horn, Pamela, *Life Below Stairs in the 20th Century* (2001).

Horn, Pamela, *Young Offenders: Juvenile Delinquency 1700–2000* (2010).

Horn, Pamela, *The Real Larkrise to Candleford: Life in the Victorian Countryside* (2013).

Howard, Ebenezer, *Garden Cities of Tomorrow* (1902).

Kidd, Alan and Terry Wyke (eds), *Manchester: Making the Modern City* (2016).

Langton, David Herbert, *A History of the Parish of Flixton* (1898).

Lawson, Richard, *A History of Flixton, Urmston and Davyhulme* (1898).

Leeming, E.L., *Road Engineering* (1964; originally published in 1924).

Leeming, E.L., *The Superelevation of Highway Curves* (1927).

Million, Ivor R., *A History of Didsbury* (1969).

Nevell, Michael et al., *Warburton* (2015).

Nicholson, John, *Folk Lore of East Yorkshire* (1890).

O'Gorman, Fr. Edmund, *A History of All Saints Church Barton-upon-Irwell* (1988).

Our Village Heritage: The Story of One Hundred Years of the Parish Church of St Clement's Urmston 1868–1968 (1968).

Page, Phil and Ian Littlechilds, *Secret Manchester* (2014).

Pegg, Bob, *Rites and Riots: Folk Customs of Britain and Europe* (1981).

Potts, Bob, *Reminiscenses of a Flixton Boyhood* (1986).

Redford, Arthur, *Labour Migration in England 1800–1850* (1926).

Royle, Cliff, *Boyhood Recollections of Flixton 1922–1938* (1994).

Russell, Jesse and Ronald Cohn, *Urmston* (2012).

Samuel, Raphael (ed.), *Village Life and Labour* (1975).

Simpson, Andrew, *The Story of Chorlton-cum-Hardy* (2012).

Smith, Peter J.C., *Luftwaffe over Manchester* (2003).

Spencer, Rev Allan, *The History of Davyhulme Wesleyan Chapel* (1898).

St Clement's Centenary (1968).

St Clement's Urmston 1868–1993 125th Anniversary Brochure (1993).

Urmston Parish Magazine 1898–99 (1899).

Tetlow, J. and A. Goss, *Homes, Towns and Traffic* (1968).

Thompson, Flora, *Lark Rise To Candleford* (1945).

Urmston Official Guide (1958; 1971).

Urmston Urban District Newsletters (from 1970).

Wilson, James Q. (ed.), *Urban Renewal: The Record and the Controversy* (1966).

Other sources have included research in Urmston library, Trafford Local Studies Centre in Sale, Manchester Central Reference Library, various websites, newspapers, census returns, births, baptisms, marriages and deaths records, OS maps, Manchester Blitz Memorials of Casualties, George Cogswell's War Dead of Trafford, Industrial Schools Act records, conversations with residents, Bob Potts's postcard collection, Alan Crossland's unpublished research on the history of Humphrey Park, Bob Potts's unpublished history of *Motor-Bus Services in Urmston and Flixton 1907–1928*, Bob Potts's unpublished *Wibberley Red Cross Hospitals Flixton 1914–1919*, Alan Lee for burial records, the pamphlet *Parish Church of St Michael Flixton: Origin, History and Guide* by Joyce Cooper, the *Welcome to St Mary's* pamphlet, the *Commemorative History of St Mary the Virgin Davyhulme 1890–1990* (Lynn Heaton, Stuart Winward and Madge Harvey) and David Smith's *A–Z of Urmston* as well as his sixteen booklets on various aspects of the history of the three townships.

APPENDICES

Appendix 1

Nineteenth-century demographics

The first census of population took place in 1801. Table 8 shows the demographics for Flixton and Urmston during the nineteenth century; the blank cells indicate that no returns were made. As can be seen, the largest township, as far as population was concerned, was Flixton right up until 1881 when Urmston finally edged ahead.

Table 8: Census data for Flixton and Urmston.

Year	Township	Inhabited	Uninhabited	Building	Male	Female	Total
1801	Flixton	_	_	_	605	488	1,003
	Urmston	_	_	_	256	276	532
1811	Flixton	210	_	_	696	691	1387
	Urmston	98	2	_	294	301	595
1821	Flixton	233	_	_	782	822	1,604
	Urmston	105	_	_	317	328	645
1831	Flixton	222	5	3	700	693	1,393
	Urmston	120	1	_	337	369	706
1841	Flixton	241	8	_	708	751	1,459
	Urmston	135	1	1	386	385	771
1851	Flixton	251	13	_	641	693	1,334
	Urmston	142	11	_	367	363	730
1861	Flixton	252	12	2	635	667	1,302
	Urmston	158	8	_	364	384	748

Year	Township	Inhabited	Uninhabited	Building	Male	Female	Total
1871	Flixton	308	9	8	716	796	1,512
	Urmston	177	7	4	444	552	996
1881	Flixton	377	45	3	811	965	1,776
	Urmston	436	65	26	987	1,255	2,242
1891	Flixton	515	21	6	1,366	1,420	2,786
	Urmston	829	42	84	1,816	2,226	4,042

Appendix 2

Today's demographics

The national census of population gives central and local government the information on the demographics of the country to better enable the provision of social amenities such as hospitals, doctors' surgeries, schools, care for the elderly, care for pre-school children and infrastructure in general. Censuses are carried out at ten-year intervals, the last one at the time of writing having been in 2011.

The 2001 census had shown that the total population of Urmston was 40,964, of which 96.8 per cent were white, 1.0 per cent Asian and 0.7 per cent black; this compared to national figures (England only) of 90.9 per cent, 4.6 per cent and 2.3 per cent respectively. Population density was recorded at 10,881 inhabitants per square mile and for every 100 females there were 93 males. A total of 19,172 households were recorded by the census, of which 39.9 per cent were married couples living together, 29.6 per cent one-person households, 7.7 per cent co-habiting couples and 8.9 per cent one-parent households.

To put the population growth into some perspective, Urmston's population at the 1801 census was 532. The 1851 census was the first to show nationally that the country's population, for the first time ever, lived in urban rather than rural areas, although this area continued to retain a predominantly rural nature. Urmston's population at this historic date was 730. The biggest leap occurred in 1881 when the 1871 figure of 996 jumped dramatically to 2,242. This can, more than likely, be put down to Urmston becoming a dormitory town for non-manual workers commuting into the city centre after the introduction of the railway.

Another dramatic leap happened in 1939 when the 1931 figure of 9,284 increased to 33,163. Due to the war years, the census was taken two years early. A steady increase followed, peaking at 44,563 in 1971 followed by a gentle fall to the 2011 figure of 40,964. It was no longer fashionable to have large families, which, possibly, is one of the reasons for this downward trend.

The Urmston figures (excluding Flixton and Davyhulme) now show the demographic split at 92.3 per cent (85.4 per cent) white, 3.2 per cent (7.8 per cent) Asian, 2.6 per cent (2.3 per cent) mixed, 1.6 per cent (3.5 per cent) black and other at 0.3 per cent (1.0 per cent). I have put the national figures in brackets for comparison.

As can be seen, there has been an increase in black and Asian figures compared to the previous census.

Table 9 uses information from the 1991 census and shows the socio-economic status of the population of Urmston as percentages compared with that of Trafford and the UK national figures.

Table 9: Data on socio-economic status from the 1991 census.

	Urmston (%)	Trafford (%)	UK (%)
Professional	6.8	9.1	6.7
Managerial	30.4	33.1	31.3
Skilled	46.8	40.2	40.6
Partially skilled	9.8	10.9	13.8
Unskilled	3.6	3.9	6.9

Table 10 is also taken from the 1991 census figures and shows the percentages of owner-occupied compared with public and private rented accommodation.

Table 10: Data on occupation from the 1991 census.

	Urmston (%)	Trafford (%)	UK (%)
Owner occupied	80.9	72.9	66.4
Public rented	13.3	19.6	31.2
Private rented	5.8	7.5	7.1

The 1991 census also showed that 82.9 per cent of the population were car owners compared with 61.3 per cent for Trafford as a whole.

Table 11 gives the 1991 age profile of the Urmston area as compared with Trafford and Greater Manchester.

Table 11: Data on age from the 1991 census.

	Urmston (%)	Trafford (%)	Greater Manchester (%)
Children (0–15)	19.8	20.2	18.8
Working age (16–59/65)	61.6	61.1	60.0
Retired	21.0	18.7	18.0

Appendix 3

Listed buildings and structures in Urmston, Flixton and Davyhulme

Church of Barton All Saints, Redclyffe Road, Davyhulme	Grade I
All Saints Presbytery, Redclyffe Road, Davyhulme	Grade II
Church of St Clement, Manor Avenue, Urmston	Grade II
The Old Rectory, 52 Carrington Road, Flixton	Grade II
Yew Tree farmhouse, 240 Davyhulme Road, Davyhulme	Grade II
Stable adjacent to 240 Yew Tree farmhouse, Davyhulme	Grade II
Church of St Michael, Flixton	Grade II
Jones chest tomb, graveyard, St Michael's church, Flixton	Grade II
Sundial, St Michael's graveyard, Flixton	Grade II
Flixton House, Flixton Road, Flixton	Grade II
Outbuilding and barn, Flixton House, Flixton	Grade II
Wall south side of gardens, Flixton House, Flixton	Grade II
Commemorative urn, Davyhulme Road, Davyhulme	Grade II
Barton aqueduct over Bridgewater canal, Davyhulme	Grade II
Barton bridge and control tower, Davyhulme	Grade II
Control tower, Barton Aerodrome	Grade II
Newcroft House, Stretford Road, Urmston	Grade II
Cenotaph at Davyhulme Circle	Grade II
Lark Rise, Nos.18–20 Carrington Road, Flixton	Grade II
No.16 Carrington Road, Flixton	Grade II
St Mary The Virgin Church, Davyhulme	Grade II
St Mary The Virgin War Memorial	Grade II

INDEX

Praise for *The Story of Urmston, Flixton and Davyhulme*

'As an Urmstonian and local historian I find Michael's book *The Story of Urmston, Flixton and Davyhulme* to be very informative with some excellent photographs and an absolute must for anyone in the area who loves to find out more about the past.'

Alan Crossland, author of *Looking Back at Urmston*.

'Michael Billington's new book is the first history of our corner of England since 1898. It is a very good read indeed and amply illustrated. I warmly recommend it to the many thousands of people who have an affinity with Urmston, Flixton, and Davyhulme.'

Bob Potts, author of *Reminiscences of a Flixton Boyhood*.

'Michael is one of those all-rounders. He is a teacher, artist, musician and now an author. I have watched as *The Story of Urmston, Flixton and Davyhulme* developed from an idea, into a major research project and now a finished book. It is part general history and also offers up fascinating glimpses of people and places which will be enjoyed by all who have links with Urmston, Flixton and Davyhulme.'

Andrew Simpson, author of *The Story of Chorlton-cum-Hardy*

Simpson Ready Foods would like to thank all those people, employees and organisations, who have contributed towards the success of the company over the last century.